CAMBRIDGE

English for Spanish Speakers

Interactive

Student's Book 2

Helen Hadkins and Samantha Lewis with Joanna Budden

CAMBRIDGE UNIVERSITY PRESS

Contents

1 That's amazing!

Present simple and present continuous
Present simple and present continuous: questions
Vocabulary: Parts of the body; The five senses
Interaction 1: Showing you're interested / not interested

A

1 Read and listen

1-B 4-C
2-D 3-A

a Read the text quickly and match paragraphs 1–4 with the pictures.

1 B

B

C

AMAZING BUT TRUE!

1 MR EAT-IT-ALL

Michel Lotito, born in France in 1950, is called Monsieur Mangetout (Mr Eat-it-all). He is famous for eating bicycles, televisions, and even a small aeroplane. He eats about one kilogram of metal or glass a day, but first he drinks oil and a lot of water. His stomach is much stronger than a normal stomach, so don't try this at home! However, Mr Eat-it-all doesn't eat bananas or eggs – they make him feel ill.

2 THE FOOT PILOT

Jessica Cox, from Arizona in the United States, was born without arms, but she can fly a plane using her feet. She is the first person in the world without arms to get a pilot's licence. Jessica can also swim, drive a car and has a black belt in tae-kwon-do. At the moment she isn't thinking of becoming a professional pilot because she is doing too many other things.

3 SNAKE-GIRL

Nokulunga Buthelezi, from South Africa, can move her body like a snake. 18-year-old Nokulunga is known as Lunga, or 'Snake-Girl', and is the star of a circus show. When she was a baby she could get into amazing positions. She slept with her legs behind her head and her hands behind her back. Lunga's great-grandmother had the same abilities.

4 DANIEL THE BRAINMAN

Daniel Tammet 'sees' numbers as colours and shapes. When he is doing mathematics, he sees a picture in his brain and he sometimes paints it. He has the best memory for numbers in Europe and he can do calculations faster than a calculator. In 2004 he spent five hours saying *Pi* π (3.1415 ...) to 22, 514 decimal places. Daniel also speaks twelve languages. When he isn't working with numbers, he's creating his own language, called Mänti.

D

b 1.1 Read the text again and listen. Write *D* (Daniel), *J* (Jessica), *L* (Lunga) or *M* (Michel).

1 M

1 B. has an unusual stomach.
2 C.. has an amazing ability with numbers and language.
3 D.. can do a martial art.
4 A.. has the same ability as other people in his/her family.
5 C.. is inventing a new language.
6 D.. isn't doing her job professionally.

c Find eight different parts of the body in the texts.

d Work in a group and answer the questions.

1 Which ability do you think is the most incredible? Why?
2 Do you think the stories are true?
3 Do you know anyone who has an amazing ability?

2 Vocabulary Parts of the body

a Look at the picture. Do you know the words for any parts of the body?

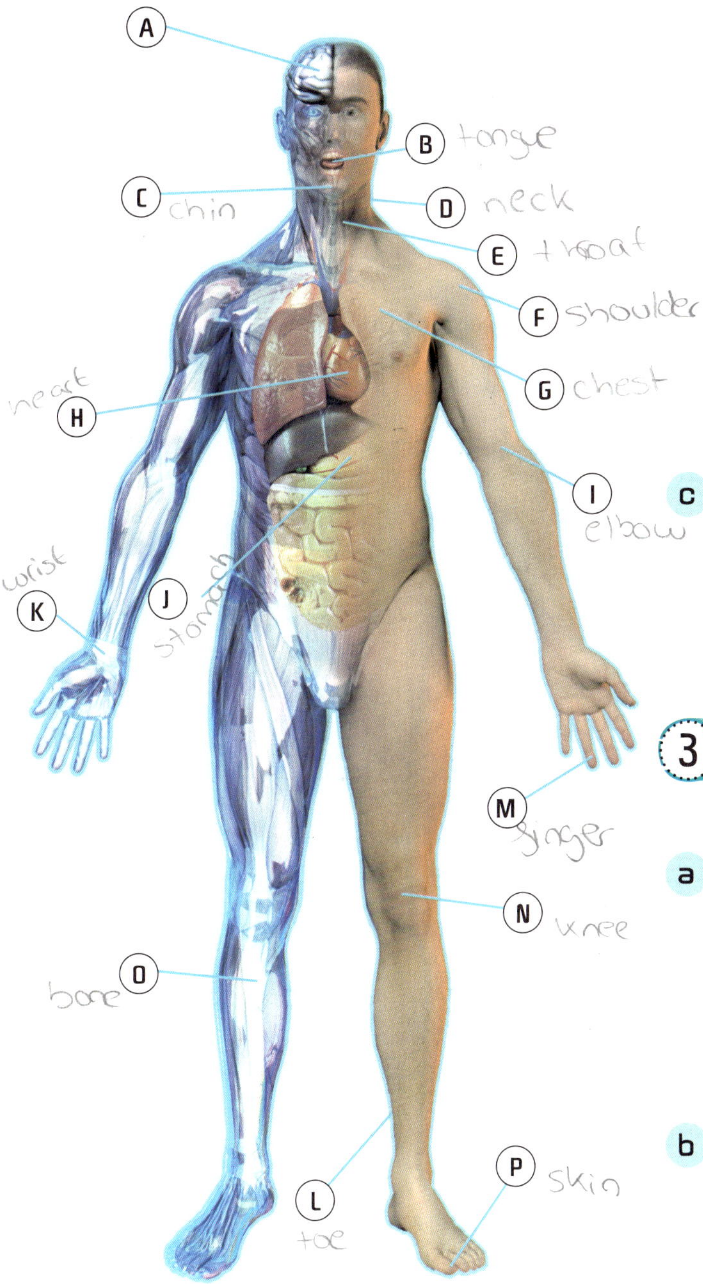

b 1.2 Match the words with the parts of the body. Then listen and check.

A 2 brain

1 bone **2** brain **3** chest **4** chin **5** elbow
6 finger **7** heart **8** knee **9** neck **10** shoulder
11 skin **12** stomach **13** throat **14** toe
15 tongue **16** wrist

Get it right!

her tongue

We use possessive adjectives with parts of the body.

✓ *She can touch her chin with **her** tongue.*

✗ *She can touch ~~the~~ chin with ~~the~~ tongue.*

c Complete the table with the words in Exercise 2b. Do it in your Workbook (page 114 Exercise 1).

internal	external
bone	*chest*

heart, stomach
tongue

3 Pronunciation DVD

Long and short vowel sounds

a 1.3 There are long and short vowel sounds in English. Listen and repeat the words.

long	short
/ɑː/ arm ...	/æ/ back ...
/uː/ tooth ...	/ʊ/ foot ...

b 1.4 Copy the table in Exercise 3a and write these words in the correct column. Listen, check and repeat.

hand shoe heart look

c Follow the words with short vowel sounds and find your way through the puzzle with your finger. You can move up or down ↕, left or right ↔. Work with a partner and say the words.

→ put	far	plan	pull	have
match	shoe	good	half	book
cook	chat	could	two	black
art	start	blue	can	would
true	do	park	bag ↓	few

d 1.5 Listen and check your answers.

Culture Vulture

Do you know what your IQ is?
IQ is your Intelligence Quotient, and is measured in points by a test. The average IQ for a 15 year-old is 100. If you have an IQ of 140–145 you are a genius! Do you think exams and tests are a good way to measure people's intelligence? Why? / Why not?

4 Grammar

Present simple and present continuous

a Look at the examples and complete the table with the correct form of the verb.

*She **sees** small changes in the body.*
*Mr Eat-it-all **doesn't eat** bananas or eggs.*
*When he **isn't working** with numbers, he**'s creating** his own language.*

Present simple

Positive

I/You/We/They **paint** He/She/It …	pictures.

Negative

I/You/We/They … He/She/It …	**paint** pictures.

Present continuous

Positive

I'… You/We/They'… He/She/It'…	**painting** pictures.

Negative

I'… … You/We/They … He/She/It …	**painting** pictures.

Choose the correct word to complete the rules.

- We use the present simple for facts, repeated actions and **temporary** / **permanent** states.
- We use the present continuous for actions happening now and **temporary** / **permanent** states.

Grammar reference: page 132

b Choose the correct word.

1. We *'re starting/start* school at 9 o'clock every day.
2. Sorry, Jason isn't here. He *'s playing/plays* basketball.
3. My teacher *'s speaking/speaks* four languages.
4. Shh! The baby *'s sleeping/sleeps*!
5. I *'m not watching/don't watch* TV in the evening.
6. Olivia*'s reading/reads* a book about animals.
7. They*'re going/go* to the cinema every Saturday.

c Complete the text with the verbs in the present simple or continuous.

1 has

THE MAGNET FAMILY

78-year-old Liew Thiw Lin from Malaysia [1]… (have) an amazing ability. Metal objects [2]… (stick) to him and he can even pull a 10.6 tonne bus along the road with his body. In the photo forks and an iron [3]… (stick) to him. Scientists [4]… (not understand) why this [5]… (happen) because 'Mr Magnet's' body [6]… (be) normal. Three of his sons and two of his grandchildren [7]… (have) the same ability.

5 Vocabulary The five senses

a 1.6 Match the parts of the body with the sense verbs. Then listen and check.

1 ears **2** eyes **3** hands **4** mouth **5** nose

A smell **B** touch **C** taste **D** see **E** hear

b Complete the sentences with the verbs in Exercise 5a.

1. Did you … Pink's new song?
2. I can't … Jon in the photo. Where is he?
3. … this perfume, it's lovely.
4. Don't … the plate. It's very hot.
5. … this soup. It's delicious!

c Work with a partner. Make word webs for things you can see, hear, taste and smell in different places. Do it in your Workbook (page 114 Exercise 4).

d Tell the class about one of your word webs.

At the beach you can hear the sea …

Get it right!

can see / hear

We usually use *can* with *see, taste, hear* and *smell.*

✓ *Listen! I can hear the sea.*

✗ *Listen! I hear the sea.*

6 Speak

a Work with a partner. Take turns to ask the questions. Can your partner do all these things in less than three minutes?

Student A: Ask Student B.

1 Can you close your eyes and write the alphabet?
2 Can you move your nose?
3 Can you say five things that taste sweet?
4 Can you say five things that smell horrible?
5 Can you touch your knee with your nose?
6 What can you hear at the moment?

Student B: Turn to page 125.

b What can your partner do in three minutes? Tell the class.

7 Read and listen

a What do you know about the human body? Work in pairs and do the quiz.

Body facts

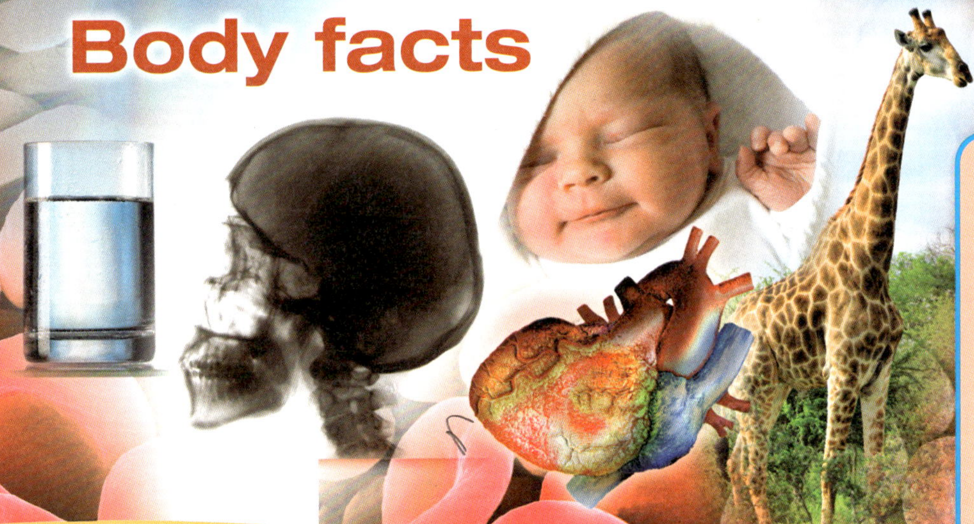

1 How much of the adult human body is water?
A 20% B 60% C 80%

2 How many litres of blood are there in the human body?
A 5 litres B 15 litres C 50 litres

3 How many times does your heart beat every day?
A 10,000 B 100,000 C 1,000,000

4 Where are most of the bones in your body?
A In your head B In your back C In your hands and feet

5 Which animal has got the same number of bones in their neck as a human?
A a horse B a panda C a giraffe

6 How much skin do you lose in one year?
A 50 grammes B 200 grammes C 2 kilogrammes

Other interesting information!

- Everyone all over the world has a mix of four colours in their skin, white, red, yellow and brown.
- Babies are born with 300 bones, but adults only have 206.
- An American woman, Lee Redmond, had the longest fingernails in the world. They were 7m 51cm long. Unfortunately, Lee lost her nails in a car accident in 2009.

Which is right? Don't look at the text!
*They were 7m 51cm **of long** / **long**.*

b 1.7 Listen and check your answers.

c 1.7 Listen again. Which facts in the quiz surprised you?

8 Grammar

Present simple and present continuous: questions

a Look at the examples and complete the tables.

→ ***Do** you **like** the exhibition? Yes, I **do**.*
*How much blood **do** we **have** in our bodies?*
***Is** Joseph **playing** a game over there? Yes, he **is**.*
*What **are** you **looking** at, Lizzie?*

Present simple

***Yes/No* questions**		**Short answers**
… I/you/we/they … he/she/it	**like** the exhibition?	Yes, I/you/we/they … . Yes, he/she/it … . No, I/you/we/they **don't**. No, he/she/it **doesn't**.

Information questions

How much blood	… **does**	I/you/we/they he/she/it	**have**?

Present continuous

***Yes/No* questions**			**Short answers**
Am **Are** …	I you/we/they he/she/it	**playing** a game?	Yes, I **am**. No, **I'm not**. Yes, you/we/they **are**. No, you/we/they … . Yes, he/she/it … . No, he/she/it **isn't**.

Information questions

What	**am** … **is**	I you/we/they he/she/it	**looking** at?

Grammar reference: page 132

b Complete the questions with the verbs in the present simple or present continuous.

1 are you doing

1 What … (you/do) at the moment?
2 What language … (you/speak) at home?
3 Listen! … (the phone/ring)?
4 Someone's in the bathroom. … (Joe/have) a shower?
5 … (they/watch) TV every day?
6 That smells good. What … (Lucia/cook) for dinner?

Get it right!

Do you live …?
Don't forget to use auxiliary verbs in present simple questions.
✓ *Do you live in Seville?*
✗ *~~You live~~ in Seville?*

c Work with a partner. Ask and answer questions. Use the present simple and the present continuous.

What Who	are do is does	do read listen to wear watch go talk to	at the moment now at the weekend in the evenings

A *What do you wear at the weekend?*
B *I usually wear jeans and a T-shirt.*
A *What's your dad doing at the moment?*
B *He's working.*

Interaction 1 DVD

Showing interest

a 1.8 Listen and write the things Jack and Lily talk about.

- blonde hair
- a horse
- a seahorse
- a star
- Japan
- blue eyes

b 1.8 Listen again and complete the phrases with the words.

you're know that's no that

Interested
1 Really?
2 … way!
3 … joking!
4 Wow, … amazing!

Not interested
5 Yeah, I …
6 Everybody knows …

c 1.9 Turn to page 124. Listen to the sentences and repeat them. Practise sounding interested or not interested.

d Work with a partner.

Student A: Turn to page 126.

Student B: Turn to page 129.

Portfolio 1

An amazing fact file

a Look at the photo and read the fact file. Why is Michael Phelps amazing?

b Look at the fact file for Michael Phelps. Match the categories in the box with the information in the fact file.

Nationality and job · Likes · Height and weight · ~~Name~~ · At the moment · Achievements · Speed · Interesting facts

FACT FILE

1 …	Michael Phelps
2 …	American/swimmer
3 …	2004 Olympic Games, Athens: 6 gold medals and 2 bronze medals 2008 Olympic Games, Beijing: 8 gold medals and 7 world records
4 …	1.93m/88kg
5 …	About 6.4 km/hour
6 …	Football, music (hip hop and rap), video games and his English bulldog, Herman.
7 …	• His body is very good for swimming. From finger-tip to finger-tip he measures 2 metres. • His feet are big and give him extra power in the water. • He trains six days a week, five hours a day. • He needs a lot of energy so he eats 8,000 to 12,000 calories a day (most men of his height need about 4,000 calories). He eats a lot of eggs, pasta, pizza and chocolate.
8 …	He's training for the next Olympics.

Which is right? Don't look at the text!
*He trains six days **a** / **in the** week.*

1 Name

c Find information about an interesting person. Make a fact file about the person. Use the categories in Exercise b.

d Work in a group. Read other students' fact files. Which person is the most amazing?

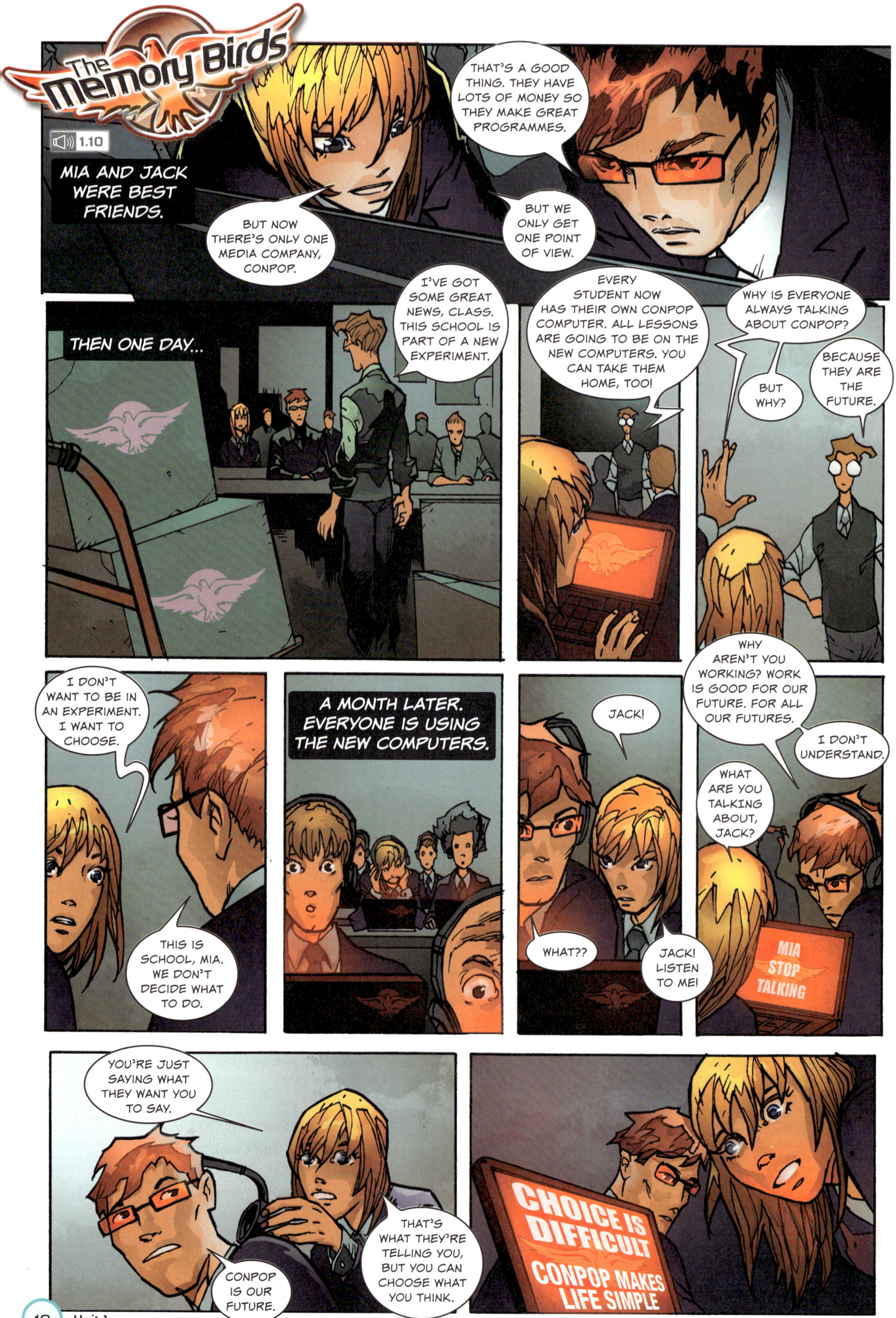
The Memory Birds
1.10
MIA AND JACK WERE BEST FRIENDS.
BUT NOW THERE'S ONLY ONE MEDIA COMPANY, CONPOP.
THAT'S A GOOD THING. THEY HAVE LOTS OF MONEY SO THEY MAKE GREAT PROGRAMMES.
BUT WE ONLY GET ONE POINT OF VIEW.
THEN ONE DAY...
I'VE GOT SOME GREAT NEWS, CLASS. THIS SCHOOL IS PART OF A NEW EXPERIMENT.
EVERY STUDENT NOW HAS THEIR OWN CONPOP COMPUTER. ALL LESSONS ARE GOING TO BE ON THE NEW COMPUTERS. YOU CAN TAKE THEM HOME, TOO!
WHY IS EVERYONE ALWAYS TALKING ABOUT CONPOP?
BUT WHY?
BECAUSE THEY ARE THE FUTURE.
I DON'T WANT TO BE IN AN EXPERIMENT. I WANT TO CHOOSE.
THIS IS SCHOOL, MIA. WE DON'T DECIDE WHAT TO DO.
A MONTH LATER. EVERYONE IS USING THE NEW COMPUTERS.
JACK!
WHAT??
JACK! LISTEN TO ME!
WHY AREN'T YOU WORKING? WORK IS GOOD FOR OUR FUTURE. FOR ALL OUR FUTURES.
I DON'T UNDERSTAND.
WHAT ARE YOU TALKING ABOUT, JACK?
MIA STOP TALKING
YOU'RE JUST SAYING WHAT THEY WANT YOU TO SAY.
CONPOP IS OUR FUTURE.
THAT'S WHAT THEY'RE TELLING YOU, BUT YOU CAN CHOOSE WHAT YOU THINK.
CHOICE IS DIFFICULT
CONPOP MAKES LIFE SIMPLE

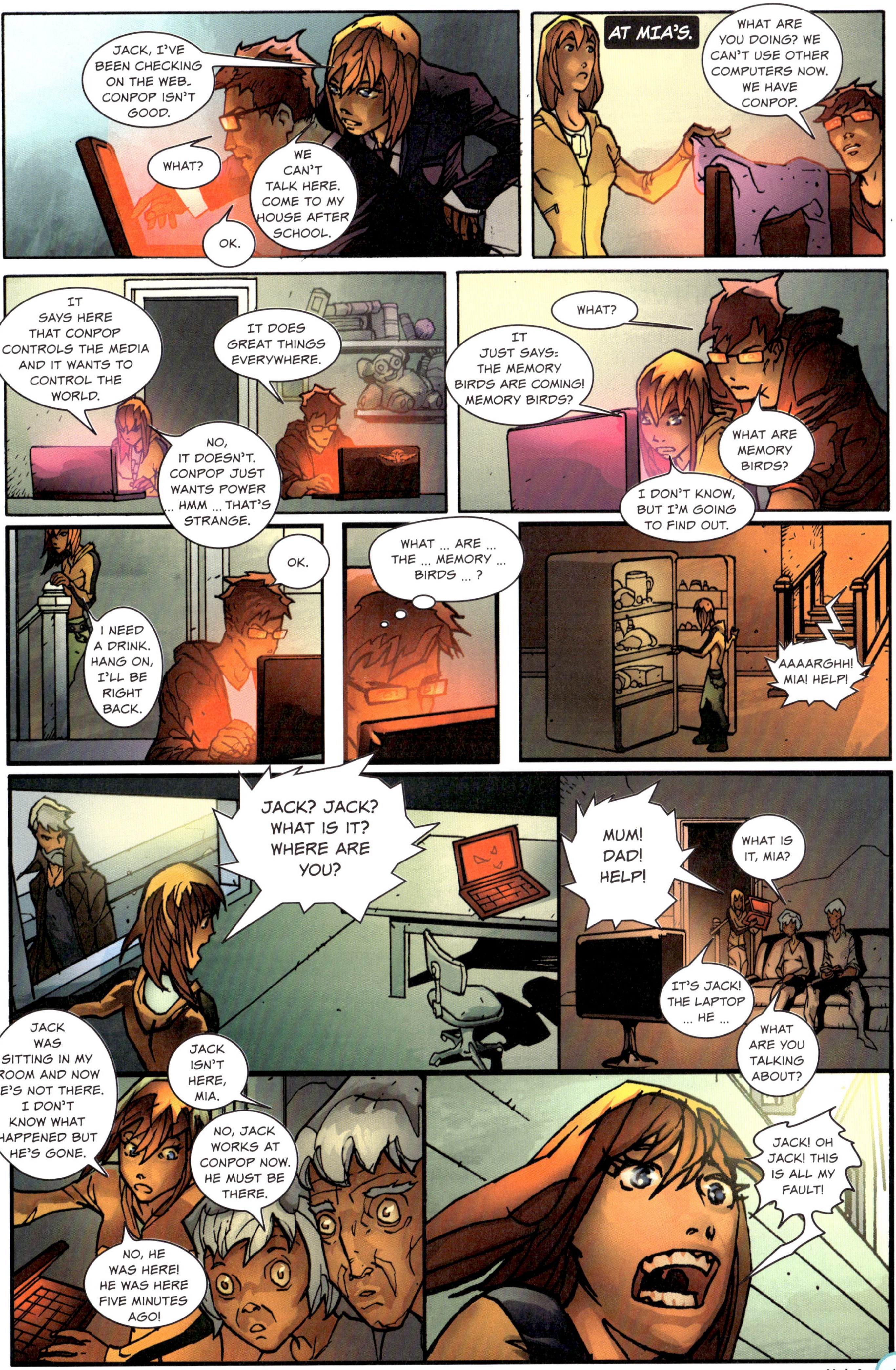
JACK, I'VE BEEN CHECKING ON THE WEB. CONPOP ISN'T GOOD.
WHAT?
WE CAN'T TALK HERE. COME TO MY HOUSE AFTER SCHOOL.
OK.
AT MIA'S.
WHAT ARE YOU DOING? WE CAN'T USE OTHER COMPUTERS NOW. WE HAVE CONPOP.
IT SAYS HERE THAT CONPOP CONTROLS THE MEDIA AND IT WANTS TO CONTROL THE WORLD.
IT DOES GREAT THINGS EVERYWHERE.
NO, IT DOESN'T. CONPOP JUST WANTS POWER ... HMM ... THAT'S STRANGE.
WHAT?
IT JUST SAYS: THE MEMORY BIRDS ARE COMING! MEMORY BIRDS?
WHAT ARE MEMORY BIRDS?
I DON'T KNOW, BUT I'M GOING TO FIND OUT.
I NEED A DRINK. HANG ON, I'LL BE RIGHT BACK.
OK.
WHAT ... ARE ... THE ... MEMORY ... BIRDS ... ?
AAAARGHH! MIA! HELP!
JACK? JACK? WHAT IS IT? WHERE ARE YOU?
MUM! DAD! HELP!
WHAT IS IT, MIA?
IT'S JACK! THE LAPTOP ... HE ...
WHAT ARE YOU TALKING ABOUT?
JACK WAS SITTING IN MY ROOM AND NOW HE'S NOT THERE. I DON'T KNOW WHAT HAPPENED BUT HE'S GONE.
JACK ISN'T HERE, MIA.
NO, JACK WORKS AT CONPOP NOW. HE MUST BE THERE.
NO, HE WAS HERE! HE WAS HERE FIVE MINUTES AGO!
JACK! OH JACK! THIS IS ALL MY FAULT!

2 All in a day's work

Past simple: regular and irregular verbs
used to
Vocabulary: Jobs; Verb/noun collocations
Interaction 2: Guessing a job

1 Vocabulary Jobs

a 1.11 Match the pictures with the words. Then listen and check.

A 5 firefighter

1 architect **2** dentist **3** engineer
4 factory worker **5** ~~firefighter~~ **6** hairdresser
7 journalist **8** nurse **9** plumber
10 police officer **11** taxi driver **12** waiter

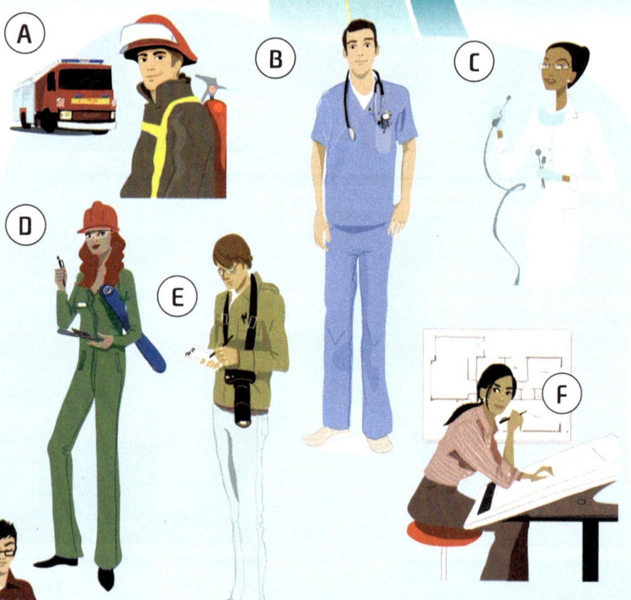

> **Get it right!**
>
> ***a journalist***
> use *a* with jobs.
> ✓ *She's a journalist.*
> ✗ *She's journalist.*

b 1.12 Listen and write the jobs.

c Do you know any more jobs? Write them in your Workbook (page 115 Exercise 1).

d Work with a partner. Which two jobs in Exercise 1a would you like to do? Which two jobs wouldn't you like to do? Why?

I'd like to be a journalist because they meet interesting people.

I wouldn't like to work as a firefighter because it's a dangerous job.

> **Check it out!**
>
> **be** + **a/an** + job = **work as** + **a/an** + job:
> *He's a photographer.* =
> *He **works as** a photographer.*

2 Pronunciation DVD

Silent consonants

a 1.13 Many words in English have silent letters. Listen to the words. The silent consonants are underlined.

arc**h**itect plum**b**er **w**riter firefi**gh**ter

b 1.14 Listen and write the words with a silent consonant.

dentist	answer	right
climb	leg	school
listen	knee	home
month	hour	talk

c 1.15 Listen, check your answers and repeat.

d 1.16 Listen and repeat.

The plumber and the architect talked for hours but didn't listen to each other's answers.

3 Listen

a 1.17 Listen to Alex, James and Natalie talk about work experience. Number the jobs in the pictures in the order you hear them.

b 1.17 Listen again. Write *A* (Alex), *J* (James) or *N* (Natalie).

1 A

1 He/she wore black trousers and a white shirt on work experience.
2 He/she thought work experience was very hard.
3 He/she answered the phone on work experience.
4 He/she thought parts of his/her work experience were boring.
5 He/she talked to children on work experience.
6 He/she thought every day of work experience was different.

c Work in a group. Ask and answer the questions.

1 Who do you think had the most interesting work experience? Why?
2 Is work experience a good idea? Why? / Why not?

4 Grammar

Past simple: regular and irregular verbs

a Look at the examples and complete the table with the correct form of the verbs *work* and *wear*.

__Did__ you __wear__ a uniform? *__Yes__, I __did__.*
What __did__ you __do__? *I __worked__ in a sports centre.*
I __wore__ different clothes for each place I worked in.
I __didn't like__ the swimming pool.

Positive	**Negative**
Regular verbs	**Regular verbs**
I/You/He/She/It/We/They … in a shop.	I/You/He/She/It/We/They … … in a shop.
Irregular verbs	**Irregular verbs**
I/You/He/She/It/We/They … a uniform.	I/You/He/She/It/We/They … … a uniform.

***Yes/No* questions**	**Short answers**
… I/you/he/she/it/we/they … in a shop?	Yes, I/you/he/she/it/we/they … .
… I/you/he/she/it/we/they … a uniform?	No, I/you/he/she/it/we/they … .

Information questions
Regular verbs Where … I/you/he/she/it/we/they … ?
Irregular verbs What … I/you/he/she/it/we/they … for work?

Choose the correct words to complete the rules.

- We use the past simple for past actions that are **finished** / **not finished**.
- We always add *-ed* to **regular** / **irregular** verbs in the positive form of the past simple.

Grammar reference: pages 132–133

Get it right!

I wore different clothes
We don't use *did* in positive sentences in the past simple.
✓ *I wore different clothes.*
✗ *I ~~did~~ wore different clothes.*

b Complete the sentences with the verbs in the past simple.

~~give~~ go not help start not tell watch

1 gave

1 They … her a new camera for her birthday.
2 I … work at 8 o'clock this morning.
3 My brother … me with my English homework.
4 … you … that programme last night?
5 Don't worry. She … me your secret.
6 Where … you … on holiday last year?

c Put the words in the correct order. Then work with a partner. Ask and answer the questions.

1 What did you buy last week?

1 did / What / you / buy / last week ?
2 last weekend / do / you / did / What ?
3 Who / you / yesterday / talk to / did ?
4 the last film you saw / was / What ?
5 What / when you were six / you / do / could ?

5 Vocabulary Verb/noun collocations

a 1.18 Match the verbs with the nouns to make six phrases. Then listen and check.

1 E answer a question

1 ~~answer~~	A work
2 help	B a photo
3 make	C a uniform
4 start	D a friend
5 take	E ~~a question~~
6 wear	F the bed

Get it right!

answer* and *help

✓ *Can you answer this question?*
✗ *Can you answer ~~to~~ this question?*
✓ *Always help a friend!*
✗ *Always help ~~to~~ a friend!*

b Complete the sentences with the verbs in Exercise 5a in the correct form.

1 My job is to … all the beds in the hotel.
2 I'm asking you a question. Can you … it please?
3 She's a nurse so she … a uniform every day.
4 Please … John with this computer programme. He doesn't understand it.
5 Enjoy your holiday. … lots of photos for me!
6 What time do you … work?

c Do you know any more nouns that go with the verbs in Exercise 5a? Make word webs for collocations you know. Do it in your Workbook (page 115 Exercise 4).

Check it out!

make	friends a phone call a mistake
do	my homework the shopping a sport
take	a photo

d Work with a partner. Ask and answer the questions.

1 Does anyone wear a uniform in your family? Why?
2 Who makes breakfast, lunch and dinner in your family?
3 Who helps you with your homework? Do you help anyone with their homework?
4 What clothes do you wear at the weekend?

6 Speak

a Work with a partner. Student A: Imagine you have a job.

Student B: Ask questions to find out Student A's job. You can only ask 20 questions and Student A can only answer *Yes* or *No*.

B *Is your job dangerous?*
A *Yes.*
B *Do you help people?*
A *Yes.*
B *Do you wear a uniform?*
A *Yes.*
B *Are you a police officer?*
A *No. That's four questions.*

b Now Student A ask questions and Student B answer.

c Tell the class how many questions you needed to ask to guess your partner's job.

7 Read and listen

a Read the text quickly and match the jobs in the box with paragraphs 1–4.

Chimney sweeps   Factory workers   Mudlarks   Mine workers

THE WORST JOBS IN HISTORY

When do you think you'll start your first job? When you are 16, 18, 22? A hundred and fifty years ago many children started work when they were 5 years old. But what did they use to do? Here are some of the terrible jobs they did.

1 ...
In the 19th century people in London used to throw rubbish into the River Thames. Mudlarks walked through the river and looked for useful things in the rubbish. Then they sold the things and bought food. The job was very dirty and freezing cold in winter.

2 ...
Factories and railways needed a lot of coal in the 19th century. Boys and girls worked in very dangerous conditions in coal mines and many died. In 1838 a lot of water flooded a mine and killed 26 young people, aged between 7 and 17. By the 1880s only boys over 12 could work in mines.

3 ...
Small boys or girls, between 5 and 10 years old, used to go up chimneys and clean them. Often the chimneys were very small so climbing up them was difficult. The children had lots of accidents and sometimes fell down the chimneys and died. When they grew too big they couldn't go up the chimneys and so they couldn't work.

4 ...
Many children and teenagers worked for sixteen hours a day in factories. They started work very early but a lot of poor families didn't use to have clocks. The workers often didn't know the time, but if they were late in the morning, they lost money. Children stood on their feet all day and this was very bad for their bones. Factories were very hot, often over 30°C, and many workers became ill.

Which is right? Don't look at the text!
Factories* / *Fabrics *and railways needed a lot of coal ...*

b 1.19 Read the text again and listen. Are the sentences *right* (✓), *wrong* (✗) or *doesn't say* (–)?

1 Cleaning chimneys was very dangerous.
2 Many adults worked as chimney sweeps.
3 Factory bosses took money from workers who arrived late.
4 Factory workers sometimes sat down to work.
5 The Thames was very clean.
6 Mudlarks made a lot of money from rubbish.
7 At the end of the 19th century, girls worked in coal mines.
8 Accidents in coal mines were unusual.

c Work in a group. Which job do you think was the worst? Why?

Culture Vulture

Did you know that the minimum age to work in the UK is 13? You can deliver newspapers or milk. When you are 15 you can work in a shop or restaurant for up to four hours a week. How old do you need to be to work in your country?

8 Grammar *used to*

a Look at the examples and complete the table with *did*, *didn't* and the verb *work*.

> *People in London **used to throw** rubbish into the River Thames.*
> *A lot of poor families **didn't use to have** clocks.*
> *But what did they **use to do**?*

Positive	**Negative**
I/You/He/She/It/We/They **used to** … in a factory.	I/You/He/She/It/We/They … **use to** … in a factory.

***Yes/No* questions**
Did I/you/he/she/it/we/they **use to** … in a factory?

Short answers
Yes, I/you/he/she/it/we/they **did**.
No, I/you/he/she/it/we/they … .

Information questions
Where … I/you/he/she/it/we/they **use to** … ?

Choose the correct words to complete the rules.

- We use *used to* for repeated actions and states in the **past** / **present**.
- The actions or states are **true** / **not true** now.

Grammar reference: page 133

Get it right!

I usually ride …

There is no present form of *used to*.
✓ *I usually ride my bike to school.*
✗ *I ~~use to~~ ride my bike to school.*

b Complete the sentences with *used to* and the correct verbs.

go have not have work

1. We … to the beach in the summer, but now we go to the mountains.
2. Before she became an actress, Jennifer Lopez … in an office.
3. In the 19th century children … many toys.
4. When you were a child, … a bike?

c Write five sentences about you. Use the ideas in the box and your own ideas.

I My brother My sister	used to didn't use to	play (with) have be like	in the park vegetables toy cars my older brother insects

d Work with a partner. Compare your sentences in Exercise 8c.

> *I used to play in the park. Did you?*
> *Yes, I did. I used to play with my sister.*

Interaction 2 DVD

Guessing a job

a 1.20 Listen to Kemi and Diana. What was Leona Lewis' job before she was famous?

b 1.20 Listen again and number the phrases in the order you hear them.

3, …

1. Did she sit down in her job?
2. Yes, that's right!
3. Did she use to wear special clothes for her job?
4. Do you want a clue?
5. Did she make something?
6. Did she work inside or outside?
7. No, that's not right. Try again.
8. Did she use to work with people?

c 1.21 Turn to page 124. Listen to the sentences and repeat them. Practise the pronunciation of *use(d) to* (/juːstə/) + verb.

d Work with a partner.

Student A: Turn to page 126.
Student B: Turn to page 129.

Portfolio 2

A blog

a Read Kate's blog. How did she feel in the morning, in the afternoon and after work?

b Find informal words or phrases in the blog and comments that mean:

1 cool

1. great *(one word)*
2. look at *(two words)*
3. yes *(one word)*
4. hate *(two words)*
5. very amusing *(two words)*
6. a lot of *(two words)*

c Write a blog about your day yesterday. Use informal language. Before you write, think about:

- what you did
- where you went
- who you saw / talked to
- how you felt

d Work in a group. Read other students' blogs and write comments on them.

Which is right? Don't look at the text!

I watched Simon ***cut her the hair*** */* ***cut her hair.***

You ***have*** */* ***are*** *so lucky.*

Kate's blog

File Edit View Insert Format Tools Actions Help

http://www.katesblog.co.uk

Last day of work experience!

Today was my last day at the hairdresser's. In the morning I helped this girl choose a new hairstyle and then I watched Simon (the boss) cut her hair. It looked really cool.

Simon's a brilliant hairdresser. He used to work for John Frieda before he opened his own salon. Check out his website for more cool hairstyles!

Boring!

This morning I thought 'Yeah, I really want to be a hairdresser when I leave school', but this afternoon was so boring that I'm not sure now. All I did was answer the phone and take messages (I don't want to be a secretary!) and I made over 30 cups of tea and coffee for customers (I can't stand tea or coffee!).

Pizza

Anyway, because it was my last day today, we all went for a pizza at Chicco's Italian restaurant to celebrate! I felt a bit sad but I'll be able to see my friends again. Listen to Simon telling his pizza joke to the waitress – very funny!

Can't believe I've got school again on Monday!

K8

Comments

24 May 18:02
You're so lucky – no exams or homework for a week. I can't wait to do my work experience next week.
Ben

24 May 20:27
All I did on my work experience was answer the phone and take messages for the whole week and it was really boring.
Liam

24 May 16:58
That's because you worked in an office Liam! Why didn't you choose a more interesting job?
Kate

25 May 21:15
OK so you answered the phone and made a few drinks! That's better than French and a Maths exam! And Miss Stevens gave us loads of Science homework yesterday morning! See you on Monday.
Sarah

A page in Ireland's history

A hard life

In the 18th and 19th centuries, most people in Ireland were very poor and often the whole family worked on the land to grow food. Large families used to live in very small houses and many people only had potatoes to eat.

In 1845 a terrible disease attacked the potato plants. For six years during 'The Great Potato Famine' there were no potatoes, so people had nothing to eat. About one million people died and many more people left Ireland to live in other countries like Canada, the USA and Australia.

Better times?

In the 1990s Ireland enjoyed a good quality of life. People from countries all over the world came to live and work in Ireland because the economy was very strong. Big companies like Microsoft, Apple and Google built new offices and there were lots of jobs for office workers, factory workers, waiters and builders. Ireland changed from one of the poorest countries in the world to one of the richest. But then, like many countries in the world, Ireland had economic problems and noone knows what the future will bring.

Sean O'Neill, 15 years old (1851)

'My family left Ireland for the USA on a big ship six months ago. Me, my parents and my six brothers and sisters lived in a small cabin for three months. We didn't have much food or water and my baby sister died before we got to New York.

Now we live in New York City, but life is still hard. My dad and I are builders and my mother and older sisters work in a factory.'

Ania Kowalski, 16 years old

'My family moved to Dublin, the capital of Ireland, from Poland three years ago. My dad worked as a builder, but then he started his own business. I love Ireland and I've got lots of Irish friends. I didn't use to speak good English, but now I'm bilingual in Polish and English!'

Traditional jobs in Ireland

The craftsman

In the past, most of the objects people used at home or to work on the land were made by craftsmen from local materials like wood, metal or glass.

Nowadays, tourists buy traditional Irish craft products, such as jewellery, glasses and jumpers as souvenirs.

The Irish dance master.

During the 18th century, the dance master was a dancing teacher who travelled from village to village. He used to wear bright clothes and taught traditional Irish dances to poor people.

Today, millions of people all over the world can enjoy traditional Irish dancing in shows like *Riverdance* and *Lord of the Dance*.

1 Culture World: Ireland

a Do the quiz about Ireland before you read the article. Choose the correct answer: A, B or C.

1 200 years ago, what was the most important food in Ireland?
- **A** bread
- **B** potatoes
- **C** fish

2 What is the capital of Ireland?
- **A** London
- **B** Belfast
- **C** Dublin

3 Which industry built offices in Ireland in the 1990s?
- **A** The computer industry
- **B** The car industry
- **C** The mobile phone industry

4 Which of these traditional gifts is Ireland famous for?
- **A** ceramics
- **B** clocks
- **C** jewellery

b Read the article quickly and check your answers.

c Read the article again and answer the questions.

1. How long was the Great Potato Famine?
2. How many people lived in Sean's room on the boat to America?
3. When were there lots of jobs for builders in Ireland?
4. What languages does Ania speak?
5. Which traditional crafts are popular today?
6. Who did the Irish dance master teach in the 18th century?

d Find words in the article that mean …

1. When people do not have any food for a long time.
2. A room on a boat.
3. Someone who speaks two languages perfectly.
4. Someone who is excellent at making things.

2 Your project

A traditional job from your country

a Work in a group. Make a list of traditional jobs in your country.

b Choose one job and make a table like in the example.

Name of job	Irish dance master
When the job was popular	In the 18th century
What he/she used to do	He taught poor people in villages how to dance traditional Irish dances.
Extra information	He used to wear bright clothes.
Today?	There are still Irish dance teachers today because Irish dancing is popular.

c Use the information in Exercise 2b to write about traditional jobs in your country. Illustrate the description with pictures.

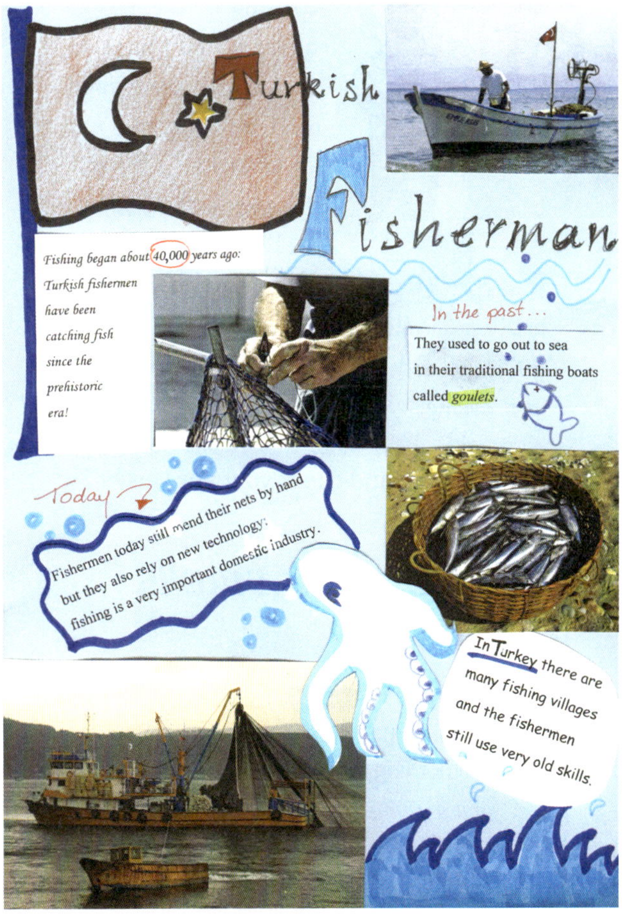

Get it right! 1 and 2

Common errors

1 Irregular verbs

Remember, not all verbs are regular in the past simple.

✓ *Harry didn't buy the toy car; it* ***cost*** *too much.* (✗ *… it ~~costed~~ too much.*)

✓ *I* ***gave*** *her a camera for her birthday.* (✗ *I ~~gived~~ her …*)

Learn the spelling of irregular verbs.

say – ✓ *said* ✗ *~~sayed~~*

can – ✓ *could* ✗ *~~coud~~*

Enjoy and *laugh* are regular.

enjoy – ✓ *enjoyed* ✗ *~~enjoied~~*

laugh – ✓ *laughed* ✗ *~~laughted~~*

a Emilio doesn't know his irregular verbs (on page 143). Correct his homework. Find nine mistakes.

Last Saturday, I buyed a new phone. I spended all my savings on it – it costed a lot of money! I taked it home to show my brother, but I coudn't find it – I losed it on the way home. My brother laughted at me and saied 'I hope you enjoied those five minutes with your new phone!'

b 1.22 Listen and check your answers.

2 That perfume smells horrible!

We use adjectives, not adverbs, to describe how something *tastes* or *smells*.

✓ *That perfume smells* ***horrible****.* (✗ *… smells ~~horribly~~.*)

✓ *He dances horribly.*

✓ *This coffee tastes too* ***sweet****.* (✗ *… too ~~sweetly~~.*)

✓ *She sings sweetly.*

Choose the correct option.

1 That soup tasted *deliciously* / *delicious*.
2 She always walks really *quickly* / *quick*.
3 Our dog needs a bath, he smells *terribly* / *terrible*!
4 They speak four languages *brilliantly* / *brilliant*.

3 *make* or *do*?

We use *make* with some expressions.

✓ *She* ***makes*** *friends easily.*

✓ *We* ***made*** *a mistake.* (✗ *… ~~did~~ a mistake.*)

We use *do* for some other expressions.

✓ *He* ***did*** *the shopping.* (✗ *… ~~made~~ the shopping.*)

✓ *I like to* ***do*** *sport.* (✗ *… ~~make~~ sport.*)

See *Check it out!* on page 14.

a Replace the underlined words with a phrase with *make* or *do*.

1 I love <u>playing football and basketball</u>.
2 My dad <u>buys the food</u> every Friday morning.
3 I <u>have met some new people</u> at my new school.
4 My sister <u>uses the phone</u> every five minutes!
5 He didn't <u>get</u> many <u>answers wrong</u> in the test.

b Work with a partner. Say a phrase from the box. Your partner makes a sentence with *make* or *do* + the phrase. Do it quickly!

the shopping · friends · a phone call · your bed · your English homework · a mistake

A: the shopping
B: I never do the shopping for my family.

4 Say it right!

/ɔː/

a 1.23 The sound /ɔː/ is common in the past simple form of many verbs. Listen and repeat these verbs in the past simple with the /ɔː/ sound.

1 bɔːt **2** brɔːt **3** cɔːt **4** fɔːt **5** thɔːt **6** tɔːt

b 1.23 Listen to the verbs in Exercise 4a again and complete them with the missing letters in your notebook. Then complete the rule.

The groups of letters … and … are pronounced /ɔː/ in past tenses.

Review 1 and 2

1 Grammar

a Complete the sentences with the verbs in the present simple or the present continuous.

listen love not play speak watch visit

1 Sophie always … to the radio.
2 They … a film right now.
3 Tim … tennis at school. There aren't any courts.
4 She … this CD. It's her favourite.
5 I … four languages.
6 We … our grandmother at the moment. [| 6]

b Match the questions with the answers. Then write the questions in the present simple or the present continuous.

1 Who / you / live / with?
2 What / he / do / now?
3 What / they / do / at the weekend?
4 Who / she / talk to?
5 Where / he / go / on holiday?

A Go out with their friends.
B To the USA. He goes every summer.
C My parents, my two brothers and my dog.
D He's playing on the computer.
E Her sister. She's on the train. [| 5]

c Complete the sentences with the verbs in the past simple.

1 They … (go) to the cinema yesterday.
2 She … (not walk), she got the bus.
3 He's tired today because he … (not sleep) well last night.
4 … she … (enjoy) the party?
5 I … (finish) that book yesterday. Do you want to read it? [| 5]

d Look at the information about Daisha and complete the sentences with *used to / didn't use to* and the information in the table.

	Ten years ago	Now
1 live	in the country ✓	in the city ✓
2 school/work	go to school ✓	work ✓
3 sport	basketball ✓	tennis ✓
4 languages	Spanish ✗	Spanish ✓

Ten years ago Daisha …
1 … , but now she lives in the city.
2 … , but now she works.
3 … , but now she plays tennis.
4 … , but now she does. [| 4]

2 Vocabulary

a Put the letters in the correct order and make words for parts of the body.

1 nihc
2 ekne
3 tehar
4 eto
5 rinab
6 tecsh
7 knsi
8 twisr
9 tmoahsc
10 torhat [| 10]

b Choose the correct words.

1 This drink *tastes / sees* of orange. It's lovely.
2 We can *smell / see* the mountains from our window.
3 Can you *taste / hear* the music?
4 That milk *sees / smells* bad. We can't drink it.
5 *Touch / Taste* the baby's skin. It feels really soft. [| 5]

c Find and write down seven more jobs in the puzzle.

F	D	T	T	A	P	A	W	R	T	P
I	E	E	H	Z	J	A	R	E	N	L
R	W	S	N	O	I	X	E	S	L	U
E	U	T	S	T	V	T	V	S	S	M
F	U	N	E	E	I	V	Z	E	V	B
I	T	R	E	T	I	S	C	R	K	E
G	C	P	C	Y	Q	D	T	D	T	R
H	K	R	W	W	E	N	U	R	S	E
T	J	O	U	R	N	A	L	I	S	T
E	T	R	E	T	I	H	U	A	A	W
R	E	E	N	I	G	N	E	H	E	H

[| 7]

d Match the two parts of the sentences.

1 We have to wear
2 My dad starts
3 My sister's a receptionist
4 I have to make
5 Could you

A so she answers the phone in a hotel.
B my bed every morning.
C a uniform for school.
D take a photo of us, please?
E work at 8 o' clock in the morning. [| 5]

3 What a hero!

Past continuous
Past simple and past continuous
Vocabulary: *-ed* and *-ing* adjectives; Ages and stages
Interaction 3: Putting pictures in order

1 Vocabulary

-ed and *-ing* adjectives

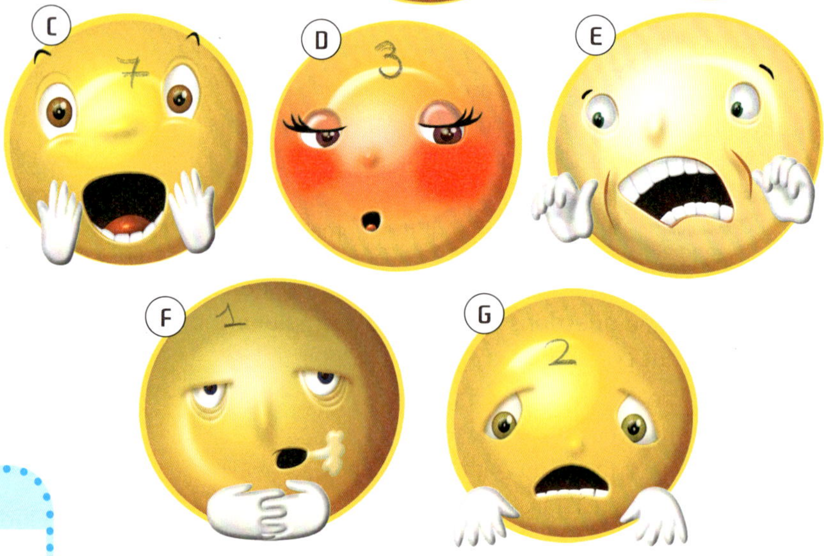

a 1.24 Match the adjectives with the pictures. Then listen and check.

A 6 interested

1 bored **2** disappointed
3 embarrassed **4** excited
5 frightened **6** ~~interested~~
7 surprised

> **Check it out!**
>
> - *-ed* adjectives describe feelings.
>   *He was bor**ed**.*
> - *-ing* adjectives describe the person or thing that causes the feeling.
>   *The game was bor**ing**.*

b Choose the correct adjectives.

1. The latest James Bond film is really *bored / boring*. I was *disappointed / disappointing*.
2. The fire was terrible but the firefighter wasn't *frightened / frightening*.
3. She read an *interested / interesting* story in the newspaper.
4. Harry didn't drive well in his driving test. He was *surprised / surprising* to pass.
5. Extreme sports like skydiving are dangerous, but *excited / exciting*.
6. Our teacher fell over in front of the whole class today. She was really *embarrassed / embarrassing!*

c Do you know any more *-ed* or *-ing* adjectives for emotions? Write them in your Workbook (page 116 Exercise 1).

d Work with a partner. Talk about:

1. a frightening film
2. an embarrassing situation
3. an interesting book
4. a disappointing present
5. an exciting day out

2 Pronunciation DVD

Intonation and emotions

a 1.25 Listen to two conversations between Milly and Ben. Who is … .

Conversation 1 … bored? … excited?
Conversation 2 … surprised? … frightened?

b 1.26 Listen to the sentences and choose the emotion.

1. I just got my exam results! *excited / frightened*
2. Oh, really. *interested / bored*
3. It's that dog again. *surprised / disappointed*
4. Can you hear that noise? *frightened / excited*
5. Hi, how was your holiday? *embarrassed / interested*
6. Oh, thank you. That's lovely. *excited / disappointed*
7. Um, I think I've lost your DVD. *embarrassed / bored*

c 1.26 Listen again and repeat.

d Work with a partner. Take it in turns to say the sentences in Exercise 2b in different ways. Can your partner guess the emotion?

excited disappointed bored interested
surprised embarrassed frightened

Oh, really.

Frightened?

Yes. OK, your turn.

3 Read and listen

a Read the text quickly. How many years were there between the two important events in the text?

Teen saves life of woman who saved him

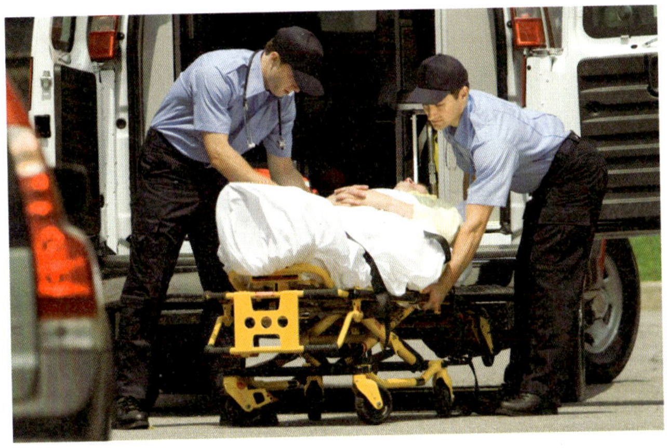

In an amazing coincidence, a New York State teenager saved the life of a woman and then discovered that she saved his life when he was a child.

Six and a half years ago, Kevin Stephan, then aged 11, was playing baseball when a player accidentally hit him with a bat. Kevin fell down and his heart stopped. Penny Brown, the mother of another player, was watching the game. Penny usually worked in the evenings as a nurse, but luckily that evening she wasn't working. Penny ran to help Kevin and saved his life.

Nearly seven years later, Kevin was washing up in the kitchen of the Hillview Restaurant in Buffalo, New York State. Normally, 17-year-old Kevin had school in the afternoon, but that week there were exams and he didn't have any classes. At about 2pm, Penny Brown was having lunch with her family in the restaurant. She was eating when some food got stuck in her throat. She was very frightened because she couldn't breathe.

Kevin was a volunteer firefighter in his free time and he ran to help. A waitress tried to help her, but the food was still stuck in Penny's throat. Kevin pulled his hands quickly into her stomach and saved Penny's life. He didn't know it was Penny, but his mother, Lorraine Stephan, was also having lunch in the restaurant. She realised that Penny was the woman who saved Kevin's life, seven years before, at the baseball game. Both Penny and Kevin were completely amazed by the coincidence!

The director of the American Red Cross in Buffalo said this story shows the importance of learning first aid. After only four hours of training, Kevin was able to save Penny's life.

First aid: how to save a life

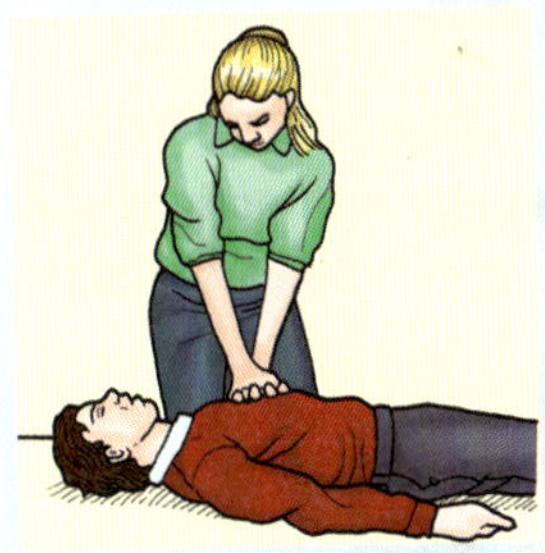

when someone's heart stops, push down on their chest.

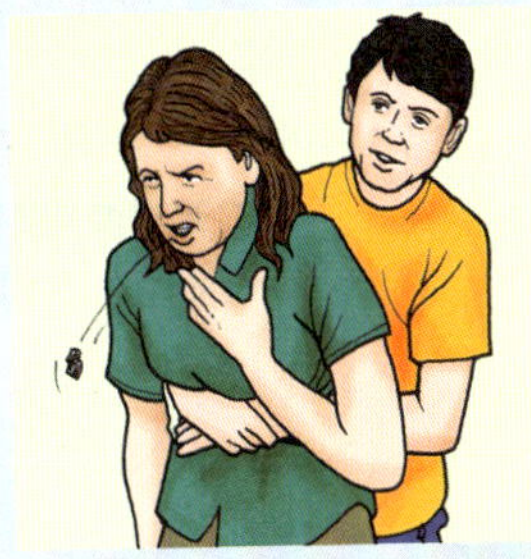

when food is stuck in someone's throat, pull back quickly with your hands into their stomach.

Which is right? Don't look at the text!
In an amazing ***casualty*** */* ***coincidence****, she saved his life.*

b 1.27 Read the text again and listen. Choose the correct answer: A, B or C.

1 During the baseball game …
 A Kevin's heart stopped.
 B Penny fell down.
 C Kevin hit someone.

2 Penny was at the game because …
 A her son was playing baseball.
 B she liked baseball.
 C she was working as a nurse.

3 When Kevin was 17 he usually … in the afternoon.
 A worked in a restaurant.
 B studied at school.
 C worked as a firefighter.

4 Penny couldn't breathe because …
 A she was frightened.
 B some food was in her throat.
 C her heart stopped.

c Work with a partner. Answer the questions.

1 Do you know any stories about lucky people?
2 Do you know any stories about real or fictional heroes?
3 What did they do? Why do you think they are heroes?

Culture Vulture

Did you know that the Red Cross and the Red Crescent are voluntary organisations? Volunteers work for them, for no money. They help people in countries all over the world. Do they, or similar groups, work in your country? Would you like to work as a volunteer? Why? / Why not?

4 Grammar

Past continuous

a Look at the examples and complete the table with the verb *play*.

> *Kevin Stephan, aged 11,* ***was playing*** *baseball.*
> ***Were*** *they* ***having*** *lunch? Yes, they* ***were****.*
> *Luckily that evening she* ***wasn't working****.*

Positive			**Negative**		
I/He/She/It	… …	baseball.	I/He/She/It	… …	baseball.
You/We/They	**were playing**		You/We/They	**weren't** …	

***Yes/No* questions**		**Short answers**
Was I/he/she/it **playing**	baseball?	Yes, I/he/she/it **was**. / No, I/he/she/it … .
… you/we/they …		Yes, you/we/they … . / No, you/we/they **weren't**.

Information questions

What … I/he/she/it … ?
What … you/we/they … ?

Choose the correct words to complete the rules.

- We use the past continuous for **actions in progress** / **completed actions** at a certain time in the past.
- We use the past simple for **completed actions** / **uncompleted actions** in the past.

Grammar reference: page 133

Check it out!

- Most verbs + *-ing*: help → help**ing**
- Verbs ending in ***-e***: move → mov**ing**
- Short verbs ending in a vowel + a consonant, double the consonant + *-ing*: ru**n** → run**ning**

b Complete the sentences with the correct verbs in the past continuous.

do   not listen   paint   ~~shine~~   watch   not work

1 was shining

1 It was a beautiful day and the sun … was shining
2 Sorry, could you repeat that? I … wasn't listen
3 A: … Ben … TV at your house last night?
B: Yes, he was. was, watching
4 My parents … the kitchen all day yesterday. were, painting
5 They … today. They were at a football match. weren't working
6 What … you … at school yesterday at eight o'clock? were, doing

c Work with a partner. Ask and answer questions about the times.

at 4pm yesterday   at 9pm last night
at 5am this morning   last Sunday at 2pm
at 11am on Saturday

> A: *What were you doing at 9pm last night?*
> B: *I was playing the guitar. And you?*

Get it right!

last night

✓ *at 6pm yesterday evening*
✓ *at 9pm last night* (✗ *at 9pm ~~yesterday night~~*)

5 Speak

a You are going to role play an interview between a journalist and Kevin Stephan from Exercise 3a the day after he saved Penny Brown's life.

Student A: You are a journalist. Make questions in the past simple or past continuous. Use *you*, the words in the box and your own ideas.

What How Where When Who	happen feel do see be talk to	yesterday? in the restaurant?

> *What were you doing yesterday? How did you feel?*

Student B: Turn to page 125.

b Student A: Interview Student B. Tell the class about any interesting questions or answers from the interview.

6 Vocabulary

Ages and stages

a 1.28 Match the words with the pictures. Then listen and check.

6 C toddler

1 baby **2** child **3** elderly
4 middle-aged **5** teenager
6 ~~toddler~~

A

B

E

F

C
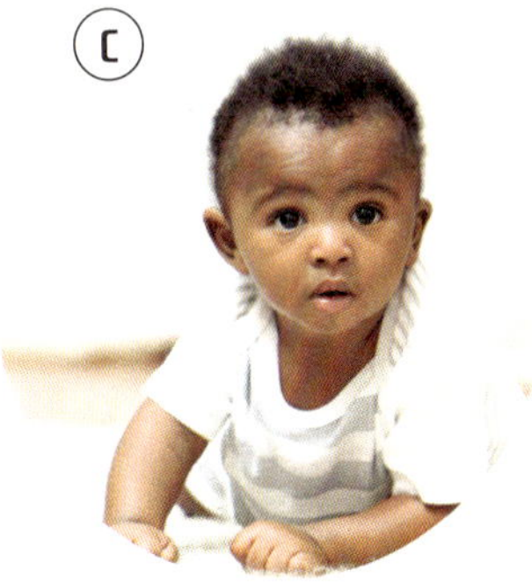
D

b Complete the definitions. Use the words from Exercise 6a.

1 child

1. You are a … from the time you are born until you are 18 years old.
2. When babies start to walk and talk they are … .
3. … people are in their 70s, 80s or 90s, etc.
4. A … is a very young child who can't walk or talk.
5. … people are in their 40s or 50s.
6. Between the ages of 13 and 19 you are a … .

Check it out!

To talk about ages, we use:
- in your **early** twenties (20–23)
- in your **mid**-thirties (34–36)
- in your **late** forties (47–49)

c Work in a group. In your country when do people usually …

start school? learn to drive?
leave home? vote in elections?
get their first job? get married?
retire?

In my country, people usually learn to drive in their late teens or early twenties.

7 Listen

a Which of these animals can attack people?

b 1.29 Listen to the story. Which animal in Exercise 7a is it about?

c 1.29 Listen again. Are the sentences *right* (✓) or *wrong* (✗)? Correct the wrong sentences.

1. The family lived in Australia.
2. The animal attacked the children.
3. Mike put his fingers in the animal's ears.
4. Mike was surprised when the animal left.
5. Juliet didn't go to hospital.

d Work with a partner. Answer the questions.

1. How did you feel when you listened to the story?
2. How would you describe Mike?
3. How do you think you would feel if you saw a crocodile?
4. How would you describe the other animals in Exercise 7a?

8 Grammar

Past simple and past continuous

a Look at the example and the timeline. Then choose the correct words to complete the rules.

Juliet ***was sitting*** *next to the river when a crocodile* ***came out*** *of the water.*

When we use the past simple and past continuous together:

- we use the past simple for **longer/shorter** actions.
- we use the past continuous for **longer/shorter** actions.
- the **past simple / past continuous** action often interrupts the **past simple / past continuous** action.

Grammar reference: pages 133–134

Check it out!

When **+ past simple:**
I was doing my homework ***when*** *my friends* ***rang****.*
While **+ past continuous:**
While I was doing *my homework, my friend rang.*

b Complete the sentences with the verbs in the past simple or the past continuous.

1 While the family … (walk) in the forest, they … (see) a snake.
2 We … (have) a rest when my phone … (ring).
3 The dog … (jump) in the water while we … (swim).
4 When the baby … (wake up), they … (have) lunch.

c Complete the text with the verbs in the past simple or the past continuous.

1 was eating

Debbie Parkhurst's dog, Toby, saved her life. Debbie [1]… (eat) an apple at her home on Friday when a piece of apple [2]… (get) stuck in her throat. She [3]… (try) to remove it herself but it [4]… (not work). While she [5]… (hit) herself on the chest, Toby [6]… (see) what was happening. He [7]… (push) her to the ground and [8]… (jump) up and down on her. The piece of apple [9]… (come out) and Debbie is now fine.

Interaction 3 DVD

Putting pictures in order

a 1.30 Look at two pictures from a story. What's happening? Listen and check.

D

H

b 1.30 Listen again and match the questions and responses.

1 Which picture do you think is first/next/last?
2 What's in picture D?
3 Is there a … in your picture(s)?
4 Do you think that's right?

A Yes, I do. / No, I don't because …
B Yes, there is. / No, there isn't.
C I think the beginning / next part / end of the story is picture D (because) …
D There's a …

c 1.31 Turn to page 124. Listen to the sentences and repeat them. Practise linking the words.

d Work with a partner:
Student A: Turn to page 126.
Student B: Turn to page 129.

Portfolio 3

A story

a What are the boys doing in the photo? What do you think the story is about? Read the story and check your ideas.

b Read the text again and match paragraphs 1–4 with the parts of a story.

the problem
the conclusion
the introduction
the solution

Mike Bloom, Joe Bloom and Sam Wilmot

Teenagers save family

1 This is a true story about three teenage heroes. Very late one summer night, Sam and Joe, both 17, and Joe's brother Mike, 16, were chatting when suddenly they saw something strange. The sky was very orange and at first, the boys thought it was the sun coming up. They were very surprised when they realised that it was a fire nearly a kilometre away.

2 The fire was at a farm outside their village and the teenagers decided to go and help. While they were running to the farm the boys rang the fire service. When they arrived, they knocked on the farmhouse door, but no one inside the house heard them because they were all sleeping.

3 The boys decided to make lots of noise to wake up the family. First, they set free the frightened sheepdog, and then they broke a window. Finally, Mr Jackson, the farmer, heard the noise and he woke up his wife and two teenage daughters. The whole farm was on fire, but luckily the family escaped.

4 Thirty-five firefighters came to put out the fire, but unfortunately it was too late to save the farm. However, Mr Jackson saved the family's three pet ducks, called Earth, Wind and FIRE!

Do you know a local hero? Call our metro desk and tell us all about them.

Which is right? Don't look at the text!
It was a fire ***nearly a kilometre away / at nearly a kilometre.***

c We use different time expressions to tell us when important things happen in a story. Read the story again and write all the expressions that help the story.

Very late one summer night
Suddenly …

d Write a story about a hero. Invent the story or write a true story (e.g. Mike and the crocodile). Use:

- the story structure in Exercise b
- time expressions
- the past simple and the past continuous
- adjectives to describe emotions

THE PLACE

Where we ride, where we love

ON THE TIP OF THE LLYN PENINSULA IN NORTH WALES, ABERSOCH IS A CHOICE SPOT FOR SURFERS, SAILORS AND WAKEBOARDERS ALIKE.

LEARN TO WAKEBOARD

Wakeboarding is one of the fastest growing sports in the world. It is very popular with youngsters as skills transfer easily from other board sports such as skateboarding or snowboarding, and you can learn the basics quickly.

At OFFAXIS our professional riders will help you find your legs and build your confidence. You'll find the atmosphere relaxed, and our instructors encouraging and inspiring. Please beware: wakeboarding is highly addictive and will change your life!

PRICES: COACHING

All OFFAXIS coaching Sessions (wakeboard / water-ski / surfing) start at £30 per person per lesson and include all necessary equipment; e.g. board/skis, wetsuit, lifejacket etc.

Wakeboard and Water ski options

GROUP SETS

Groups of four people can share a 2 hour session. During the session, each person has a 15 minute set of one-on-one coaching session in the water. Contact the OFFAXIS shop 01758713407 to book a group session.

PRIVATE FRIENDS/FAMILY SET

You can also book all four sessions for just your friends / family. This provides more flexibility in terms of your time on the water. A maximum of four people per session is permitted.

For all coaching sessions, advance booking is essential, and a non-refundable deposit is also required.

The longest station name in the UK!

Hero saves man from drowning at Rhyl after spotting mobile phone flash

by Hywel Trewyn, Daily Post

Durell Faulkner

A HERO dived into the sea to rescue a drowning man after spotting the light of his mobile phone flashing on a beach at night.

Durell Faulkner swam out to the man, and dragged him to shore at Splash Point, Rhyl.

The 25-year-old said he had seen the light on a mobile phone the man had left on the beach, which was flashing because it had an incoming call.

Last night Durell's actions were praised by North Wales Police, who have recommended him for an award. Inspector Steve Williams said: "We would like to thank Durell for his bravery. His quick-thinking saved this man's life.

The modest rescuer said: "He was lucky. Anyone would have done the same thing."

The man was taken by ambulance to hospital, where he was treated for mild hypothermia.

Beddgelert Village, Snowdonia
The legend of Gelert

Beddgelert was the site of a palace of Prince Llewelyn in the thirteenth century. One day he went hunting without his faithful dog, Gelert, who stayed at the palace.

When Prince Llewelyn returned his dog came to meet him, covered in blood. The prince ran to the room of his baby son, and saw the infant's bed was empty and the floor was covered with blood.

The prince killed the dog with his sword because he thought it had killed his child. However, as he was doing so, he heard a baby's cry. He searched the palace and found his son unharmed. Next to the baby was the body of a huge wolf which the dog Gelert had fought to protect the Prince's baby.

Gelert's body was buried with a beautiful stone as a memorial to the brave animal. Nowadays, visitors come from all over the country to visit the dog's grave.

The pop star Duffy grew up in the village of Nefyn in north Wales. Her first language is Welsh: people in the village didn't speak English very much.

1 Culture UK: North Wales

a Look at the information about North Wales and answer the questions.

1. How many letters are in the longest place name in Britain?
2. Who was looking after a baby while the Prince went hunting?
3. What's the name of a seaside town popular with surfers and wakeboarders?
4. Why did Durell Faulkner notice a mobile phone on the beach at Rhyl?
5. What's the name of Duffy's first album?
6. Do you need your own equipment for an OFFAXIS coaching session?
7. How can you win a prize on 30th/31st October or 1st November?
8. What's the name for the part of North Wales which includes Beddgelert and Ffestiniog?

b Copy and complete the puzzle and find the mystery word.

1. A first performance or film, album, etc
2. A teacher (usually of a special skill)
3. Rails that trains run on
4. Noticing or seeing somebody or something
5. A type of wild animal similar to a dog
6. A festival on the 31st October

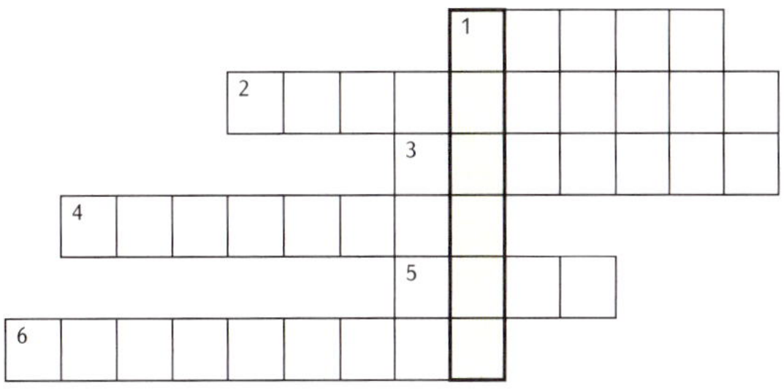

c Work with a partner. What would you most like to do in North Wales?

2 Your project

A historical hero

a Work in a group. Think of a historical hero or heroine from your country. It could be a person (e.g. Robin Hood) or an animal (e.g. Gelert). Make notes about:

- Where he/she it was from
- When he/she/it lived
- Who he/she/it was
- What he/she/it did
- Why he/she/it is still important

b Write about your hero/heroine. Illustrate the description with pictures.

4 Memorable meals

Comparative and superlative adjectives
Modifiers
Vocabulary: Adjectives; Eating out
Interaction 4: In a restaurant

1 Read and listen

a Look at the pictures. Read the text quickly and match paragraphs 1–4 with the pictures (A–D).

The weirdest restaurants in the world

1 Al Mahara, Dubai
The Al Mahara is one of the most amazing restaurants in the world. You take a submarine ride from the reception to your table. The dining room is inside a giant aquarium so you can see tropical fish swimming past you as you enjoy your delicious meal. The menu is mainly fish dishes but it is a lot more expensive than a normal fish and chips dinner!

2 Coolbaby Pet, Beijing
This has to be one of the craziest restaurants on the planet. It is the first restaurant in the world where pets are the main customers! Your dog, cat, hamster or even your rabbit can sit at your table and enjoy a meal with you. All the dishes for animals are specially designed to be a lot tastier than normal pet food. Their food will be as delicious as yours!

3 Dans le Noir, Paris
Dans le Noir (In the dark) restaurant in Paris is one of the weirdest eating experiences in the world. All the waiters and waitresses are blind and you eat in total darkness. Your meal is more memorable if you eat in the dark as your senses of smell and taste are more sensitive. However, it is a bit more difficult to remember what you eat when you can't see it, as our memories are 83% visual!

4 Duvet Restaurant, New York
Do you like eating in bed? In the Duvet Restaurant in New York you can relax and enjoy your meal in one of their thirty luxurious beds. The beds are bigger than normal and it is more comfortable than sitting at a table. It's also one of the trendiest restaurants in the 'Big Apple', so make a reservation today!

Which is right? Don't look at the text!
Your senses of smell and taste are more ***sensitive / sensible****.*

A

B

C

D

b 2.1 Read the text again and listen. Which restaurant would the people A–D like the most?

A My ideal morning is to have breakfast in bed.
B I want to work with blind people in the future.
C I want to be a vet when I leave school. I love all animals.
D I've got a fish tank of tropical fish. Fish is my favourite food too.

c Work with a partner. Which restaurant would you most like to go to? Why?

2 Vocabulary Adjectives

a 2.2 Match the adjectives with the definitions. Then listen and check.

1 H weird

1 a bit different and strange	**A** amazing
2 really tasty	**B** crazy
3 extravagant and expensive	**C** delicious
4 really different and strange	**D** disgusting
5 very fashionable	**E** luxurious
6 tastes horrible	**F** memorable
7 something you don't forget	**G** trendy
8 incredible and fantastic	**H** ~~weird~~

b Choose the correct words.

1 weird

1 My brother likes playing with spiders. He's *tasty / weird*!
2 The clothes in *Vogue* magazine are always so *trendy / disgusting*.
3 My friend bought a silk dress to wear to a party. It's so *luxurious / crazy*.
4 Have you seen that *amazing / delicious* film set in the Amazon jungle?
5 I had a *delicious / disgusting* sandwich for lunch yesterday. It had an insect in it! Yuck.
6 My grandmother always says her wedding was the most *memorable / trendy* day of her life.

c Work with a partner. Decide on one thing you can describe with each adjective from Exercise 2a. Make sentences.

My sister's new laptop is amazing.

Chocolate ice cream is delicious.

3 Grammar Comparative and superlative adjectives

a Look at the examples and complete the table.

It is one of ***the weirdest*** *eating experiences in the world. Your meal is* ***more memorable*** *if you eat in the dark.*
This has to be one of ***the craziest*** *restaurants on the planet. The beds are* ***bigger*** *than normal.*

Regular adjectives		**Comparative**	**Superlative**
1 syllable	weird	weirder	the weird…
2 or more syllables	memorable	… memorable	the … memorable
ending in -*y*	crazy	crazier	the craz…
ending in a consonant	big	bigg…	… biggest
Irregular adjectives	bad	worse	the worst

Choose the correct words to complete the rules.

- To make a comparative adjective of two or more syllables we add **more / most** before the adjective.
- To make a superlative adjective we often add **the / than** before the adjectives.

Grammar reference: page 134

b Complete the sentences. Use the comparative or superlative form.

1 the weirdest

1 That was … (weird) film ever! I didn't understand it at all.
2 You're … (good) me at cooking. You're quite a good cook and I'm terrible.
3 The cheese pizza is … (tasty) the ham one.
4 He's … (interesting) person I've ever met.
5 My cousin is very small for her age. My aunt says she's … (small) student in her class.

Get it right!

than

We use *than* in comparative sentences.

✓ *My sister is taller than me.*

✗ *My sister is taller ~~that~~ me.*

c Work with a partner. Ask and answer the questions.

1 What's the worst film you've seen recently?
2 Who's the best actor in the world?
3 What's the tastiest thing you've eaten today?
4 Which is the coolest computer game at the moment?
5 What's the most delicious meal you've had this week?

4 Pronunciation Word stress DVD

a 2.3 The stress in adjectives is often strong. Listen to the sentence.

This is the most *delicious* cake in the world!

b 2.4 Copy the adjectives. Then listen to the sentences and underline the stressed syllables in them.

1 coolest

1 That's the *coolest* jacket.
2 I think Geography is much more *interesting* than Chemistry.
3 His brother is the *craziest* person in our school.
4 That soup is the most *disgusting* thing ever!
5 She's got the *weirdest* hairstyle.
6 What's the most *difficult* subject for you at school?

c 2.4 Listen, check your answers and repeat.

d 2.5 Listen and repeat. She's the weirdest, craziest, coolest, most interesting person I know!

5 Listen

a 2.6 Listen to three teenagers on a radio phone-in programme. Number the meals in the order you hear them.

A

B

C

b 2.6 Listen again. Are the sentences *right* (✓) or *wrong* (✗)? Correct the wrong sentences.

1 Jazzy met a famous singer while she was having her most memorable meal.
2 Chloe's most memorable meal was at a restaurant.
3 For Michael and Jazzy, the people they shared the meals with were much more important than the food.
4 Chloe didn't enjoy her birthday meal.
5 Michael's most memorable meal was fast food.

c Which meal would you prefer? Why?

d Work with a partner. Take it in turns to describe your most memorable meal.

Culture Vulture

Did you know that people in the UK love eating food from other countries? Indian, Thai, Italian and Chinese food are all very popular. Do you like food from other countries? Which international cuisines are popular in your country? Why do you think they are popular?

6 Speak

a Work with a partner. Use the language to talk about your favourite things.

b Tell the class two things about your partner.

7 Grammar Modifiers

a Look at the examples and choose the correct words to complete the rules.

*It was **a bit** colder than the day before.*
*It was **much** more expensive than the restaurants I usually go to.*
*It was **a lot** better than any duck I've had before.*

- *Much* and *a lot* express a **big** / **small** difference between two things.
- *A bit* expresses a **big** / **small** difference between two things.

Grammar reference: page 134

b Read the sentences. Choose the correct answer: A, B or C.

1 The Italian restaurant is a lot ...... than the French café.
A expensive B very expensive C more expensive

2 The new disco in the centre of town is ...... than the old one.
A much trendier B trendy C the trendiest

3 For me, cooking is a lot ...... than learning English.
A most difficult B more difficult C bit difficult

4 It's only ...... more expensive but it's much better quality.
A a bit B much C very

5 The new sofa is a lot ...... than our old sofa.
A more comfortable B the most comfortable
C most comfortable

Check it out!

- ***Much*** + comparative = ***a lot*** + comparative
*He's **much** better than me.* *He's **a lot** better than me.*

Get it right!

... in the world
Remember:
✓ *He's the best-looking actor in the world.*
✗ *He's the best-looking actor ~~of~~ the world.*

c Look at the picture and put the words in the correct order.

1 taller / woman / the / is / a / the / than / man / lot
2 bit /than / his / is / a / smaller / pizza / hers
3 than / a / bit / him / she / older / is
4 her / a / delicious / food / is / lot / than / more / food / his
5 is / than / his / hers / longer / hair / much

8 Vocabulary Eating out

a 2.7 Match the words with the definitions. Then listen and check.

1 D glass

1 you drink from this
2 the knife, fork and spoon you eat with
3 a piece of paper that tells you how much your meal costs
4 you eat off this
5 paper or material to clean your mouth
6 a starter, main course or dessert
7 you cover a dining table with this

A bill 3
B course 6
C cutlery 2
~~**D** glass~~ 1
E napkin 5
F plate 4
G tablecloth 7

b Complete the table with the words in Exercise 8a. Do it in your Workbook (page 117 Exercise 3).

Courses	Things on the table
course	*cutlery*

c Do you know any more words for eating out? Write them in your Workbook (page 117 Exercise 4).

d Work with a partner. Ask and answer the questions.

1 Do you like eating in restaurants? Why? / Why not?
2 How many courses do you usually eat in a meal?
3 What is your favourite course in a meal? Why?

Check it out!

- Some food words are different in the UK and the USA.

UK	starter	bill	chips
USA	entrée	check	fries

Interaction 4 DVD

In a restaurant

a 2.8 Listen to the conversation. Choose the correct picture for each problem: A, B or C.

Problem 1

A
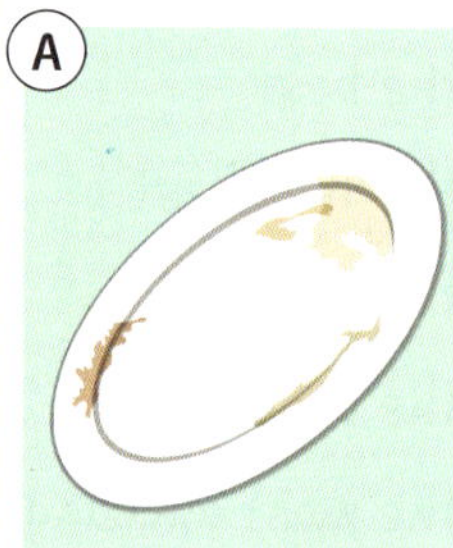
B
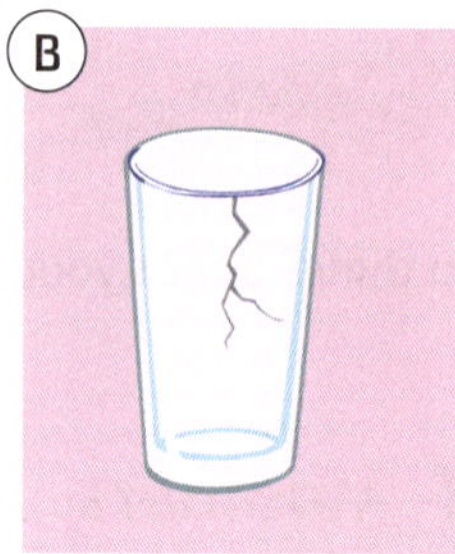
C

Problem 2

A

B

C

b 2.8 Listen to the conversation again. Who says the phrases, the customer (*C*) or the waitress (*W*)?

1 C

1 This glass is dirty.
2 I'll change it immediately.
3 Are you ready to order?
4 Enjoy your meal!
5 Excuse me, but I haven't got a fork.
6 Anything else?
7 Could we have the bill, please?

c 2.9 Turn to page 124. Listen to the sentences and repeat them. Practise the sentence stress and rhythm.

d Work with a partner.

Student A: Turn to page 126.
Student B: Turn to page 129.

Portfolio 4 Planning an ideal restaurant

a Look at the webpage and answer the questions.

1 What do you have to do to enter the competition?
2 What is the prize?
3 What do you think about Sam's entry from last year's competition?

Fab Mag

File Edit View Insert Format Tools Actions Help

http://www.fabmag.co.uk/competitions/ideal_restaurant

Win a two-week trip to the UK's coolest eating places by designing your ideal restaurant!

Last year Sam McCormick won the competition! Here's his entry for a restaurant called 'Cyberfun and Food'.

1 This is my ideal restaurant. It's called 'Cyberfun and Food' and it's a very special restaurant because you can play computer games and eat tasty food at the same time! It's a paradise for gamers.

2 The restaurant is divided into three zones. In one zone there are comfortable chairs so you can play games and have a snack. This area is perfect if you are on your own. You can choose a game to play, or you can read a computer magazine. All the snacks are easy to eat with your fingers so you don't miss a minute of gaming while you eat! The second zone has a table with computer screens on it! Here you can play games with your friends and enjoy a meal at the same time. The third area is a technology-free zone where you can talk to your friends and spend time thinking about real life!

3 The waiters and waitresses dress as characters from computer games and the big screen on the wall shows previews of new games that are going to appear in the shops soon. It's my ideal restaurant because I love gaming!

All entries must include:

- **a picture of the restaurant**
- **a description of the restaurant**

Here's a photo of Sam enjoying his trip to the UK last summer! This year, it could be you! Send your entries to:

idealrestaurantcomp@fabmag.co.uk

Which is right? Don't look at the text!

*You can talk to your friends and **spend** / **pass** time thinking about real life.*

b Which paragraphs on the webpage give us this information?

a why it's Sam's ideal restaurant
b the design of the restaurant
c the name and the general idea behind the restaurant

c Plan your own ideal restaurant. Draw and label the plan of the restaurant and write a description in three paragraphs.

Afternoon Tea

1 Song

a What do you know about afternoon tea in the UK? When do people have it? What do they eat and drink?

b 2.10 Listen to the first verse of the song. How does the singer feel?

1 He's happy because he's about to meet Donna for tea.
2 He's sad because he doesn't meet Donna any more for tea.
3 He's angry because Donna didn't come for tea today.

c 2.10 Listen to the first verse of the song again. Match the words in the two columns.

1 tea	**A** café
2 afternoon	**B** awake
3 small	**C** day
4 lie	**D** time
5 each	**E** tea

d 2.11 Listen to the whole song and put the lyrics in the correct order.

A 2

A
That's where we used to meet each day
And then we used to sit a while
And drink our afternoon tea

B
I take sugar with tea (afternoon tea)
You take milk if you please (afternoon tea)
Like you talking to me Because you ease my mind

C
They said that Donna walked away
You'd think at least she might have stayed
To drink her afternoon tea

D
Tea time won't be the same without my Donna
At night I lie awake and dream of Donna
I think about that small café

E
I take afternoon tea (afternoon tea)
Every day of the week (afternoon tea)
Please come along if you like Because I like you, girl

F
Tea time still ain't the same without my Donna
At night I lie awake and dream of Donna
I went to our café one day

G
I'll take afternoon tea (afternoon tea)
If you take it with me (afternoon tea)
You take as long as you like 'Cause I like you, girl

e Work in small groups. Ask and answer the questions.

1 Do people meet in your country for afternoon tea? Why / Why not?
2 Do you ever meet people to have a drink or a snack together?
3 Where do you usually meet and what do you have?

2 Sound check

a 2.12 Listen to the first line of the song and choose the correct number of syllables.

10 11 12

b 2.13 Listen to the rest of the first verse and write the correct number of syllables for each line.

1 At night I lie awake and dream of Donna
2 I think about that small café
3 That's where we used to meet each day
4 And then we used to sit a while
5 And drink our afternoon tea

c 2.13 Listen again and repeat.

3 Musical notes

a 2.14 Listen to the types of British music. Match the music (1–4) with the styles.

punk Britpop
rock folk

b Do you know any other types of famous British music? What types of music is your country famous for?

Punk

Folk

THE KINKS

The Kinks were an English rock band which formed in London in 1964 and stayed together for 32 years! The Kinks were one of the most influential bands of their time and they inspired Britpop bands Oasis and Blur in the 1990s. In the USA they were known as a 'British Invasion Band' as they often used to sing about things that culturally linked to the UK such as afternoon tea, London landmarks and fashion in the 1960s.

ROCK

Britpop

Get it right! 3 and 4

Common errors

1 It was a bit colder ...

Make sure you use modifiers and comparative adjectives correctly.

✓ *It was a **bit colder** yesterday.*

✗ *It was a bit ~~more~~ colder yesterday.*

Complete the sentences with the word in brackets and a comparative form of the adjective in **bold**.

1 **A:** It was **hot** in my house yesterday.
B: It was ... in *my* house! (much)

2 **A:** It's **quiet** in my town.
B: It's ... in *my* town! (a lot)

3 **A:** I like this watch, it's **cheap**.
B: Look at this one, it's ... . (a bit)

4 **A:** Listen to my brother's music. It's really **loud**.
B: *My* brother's music is ... than that! (much)

2 See you on Saturday!

Make sure you put time expressions in the correct place in a sentence. Don't put them in the middle.

✓ *I'm going to the cinema **next Saturday**.*

✓ ***Next Saturday** I'm going to the cinema.*

✗ *I'm going ~~next Saturday~~ to the cinema.*

a Correct the text.

What a crazy week!
On Monday I saved a cat from a tree.
I rang on Tuesday the fire service because the neighbours' house was on fire.
I found yesterday a toddler alone in the street.
I had to go last night to the hospital – my sister accidentally hit me with a bat!
I hope things will be calmer next week!

b 2.15 Listen and check your answers.

3 plates, meals and courses

Don't confuse these food words.

✓ *She only eats vegetarian **food**.*

✓ *I have three **meals** a day.*

✗ *I have three ~~foods~~ a day.*

✓ *He put his food on his **plate**.*

✓ *I'd like chicken for the main **course**.*

✗ *I'd like chicken for the main ~~plate~~.*

a Complete the sentences with words from the box.

course meal plates food

1 Do you like fast ... ?
2 Which is your favourite ... of the day? Why?
3 When was the last time you ate food on paper ... ?
4 In an Italian restaurant, what would you choose for your main ... ?

b Now ask and answer the questions with a partner.

4 Say it right!

/ʌ/

a 2.16 Listen and repeat the words.

1 s /ʌ/ mmer
2 br /ʌ/ ther
3 y /ʌ/ ng
4 an /ʌ/ ther
5 disg /ʌ/ sting
6 b /ʌ/ t
7 l /ʌ/ ve

b 2.16 Listen again and complete the words with the missing letters in your notebook. Then complete the rule.

The spelling for /ʌ/ can be ..., ... or ... .

c 2.17 Work with a partner and read these sentences. Then listen and check.

1 Lovely young Sam loves to run in the sun.
2 My brother spends money in London in summer.
3 Mum, have I done enough?

Review 3 and 4

1 Grammar

a Look at the picture of what Ella and Jake were doing yesterday. Complete the sentences with the verbs in the past continuous (positive or negative).

1 Ella … (walk) her dog.
2 Jake … (talk) on his mobile.
3 They … (play) football.
4 Ella … (have) a drink.
5 The sun … (shine).
6 Jake … (ride) a bike.

6

b Choose the correct words.

1 Yesterday Megan *shopped / was shopping* in town when she *saw / was seeing* her friends.
2 When Antonio's computer *broke / was breaking* he *played / was playing* a new computer game.
3 Leon and Anna *did / were doing* their homework when their mum *rang / was ringing* them.

6

c Complete the sentences with the comparative or superlative form of the adjective.

1 Cities are … … towns. (big)
2 I think motorbikes are … … … form of transport. (dangerous)
3 The weather in Spain is … … in Britain. (hot)
4 The cheetah is … … animal in the world. (fast)
5 I think the violin is … … … instrument to play. (difficult)

5

d Complete the sentences with *a lot* or *a bit* and the comparative form of the adjectives.

1 I'm 1.9 m tall. You're only 1.4 m tall. I'm … (tall) you.
2 My pizza is €12, yours is €11. My pizza is … (expensive) yours.
3 The sea is very big. A pond is very small. A pond is … (small) the sea.
4 Today it's 15°C in London and 16°C in Liverpool. Liverpool is … (warm) London.
5 My dad is very serious, but my brother is very funny. I think my brother is … (funny) my dad.

5

2 Vocabulary

a Match the numbers (1–6) with the words for ages (A–F).

1 6 months
2 5 years
3 14
4 46
5 82
6 2 years

A teenager
B middle-aged
C elderly
D baby
E child
F toddler

6

b Complete the adjectives in the sentences.

1 That boy only talks to dogs. He's w… .
2 She's c… about football. She plays every day.
3 My most m… holiday was when we went to Greece. I'll never forget it.
4 Potato ice cream – that's d… !
5 I think the most d… chocolate in the world comes from Switzerland.
6 We had an a… time at the theme park. I can't wait to go again.
7 She's so t… . She always wears fashionable clothes.

7

c Complete the adjectives with *-ed* or *-ing*.

1 The children are excit… because they're going to a party.
2 Isabella's really frighten… of the dark!
3 I think Science is bor… !
4 Victor was disappoint… because his football team lost the match.
5 I don't want to be an actress. It's embarrass… when everyone watches you.
6 I'm surpris… to see you. Why are you here?

6

d Put the letters in the correct order and make restaurant words.

1 sagls
2 lptea
3 lilb
4 frko
5 rtersta
6 sstrdee
7 utelcry
8 rcsoeu
9 pikann

9

5 Tomorrow's world

Future predictions: *will/might*
***going to* for future plans**
Vocabulary: Transport; Computers
Interaction 5: Giving instructions

1 Vocabulary

Transport

a 2.18 Match the words with the pictures. Then listen and check.

A 8 ship

1 boat **2** ferry
3 helicopter **4** lorry
5 motorbike **6** plane
7 scooter **8** ~~ship~~ **9** tram

b Complete the table with the words in Exercise 1a. Do it in your Workbook (page 118 Exercise 1)

by land	by sea	by air
lorry	boat, ferry	helicopter, plane, ship

c Do you know any more words for transport? Add them to the table in your Workbook (page 118 Exercise 2).

d Which words are the odd ones out? Why?

1 boat lorry ship ferry
2 helicopter tram bus car
3 scooter motorbike bicycle taxi (taxi or bycicle
4 train plane lorry car

Get it right!

by plane
Use *by* + transport.
✓ *He's coming by plane / car, etc.* (✗ … ~~*in*~~ *plane / car, etc.*)
Use *on* + *foot* or *to walk*.
✓ *He's coming on foot.* (✗ ~~*by*~~ *foot*)
✓ *I walk to school.* (✗ *I* ~~*go to school walking.*~~)

e Work with a partner. Ask and answer the questions.

How do you usually travel …
1 to school?
2 in your town?
3 when you go on holiday?

⋯> *I usually walk to school but sometimes I go by bus.*

2 Pronunciation DVD

Consonant clusters

a 2.19 Some words have more than one consonant sound at the beginning. Listen to these words.

plane	**tr**ain	**sch**ool	**qu**een	**str**eet
/pl/	/tr/	/sk/	/kw/	/str/

b 2.20 Listen and choose the word you hear.

	A	B
1	plane	pain
2	train	rain
3	school	cool
4	queen	keen
5	street	seat
6	slow	low
7	square	wear
8	price	rice

c 2.21 Listen and repeat.

He rode his green scooter quietly down the street to the train station.

3 Read and listen

a Read the text quickly. Complete the sentences in paragraphs 1–4 with the names of the inventions.

Travelling in the future

Cars without drivers, cars that turn into planes, motorbikes that travel at 500km/hour and a man who can fly without a plane. Is this science fiction or the future?

1 The ... car doesn't need a driver.

Dr Matt Barth, of the University of California, thinks we might have automatic cars very soon. He is working on the Ce-Cert car which won't need a human driver. It will use two cameras as 'eyes' to prevent accidents and a computer to talk to other cars. In the future we might not have many traffic problems because automatic cars will move very quickly and intelligently.

2 Not an egg, a ... motorbike.

There will also be many new types of motorbike. The Dodge Tomahawk is the fastest motorbike in the world. It can travel at an amazing 480 km/hour, but it costs $3 million so not many people will be able to buy it. A cheaper option is the Monotracer. It looks like an egg and is very light. At the moment it costs about $70,000, but it will probably be a lot cheaper in the future.

3 Is it a plane? Is it a car? The ... is both!

We might be able to drive over the traffic in a flying car in the future. Canadian Chris Milner has invented the AirCar, which you might be able to buy soon. At first it just looks like a very modern car, but in a few seconds it can turn into a small plane and fly at a height of 7,500 metres.

4 Yves Rossy used a ... to cross the Alps.

How about flying without a plane with the Jet Pack? In 2006 Yves Rossy became the first person to fly long distance like a bird, using a jet engine attached to a rucksack and carbon wings 2.4 metres long. In 2008 he flew across the Alps at 300km/hour.

Finally, how about travelling between two places in a second, like Hayden Christensen in the film *Jumper*? Scientists are working on teleportation at the moment, so in the future we might not need transport at all!

b 2.22 Read the text again and listen. Are the sentences *right* (✓), *wrong* (✗) or *doesn't say* (–)?

1 Some people have cars which drive themselves now.
2 Driving will be safer because of cameras and computers.
3 The AirCar is very fast.
4 A lot of people will have the Dodge Tomahawk.
5 Yves Rossy flew over the Alps without a plane.
6 Scientists will soon invent teleportation.

c Work with a partner. Which way(s) of travelling would you like to try? Why?

4 Grammar

Future predictions: *will/might*

a Look at the examples and complete the table with *will/might* and the verb *buy*.

> **Get it right!**
>
> ***will* and *might***
>
> After the modal verbs *will* and *might* we use the infinitive without *to*.
>
> ✓ *I might / will come with you.*
>
> ✗ *I might / will ~~to~~ come with you.*

*We **might have** automatic cars very soon.*
*In the future we **might not need** transport at all!*
*There **will** also **be** many new types of motorbike.*
***Will** you **get** a Monotracer? Yes, I **will**. / No, I **won't**.*

Positive			**Negative**		
I/You/He/She/ It/We/They	… ('ll) **might**	**buy** a flying car.	I/You/He/She/ It/We/They	… **might not**	**buy** a flying car.

***Yes/No* questions**	**Short answers**
… I/you/he/she/ it/we/they … a flying car?	Yes, I/you/he/she/it/we/they … / **might**.
Might	No, /you/he/she/it/we/they … / **might not**.

Information questions

When … I/you/he/she/it/we/they … a flying car?

Choose the correct words to complete the rules.

- We use *will* to make predictions about the future when we are **sure** / **not sure** about something.
- We use *might* to make predictions about the future when we are **sure** / **not sure** about something.

Grammar reference: pages 134–135

b Choose the correct words.

1 We don't know where we're going in July yet, but we *might / will* go to Greece.
2 I'm sure that robots *might / will* work as bus drivers in the future.
3 Paula's got a broken leg so she *might not / won't* be able to run in the race next week.
4 There *will / won't* be more types of automatic transport in the future if scientists keep inventing new cars.
5 They're very busy so they *might not / won't* come out. It depends when they finish.

c Complete the sentences with *will / won't / might / might not* and the verb.

1 I … (go) to university next year if I get good exam results.
2 She … (go) to the party on Friday, but she will if she finishes her homework.
3 Jon … (be able) to come to the match because he's working in the evening.
4 Scientists are sure that in the future cars … (need) petrol. They … (use) electricity.
5 We … (go) to the beach tomorrow. It depends on the weather.

d Complete the sentences about the future for you.

1 I think I'll …
2 I don't think I'll …
3 I might …
4 I might not … , I'm not sure.

5 Speak

a How will things change in the next 20 years? Student A: Look at the topics. Make notes about your opinions.

school clothes holidays transport

Student B: Turn to page 125.

b Work with your partner. Tell him/her your opinions. Does he/she agree?

I don't think people will go to school, they'll have classes at home through the internet.

I agree / I don't think so. I think …

c Tell the class your opinions.

> **Get it right!**
>
> ***I don't think …***
>
> ✓ *I don't think I'll be rich.*
>
> ✗ *I ~~think I won't~~ be rich.*

6 Listen

a 2.23 Listen to the students. Match the name with the plan for the future.

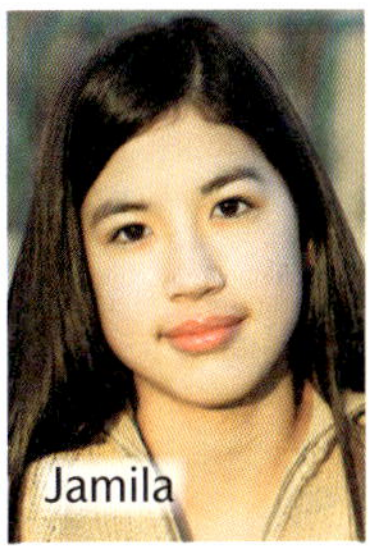

A Start a business
B Live in another country
C Become a doctor
D Work with cars and motorbikes

b 2.23 Listen again. Choose the correct answer: A, B or C.

1 Ryan wants to … when he's sixteen.
  - **A** take exams
  - **B** get a job
  - **C** go to college

2 Connor wants to …
  - **A** do a course online.
  - **B** learn another language.
  - **C** be a mechanic.

3 Libby … go to university.
  - **A** doesn't want to
  - **B** will definitely
  - **C** might

4 Jamila … about what she wants to do.
  - **A** is sure
  - **B** has two ideas
  - **C** isn't sure

c Work in a group. Talk about your plans for the future. Are your plans the same? Who is sure about their future? Who isn't sure?

7 Grammar *going to* for future plans

a Look at the examples and complete the table.

*What **are** you **going to do** next year?*
*I**'m** also **going to do** a computer course online.*
*Next year I**'m not going to stay** at school.*
***Are** you **going to go** back to school next year?* ***Yes**, I **am**.*

Positive		**Negative**	
I'… He/She/It'… You/We/They'…	**going to get** a job.	I'm not He/She/It … You/We/They …	**going to leave** school.

***Yes/No* questions**		**Short answers**
… I … he/she/it … you/we/they	**going** … **get** a job?	Yes, I … . / No, I'm not. Yes, he/she/it … . / No, he/she/it … . Yes, you/we/they … . / No, you/we/they … .

Information questions

What	am I … he/she/it … you/we/they	**going to do** next year?

Choose the correct word to complete the rule.

- We use *be going to* + infinitive to talk about future plans. We usually make the plans **before** / **at** the moment of speaking.

Grammar reference: page 135

b Complete the sentences with *be going to* and the verbs.

1 They … Spanish in the evenings next year. (learn)
2 Lee … at school. He wants to get a job. (not stay)
3 … you … a party for your birthday? (have)
4 I … to university in London in September. (go)
5 Ellie … around Australia next year. (travel)

c Put the words in the correct order.

1 tomorrow / are / going to / do / What / you ?
2 are / leave / you / When / school / going to ?
3 are / you / What / going to / do / this summer ?
4 going to / are / How / celebrate / you / your next birthday ?
5 are / going to / When / you / with your friends / go out ?

d Work with a partner. Ask and answer the questions in Exercise 7c.

Culture Vulture

Did you know that you can leave school at 16 in Britain, but 78.7% of British 16–18 year olds are in education or training? What do most 16–18 year olds do in your country?

8 Vocabulary

Computers

a 2.24 Match the words with the parts of the computer. Then listen and check.

A 2 keyboard

1 disc drive **2** ~~keyboard~~
3 laptop **4** mouse
5 printer **6** screen
7 speakers
8 memory stick
9 USB port **10** webcam

b 2.25 Match the words with the definitions. Then listen and check.

1 A click on something

1. press on the mouse and give the computer an instruction
2. this helps you find information on the internet quickly and easily, e.g. Google and Yahoo
3. a place online where you communicate with your friends, e.g. Facebook and MySpace
4. a symbol on a computer screen that you select to give the computer an instruction
5. information saved on a computer with one name
6. move words or pictures from one place to another in a computer document

A click on something
B cut and paste
C file
D icon
E search engine
F social networking site

c Do you know any more computer or internet words? Write them in your Workbook (page 118 Exercise 5).

d Work in a group. Ask and answer the questions.

1. Where do you use a computer? (at home, at school, at the library, etc.)
2. How often do you use the internet?
3. Which search engines do you use?
4. Which social networking sites are you a member of?

Interaction 5 DVD

Giving instructions

a 2.26 Rajiv is explaining to his mum how to use a memory stick. Listen and put the pictures into the correct order.

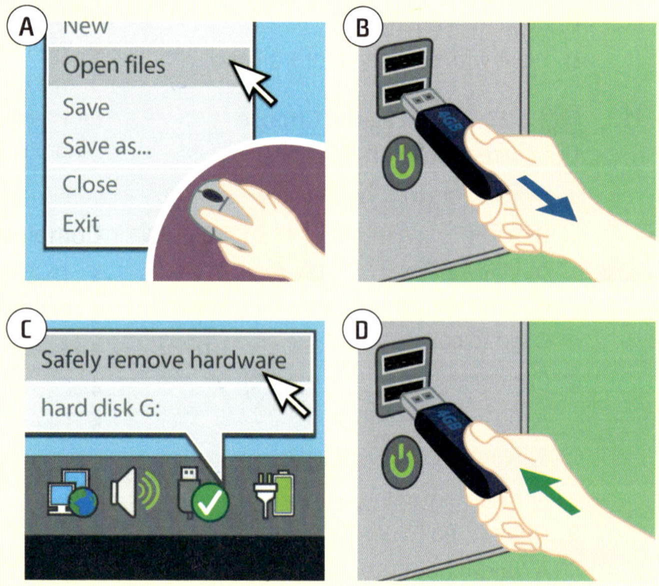

b 2.26 Listen again. Who says the phrases? Write *R* (Rajiv) or *M* (Mum).

1 M

1 What do I do first/next?
2 First/Then you have to …
3 What's that?
4 OK, next … .
5 Is there anything else?
6 Look, here it is …

c 2.27 Turn to page 124. Listen to the sentences and repeat them. Practise stressing the important words. Speak clearly!

d Work with a partner.

Student A: Turn to page 127.
Student B: Turn to page 130.

Portfolio 5

An opinion essay

a Read Kirk's essay. Write the numbers of the activities he thinks robots will do in the future.

Robots in the future

Today we use robots for lots of jobs and in the future I believe there will be lots more of them.

First of all, robots are very important in our lives today. All the machines we use to wash clothes and to cook in our homes are like robots. I believe we will have more robots in the future to do other jobs. They might walk the dog or make the beds.

Secondly, I think robots in the future will be more like people. Today scientists are making androids (robots that look like humans) and in the future we will have androids at home and at work. They will do a lot of jobs that humans do today. For example, they will do the cooking, drive buses or answer the phone in an office.

To sum up, I think there will be lots more robots in the future and they will be like humans, not machines.

Which is right? Don't look at the text!
We will have androids ***at*** */* ***in*** *home and* ***in the*** */* ***at*** *work.*

b Read the essay again. Put the opinion essay plan in the correct order.

conclusion   second idea   introduction   first idea

1 …
2 …
3 …
4 …

c Write the expressions in the essay which:

1 give your opinion
2 give examples
3 introduce the first idea
4 introduce the second idea
5 introduce the conclusion

d Write an opinion essay about the future. Before you write, choose a subject from the box and think about your ideas. Use the essay plan in Exercise b and the expressions in Exercise c to help you.

computers   transport   entertainment
houses   school   holidays

The Memory Birds

2.28

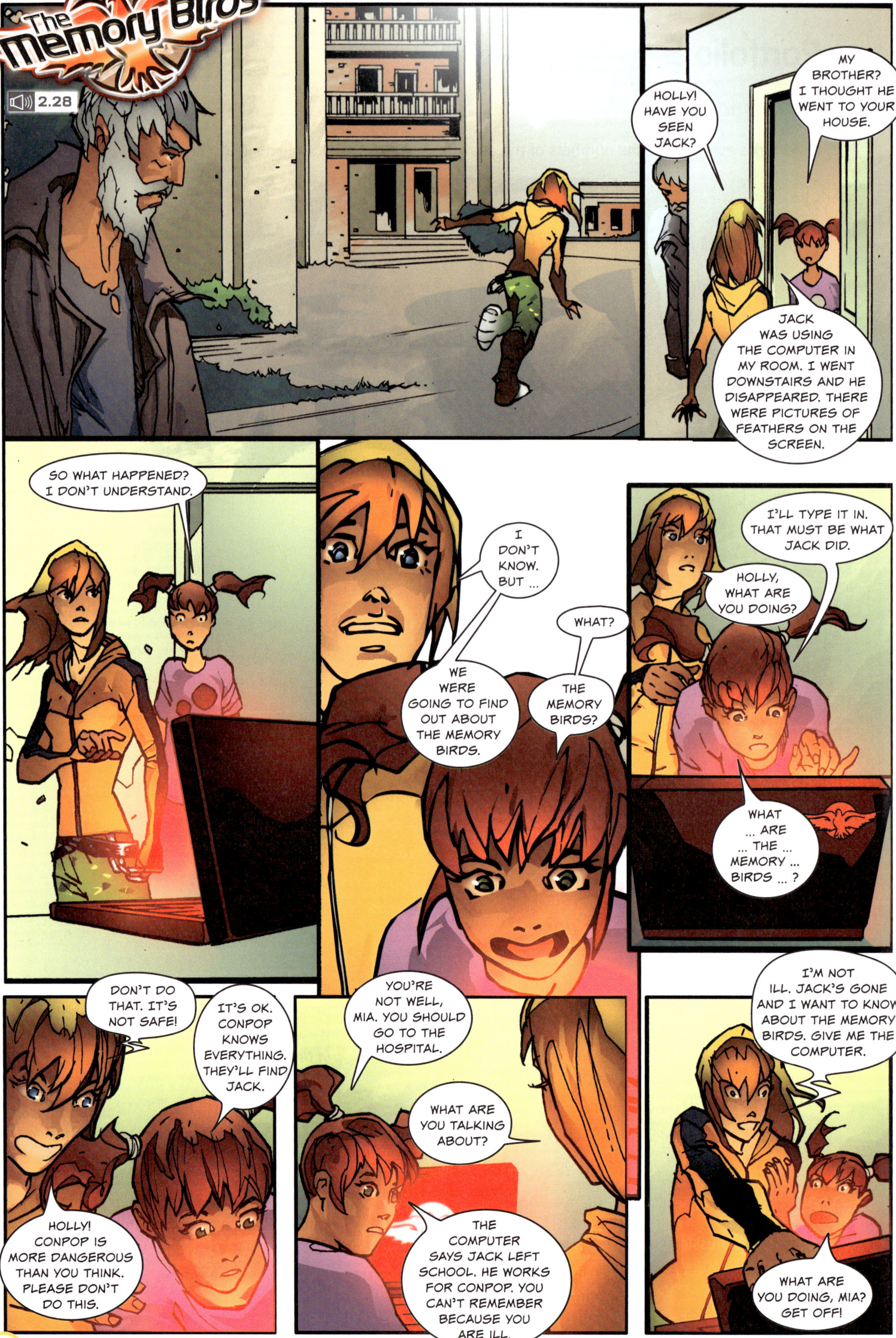

HOLLY!
HELP ME! MIA!
IT'S NOT HER YOU WANT. IT'S ME!
WHAT? WHO?
WHO ARE YOU? WHY ARE YOU WATCHING ME?
THE MEMORY BIRDS HAVE TAKEN YOUR FRIENDS. THEY'LL GET YOU NEXT.
COME WITH ME. YOU DON'T HAVE MUCH TIME. THEY'RE WATCHING US.
HOW DO YOU KNOW ABOUT THE MEMORY BIRDS?
WHERE ARE WE GOING?
WHAT ... JUST ... HAPPENED? WHERE HAVE YOU BROUGHT ME?
DO YOU SEE THAT BUILDING? THE HEART OF CONPOP IS IN THERE. THAT'S WHERE THEY USE PEOPLE'S MEMORIES TO CREATE THE ENERGY FOR ALL THEIR COMPUTERS.
CONPOP HAS YOUR FRIENDS IN THERE. YOU HAVE TO GO IN AND BRING THEM BACK BEFORE THEY FORGET EVERYTHING.
HOW DO YOU KNOW ALL THIS? WHO ARE YOU?

6 Xtreme

should* and *shouldn't
have to* and *don't have to
Vocabulary: Extreme sports; Verbs of movement
Interaction 6: Describing rules

1 Listen

a 2.29 Listen to Felicity talking to Ben about Parkour. Where does she practise?

b 2.29 Listen again and choose the correct words in the text.

c Have you tried Parkour? Would you like to? Why/Why not?

PARKOUR

THE FACTS

1 Parkour began in **Britain / France**.
2 At the moment, Parkour is more popular with **girls / boys**.
3 Parkour is **difficult / easy** at the beginning.

Parkour is dangerous. Follow the rules!

4 Practise first on sand and **grass / the pavement**.
5 Wear good running shoes and **comfortable / special** clothes.
6 Get information from **sports centres / websites**.

Remember, if you can't do it, don't try it! Parkour is not about jumping off tall buildings. It's about the way you move.

2 Grammar

should and *shouldn't*

a Look at the examples and complete the table with *should* and *shouldn't*.

*You **should have** some lessons at the beginning.*
*You **shouldn't jump** in the street at first.*
***Should** I **practise**? Yes, you **should**. Where **should** I **practise**?*

Positive
I/You/He/She/It/We/They … **have** some lessons.

Negative
I/You/He/She/It/We/They … **jump** in the street at first.

***Yes/No* questions**
… I/you/he/she/it/we/they **practise** first?

Short answers
Yes, I/you/he/she/it/we/they … .
No, I/you/he/she/it/we/they **shouldn't**.

Information questions
Where … I/you/he/she/it/we/they **practise** first?

Choose the correct words to complete the rules.

- We use *should* for actions that **are / aren't** a good idea.
- We use *shouldn't* for actions that **are / aren't** a good idea.
- After *should(n't)* we use the infinitive **with / without** *to*.

Grammar reference: pages 135–136

Check it out!

Use ***must*** and ***mustn't*** for **strong obligation** and **rules**.
*You **must be** 18 to go skydiving.*
*Skiers **mustn't ski** at night.*

b Choose the correct words.

1 should

1 You *should / shouldn't* try water skiing. It's great fun!
2 They *should / shouldn't* skateboard in the playground. It's dangerous.
3 Which website *should / shouldn't* I look at to learn about Parkour?
4 Harry *should / must* learn to swim if he wants to go scuba diving!
5 You *should / shouldn't* wear sunglasses when you go skiing. The sun can be very strong.
6 My sister wants to learn how to snowboard. *Should / Must* she have lessons?

c A penfriend from another country is coming to stay with you. Tell him/her about things in your country. Use *should and shouldn't*.

You should visit Córdoba.
You should bring sunglasses with you.

3 Vocabulary

Extreme sports

a 2.30 Match the extreme sports with the pictures. Then listen and check.

A 3 mountain biking

1 bungee jumping **2** motor racing **3** ~~mountain biking~~
4 scuba diving **5** skateboarding **6** skydiving
7 snowboarding **8** water skiing

b Which extreme sports in Exercise 3a can you do in these places?

- *on/in the water*
- *on a mountain*
- *in the countryside*
- *in the city*
- *in the air*
- *other*

c Do you know any more extreme sports? Write them in your Workbook (page 119 Exercise 1).

d Work in a group. Ask and answer questions.

1. Which of the extreme sports in Exercise 3a do you do?
2. Which sports would/wouldn't you like to do? Why? / Why not?

Check it out!

- **Compound nouns** are two words together. We often write them as **two words**: *water skiing*. We sometimes write them as **one word**: *skateboarding*. There are no rules but you can check in a dictionary.

4 Speak

a Imagine you do an extreme sport, but don't tell your partner its name. Put the words in the correct order.

1 Where do you do the sport?

1. you / do / Where / do / the sport ?
2. it / or / difficult / Is / easy ?
3. it / dangerous / Is ?
4. lessons / have / Should / people ?
5. you / wear / What / clothes / should ?
6. should / you / often / practise / How ?

b Work with a partner. Take turns to ask and answer the questions. Can you guess your partner's sport?

c Tell the class. What was your sport? Did you guess your partner's sport?

Where do you do the sport?

Outside.

Is it skiing?

No.

5 Vocabulary Verbs of movement

a 2.31 Match the verbs with the pictures. Then listen and check.

A 4 jump

1 climb **2** dive **3** fall **4** ~~jump~~ **5** roll **6** spin

A

B

C

D

E

F

b Match the two parts of the sentences.

1 Look at David. He's climbing
2 He can spin around
3 People doing Parkour roll on
4 Can you jump
5 When you learn how to ski
6 When you dive into the water

A over this chair?
B up the wall.
C your head goes into the water first.
D you fall onto your side a lot.
E on the back wheel of his bike.
F the ground when they land.

c We can use different prepositions with the same verb. Choose the two options which are possible in each sentence.

1 climb — **up** a mountain / **over** the wall / **down** the ground
2 fall — **down** the stairs / **up** the water / **off** a bike
3 dive — **off** the diving board / **out of** the water / **into** the water
4 jump — **over** the chair / **off** the table / **onto** the water

d Do you know any more verbs of movement? Write them in your Workbook (page 119 Exercise 4).

e Which of these things can you do? Tell your partner.

* jump in the air on a snowboard, a skateboard or a bike
* dive off a diving board into the swimming pool
* climb up a tree
* spin around on inline skates or ice skates

Culture Vulture

Did you know that the five most popular urban sports in the UK are rollerblading, skateboarding, mountain biking, cycling and paintball? What are the most popular urban sports in your country? Do you do any of them?

Get it right!

dive

✓ *She **dived** into the pool.*
✗ *She ~~threw herself~~ into the pool.*

6 Pronunciation DVD
Linking sounds

a 2.32 A word that ends with a consonant sound links to a word that starts with a vowel sound. Listen to these words.

fall_off climb_up
dive_into jump_over

b 2.33 Copy the sentences, then draw a line to link the words. Then listen and check.

1 Climb onto the diving board and dive into the water.
2 I jumped off the wall and rolled on the ground.
3 Get on your skateboard and spin around.
4 He rode over the hill, then fell off his bike.
5 We jumped out of the plane and landed in a field.

c Work with a partner. Practise saying the sentences.

7 Read and listen

a Read the text quickly and choose the correct title for the webpage.

1 Zorbing is fun! **2** Extreme sports for beginners **3** Courses for experts

Extreme sport

File Edit View Insert Format Tools Actions Help

http://www.extremesports.co.uk

ZORBING

Come and try this new extreme sport. A Zorb is a giant ball, or sphere, about 3m tall, with one or two people inside. The 'Zorbanauts' put on harnesses to hold them to the inside of the sphere and protect them, then they roll down a hill! Don't be frightened – you don't have to wear a helmet, it's completely safe and really good fun!

Zorbing FAQs

- ***Do I need to be sporty?***
  No, you don't have to be sporty to go zorbing, but people with health problems should check with their doctor first.
- ***What's the minimum age?***
  You have to be over 12 years old.
- ***Do I need special clothes?***
  Special clothes aren't necessary, but you mustn't wear shoes inside the Zorb.
- We also offer hydro zorbing: you don't wear a harness, and there's water inside the Zorb. It's a fantastic experience but you'll get very wet!
- Harness zorbing and hydro zorbing are both £45.00 per ride.

MOUNTAIN BOARDING

Mountain boarding is an exciting combination of skateboarding, surfing and snowboarding. It's one of the most popular extreme sports in the UK right now and you can learn it very quickly! Our fantastic downhill course, right next to the beach, is the perfect place to learn all the basic skills. Our instructors will teach you all you need to know.

Mountain boarding FAQs

- ***Do I have to bring my own board?***
  No, you don't have to bring your own board, we provide all the equipment.
- ***Is it dangerous?***
  No, not if you wear protection. You must wear knee and elbow pads, wrist supports and a helmet to protect your head.
- ***Can my seven-year-old brother come with me?***
  Sorry! You must be over eight years old. Children under 16 years of age have to be accompanied by an adult.
- Prices from £30.00 for half a day.

Click on the photos for info about other beginners' courses.

KITE SURFING

PARAGLIDING

CANYONING

Which is right? Don't look at the text!
*It's a ball about **3m of** / **3m** tall.*

b 2.34 Read the text again and listen. Write *Z* (zorbing), *M* (mountain boarding) or *B* (both zorbing and mountain boarding).

1 B

1 You move down a hill in this sport.
2 Two people can do this sport together.
3 You need to wear protection on your arms and legs.
4 You need an instructor to do this sport.
5 This sport is similar to other sports.
6 Children under eight years old can't do this sport.

c Would you like to do any of the sports on this webpage? Why? / Why not?

must / mustn't → rule   have to → necesidad to
should → recomendación

8 Grammar

have to and *don't have to*

a Look at the examples and complete the table with *have to* and *don't have to.*

→ *You* ***have to*** *be over eight years old.*
You ***don't have to*** *be sporty.*
Do *I* ***have to*** *bring my own board?*

Positive

I/You/We/They	… …	**be** over eight.
He/She/It	**has to**	

Negative

I/You/We/They	… … …	**wear** a helmet.
He/She/It	**doesn't have to**	

***Yes/No* questions**

…	I/you/we/they	**have to pay**?
Does	he/she/it	

Short answers

Yes, I/you/we/they … . / No, I/you/we/they … .
Yes, he/she/it **does**. / No, he/she/it … .

Information questions

Where	**do**	I/you/we/they	**have to pay**?
	…	he/she/it	

Choose the correct words to complete the rules.

- We use *have to* for actions that are **necessary** / **not necessary**.
- We use *don't have to* for actions that are **necessary** / **not necessary**.

Grammar reference: page 136

Check it out!

- ***Don't have to*** is different from ***mustn't***.
  You ***mustn't*** *wear shoes inside the Zorb.*
  (= don't wear shoes)
  You ***don't have to*** *wear a helmet.*
  (= it isn't necessary to wear a helmet)

b Choose the correct words.

1 They *have to* / *don't have to* go to school tomorrow. It's a holiday.
2 He *has to* / *doesn't have to* pay the full price because he's over 18.
3 You *mustn't* / *don't have to* use your phone in class.
4 You *have to* / *don't have to* wear elbow pads when you go skateboarding, but it's a good idea.
5 I *mustn't* / *don't have to* forget Mum's birthday tomorrow.

c Complete the sentences so they are true for you.

1 At home I don't have to … but I have to …
2 At school we mustn't … and we have to …
3 At the weekend I don't have to …
4 Tomorrow I have to …
5 Today I mustn't forget to …

d Work with a partner. Are any of your sentences the same?

Interaction 6 DVD

Describing rules

a 2.35 Listen to Dave and Morgan talking about bungee jumping. Is Morgan interested in the sport?

b 2.35 Listen again. Which questions does Morgan ask?

How much is it?
Where do you do it?
Do you have to wear special clothes?
Do you have to have lessons?
What do you do?
How old do you have to be?

c 2.36 Turn to page 124. Listen to the questions and repeat them. Practise the pronunciation of *do you have to … ?* (/dʒəhaftə/).

d Work with a partner.
Student A: Turn to page 127.
Student B: Turn to page 130.

Portfolio 6

Formal and informal messages

a Read the messages. Match A–D with 1–4.

1 thanks someone
2 gives permission to do something
3 invites someone to do something
4 asks for information

b Which messages are formal and which are informal?

Check it out!

We use different language for formal and informal letters.

- **Formal letters**: to people in authority, e.g. teachers
- **Informal letters**: to friends or family

A

Hi Tim,
Do you want to come Zorbing on Saturday? You get inside a big ball and you roll down a hill. It's really good fun and very easy. We're going to leave at 9:30 in the morning.
See you soon,
Jake

B

Dear Sir/Madam
I am writing to ask for information about rollerblading lessons. Please could you answer these questions:
- What days are the lessons?
- How much is one lesson?
- Is there a minimum age?
- Do I need to wear special clothes?
Thank you for your help.
Yours faithfully
Drew Blake

C

Dear Jessica
Sorry, I can't come skateboarding on Sunday, but thanks for asking me. We're going away for the weekend. I'd really like to come with you next weekend, but my board is broken. Can I use your brother's board?
Love Emily

D

Dear Miss Freeman
My daughter, Grace Mitchell would like to go on the adventure sports trip on Saturday 17 May. I am writing to give my permission for Grace to go hang-gliding.
Yours sincerely
Julia Mitchell

Which is right? Don't look at the text!
You get ***inside / inside of*** *a big ball.*

c Read the messages again and copy and complete the table with the words.

Dear Sir/Madam   would like to …   Love X   I'm …   thank you
Yours faithfully   thanks   Yours sincerely   Hi X   want to …
Dear Mr/Mrs X   See you soon

Informal language	Formal language
	Dear Sir / Madam

d Write a formal message to ask for information about a sport. Ask questions about:

- the clothes and equipment
- the cost
- the time and place
- anything else

e Swap messages with a partner. Read your partner's message and write a reply.

New Zealand: Paradise on earth

New Zealand is the youngest country on earth. One thousand years ago there were no people living there. Then Maori people set off in boats from Polynesia, discovered New Zealand and decided to stay there. After that people came from all over the world to live in this beautiful country.

New Zealand has a spectacular landscape, including huge mountain ranges, active volcanoes, fjords and rainforests. The country is the same size as the UK or California, but it has 13 national parks and a population of only four million people. This combination of amazing landscape and very few people has made New Zealand very popular with tourists and film-makers. New Zealand film director Peter Jackson made the *Lord of the Rings* trilogy there. Tourists can visit the locations of the three films, including hobbit houses!

New Zealand is also the adventure capital of the world. Thousands of extreme sports fans come here every year to go bungee jumping, white-water rafting or go on the world's fastest ride: a rocket ship that flies at 170 km/hour. You can also ski down a volcano or learn to snowkite (a combination of kite surfing and snowboarding). For people who don't like danger there are lots of other activities. How about black-water rafting, horse trekking or swimming with dolphins?

Five 'must-do's' in New Zealand

- You must visit Queenstown, the centre for extreme sports.
- Spend time on New Zealand's fantastic beaches.
- Check out the Maori Matariki (New Year) festivals in June and July.
- You should relax in natural hot pools on North Island.
- Stay on a farm with good food and lots of animals.

Do's and don'ts for extreme sports

- You must wear a high factor sun cream – the sun is very strong in NZ.
- You must also protect your eyes from the sun.
- Make sure you are fit before your adventure holiday.
- You should wear the right clothes for the sports activity.
- You have to get your parents' permission for some sports.

A Maori face tattoo

Warning: active volcano!

Visit the hobbit houses

New Zealand facts

- Its nearest neighbour, Australia, is 2,000 km away.
- New Zealand people are called 'Kiwis', after the kiwi bird.
- The highest bungee jump in the world was done in New Zealand in 1998. A.J. Hackett jumped 180m.
- The All Blacks, the New Zealand rugby team, do a Maori war dance, or haka, before rugby matches. They try to frighten the other team.
- There are several active volcanoes in New Zealand and they often erupt. Be careful when you do your extreme sports!

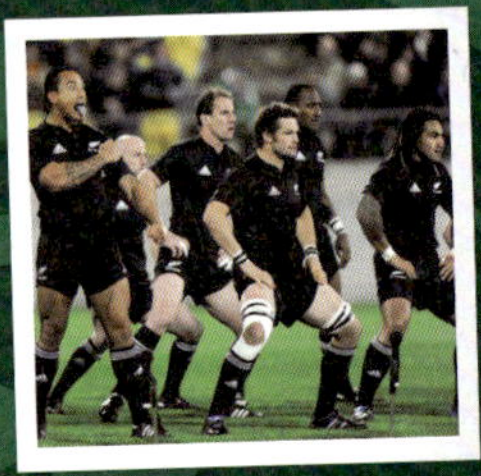

The Maori war dance – are you frightened?

Go snow kiting for the ultimate adrenaline rush!

The kiwi bird, the symbol of New Zealand

1 Culture World: New Zealand

a How much do you know about New Zealand? Work with a partner and do the quiz before you read the article.

New Zealand Quiz

1 The first people who lived in New Zealand were the ...
A Australians
B Aborigines
C Maoris

2 People started living in New Zealand about ...
A 1,000 years ago
B 10,000 years ago
C 5,000 years ago

3 New Zealand is famous for its ...
A computer industry
B football team
C beautiful landscape

4 The most famous films made in New Zealand were the ...
A *Star Wars* films
B *Lord of the Rings* films
C *Star Trek* films

5 Tourists usually like going to New Zealand to ...
A visit museums
B go shopping
C do extreme sports

6 People who live in New Zealand are sometimes called ...
A All Blacks
B Kiwis
C bungee jumpers

b Read the article and check your answers.

c Find words in the article that mean …

1. leave a place (paragraph 1)
2. natural features in the countryside, e.g. mountains and lakes (paragraph 2)
3. two or more things together (paragraph 2 and paragraph 3)
4. a slow journey made on a horse or on foot. (paragraph 3)

d Read the article again. Write two quiz questions on New Zealand. Swap your questions with your partner. Can they answer the questions?

2 Your project

An extreme map

a Work in a group. Write information for your country like in the example.

	New Zealand
Highest mountain	Mount Cook (3,754 m)
Longest river	Waikato River (425 km)
Largest lake	Lake Taupo (606 km)
Biggest city	Auckland
Most important city	Wellington
Most interesting extreme sports	snowkiting
Best festival	Matariki festivals in June/July

b Draw a map of your country and put the information from the table on your map. Add lists of 'must-dos' for tourists and 'dos and don'ts' for sports.

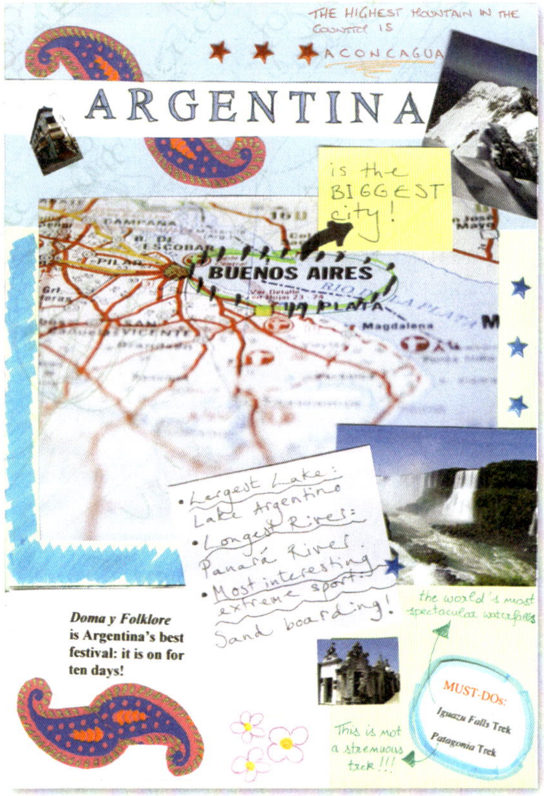

Get it right! 5 and 6

Common errors

1 Modals without *to*

With *must*, *will*, *might*, *can*, *could* and *should*, we don't use *to*.

✓ *You **shouldn't do** that.* (✗ *… shouldn't ~~to~~ do that.*)

✓ *I **must go** now.* (✗ *… must ~~to~~ go now.*)

With *need* and *want*, we use *to*.

✓ *I **need to do** more sport.*

✓ *I really **want to see** you soon.*

And remember *have to*:

✓ *I **have to leave** early today.*

a Complete Clara's email to her Canadian boyfriend Ethan with *to* or – (nothing).

From Clara
Send To Ethan
Subject

I'm in my computer class (don't you call it IT?) so I can [1] … write to you when the teacher isn't looking. ☺ We have [2] … arrange a date for my visit (we've just done 'arrangements' in English! LOL), so I need [3] … know when you are on holiday. Can you [4] … send me the info tonight? I really want [5] … see you! I need [6] … book my tickets to Vancouver as soon as possible. Must [7] … go – teacher's looking!
Clara

b 2.37 Listen and check your answers.

2 Spelling modals

Remember how to spell modal verbs!

✓ *You **mustn't** go without a helmet.* (✗ ~~musn't~~)

✓ *Ellie **should** put on a harness.* (✗ ~~shold~~ / ~~shoud~~)

✓ *We **might** try zorbing.* (✗ ~~migth~~)

✓ *They **won't** arrive late.* (✗ ~~wount~~ / ~~wont~~)

✓ *He **couldn't** try zorbing.* (✗ ~~coudn't~~)

Read the chat between Clara and her friend Emilia and correct the mistakes.

ClaiR: Oh Emmy, why did Ethan go zorbing with another girl? It's not fair. I coudn't get here any earlier – the plane didn't leave until 11 o'clock. I wount speak to him again!

Emmy2: You musn't be upset, Clara. Ethan really likes you. I'm sure he went zorbing with Jenny because you weren't here! You shoud go and talk to him. You sholdn't worry, it'll all be OK.

ClaiR: I don't know. Well, I migth go later, but I wont speak to him.

Emmy2: Really Clara, don't worry! You shoudn't get upset. He'll be really happy to see you.

3 *I don't think …*

Remember where we put *not* in negative predictions.

✓ *I **don't think** they will go.*

✗ ~~*I think they won't go.*~~

a Correct the sentences.

1 I think I wouldn't like skydiving.
2 I think I can't learn to speak perfect English.
3 I think I won't go to university one day.
4 I think Spain isn't going to win the next World Cup.

b Work with a partner. Discuss the sentences. Make them true for you.

4 Say it right!

Stress in Compound Nouns

a 2.38 Listen to the compound nouns. Then complete the rule with *first* or *second*.

bungee jumping motor racing scuba diving snowboarding skydiving

In compound nouns, the … word is stressed.

a 2.38 Listen to the words again and repeat them.

Review 5 and 6

1 Grammar

a Complete the sentences with the words.

might will (x2) won't probably

1 Joe doesn't know what he's going to do when he leaves school, but he … work in a restaurant.
2 When … you take your exams?
3 They say it … rain this afternoon, but I'm going to take an umbrella anyway.
4 She's very busy at work so she… probably be home late tonight.
5 I think people will … use more public transport in the future.

[ ] 5

b Complete the sentences with *going to* and the verbs.

buy learn meet not come see

1 I want to live in Brazil so I … Portuguese.
2 Which film … you … at the cinema tonight?
3 She … a car when she's eighteen.
4 They … to the park because they're tired.
5 … he … us at the café this afternoon?

[ ] 5

c Maria wants to learn how to scuba dive. Write sentences with *must(n't)* or *should(n't)* that mean the same as sentences 1–5.

1 It's necessary to carry an oxygen tank on your back. You …
2 It's a good idea to practise in a swimming pool before you go in the sea. You …
3 Don't dive alone before you have classes. You …
4 It's not a good idea to go diving if you are tired. You …
5 Don't swim up too quickly when you finish diving. You …

[ ] 5

d Complete the sentences about Blake's skiing holiday in France with the correct form of *have to* or *don't have to*.

1 The hotel has extra skis so Blake … buy his own skis.
2 Blake can't ski so he … have lessons.
3 The weather is very cold so Blake … wear warm clothes.
4 Blake hasn't got any euros so he … go to the bank.
5 There are free drinks at the hotel so Blake … pay for drinks.

[ ] 5

2 Vocabulary

a Put the letters in the correct order and make transport words.

1 tobkmoier
2 mtar
3 yrfre
4 psih
5 cltohpiere
6 lnpea
7 orrly
8 aotb
9 ostroce

[ ] 9

b Match the two parts of the sentences.

1 A laptop is a computer
2 Use the mouse
3 Put the memory stick
4 If you want to print a copy
5 Which search engine do you use
6 You've got lots of icons
7 This music sounds great
8 It's easy to write

A into the USB port.
B you can take with you.
C on your computer screen.
D on this keyboard.
E I've got a printer.
F to click on information.
G to look for information online?
H on these new speakers.

[ ] 8

c Write the words.

1 A snow sport. You go down a mountain with both feet on a single board.
2 An urban sport. You move or jump on a board with four wheels.
3 A sport where you jump from a plane and fall through the air.
4 A sport where you swim under water with a special oxygen tank.
5 A sport where you ride a bicycle off the road in the countryside.
6 A sport where you jump from a high place with an elastic rope tied to your legs.

[ ] 6

d Choose the correct words.

1 I'm going to climb *up / off* that mountain.
2 Can you spin *out / around* on your skateboard?
3 He doesn't want to dive *off / into* the water.
4 You have to jump *up / out* high in basketball.
5 When he was skiing down the mountain, he fell *down / off*.

[ ] 5

7 Sounds good!

Present perfect and past simple
Present perfect with *for* and *since*
Vocabulary: Music; Music online
Interaction 7: Talking about songs

1 Vocabulary Music

a 3.1 Match the words with the definitions. Then listen and check.

1 B band

1 a group of musicians who sing and play music together
2 one song which a music company sells to the public
3 the words to a song
4 a collection of songs which a music company sells as a CD, etc.
5 a person who likes a singer or musician a lot
6 the list of best-selling singles and albums
7 to sing, dance or play an instrument in public
8 to save music electronically
9 a song which is very successful
10 a room where musicians and producers make albums

A album	B ~~band~~
C charts	D fan
E hit	F lyrics
G perform	H record
I single	J studio

b Do you know any more music words? Write them in your Workbook (page 120 Exercise 1).

c Work in a group. Answer the questions.

1 What's your favourite single/album/band?
2 Do you know the lyrics to your favourite songs?
3 What's in the charts in your country at the moment?
4 Do you sing or play an instrument? What kind of music do you sing/play?

Get it right!

✓ *I know the **lyrics** to that song.*
✗ *I know the ~~letter~~ to that song.*

Culture Vulture

Did you know that the UK singles chart started in 1952? Now the charts include information about top downloads and online music, as well as CDs people buy in shops. Do you have music charts in your country? How often do you listen to the charts on TV / the internet / the radio?

2 Pronunciation /s/ and /z/ DVD

a 3.2 Listen to the sounds /s/ and /z/ in these words.

/s/ song producer   /z/ music president

b 3.3 Listen and choose the correct sound: /s/ or /z/

1 musician 4 house 7 hasn't
2 voice 5 science 8 pencil
3 easy 6 these 9 listen

c 3.4 Listen, check your answers and repeat.

d Follow the /s/ sounds with your finger to find a way through the puzzle. You can move up or down ⇕, left or right ⇔. Work with a partner and say the words.

→ first	course	museum	postcard	message	race
choose	mistake	whose	single	because	police
isn't	disc	mouse	star	please	concert
cousin	those	busy	wasn't	present	answer ↓

e 3.5 Listen and check your answers.

3 Read and listen

a Do you know who Rihanna is? How much do you know about her? Are the sentences true or false? Read the text quickly and check your ideas.

1 Rihanna is from Jamaica.
2 Her first hit single was 'Umbrella'.
3 She works with a lot of famous hip-hop stars.
4 She has been to university.

A girl like RIHANNA

In 2003 Rihanna was an ordinary 15-year-old schoolgirl on the Caribbean island of Barbados. Then a meeting with a music producer gave her the opportunity to become a professional singer. In only a few years, Rihanna has become one of the biggest stars of the twenty-first century.

Rihanna met Evan Rogers, the producer of stars like Cristina Aguilera, when he was on holiday in Barbados. After he heard Rihanna's voice, he immediately knew that she was going to be a star and decided to help her. Over the next year Rihanna and her mother flew many times to Rogers' studio in the USA. Her singing improved and she started to record songs.

In 2005 Rogers sent four songs by Rihanna to important record companies. A few weeks later she had a meeting with the hip-hop star Jay-Z, also President of the Def Jam record label. Twelve hours later, Rihanna signed a contract with Def Jam and her life changed completely.

Her first album *Music of the Sun* sold a million copies. 'Pon De Replay', the first single from the album, was number two in both the UK and US charts, and made her a star.

Her second album, *A Girl Like Me*, included the number one US hit *SOS*.

For her third album, *Good Girl Gone Bad*, Rihanna had help from Jay-Z, Timbaland, Ne-Yo and Justin Timberlake. There have been eight hit singles on this album, including Rihanna's biggest hit: 'Umbrella'. It was number one in the UK charts for 10 weeks.

Seven things you didn't know about Rihanna!

- Her full name is Robyn Rihanna Fenty and her friends call her RiRi.
- She's a fan of Beyoncé and Alicia Keyes.
- She loves Bajan food (from Barbados) like flying fish and mango.
- She's had a lot of different hairstyles.
- She hasn't studied at university, but she's very interested in Psychology.
- Rihanna has worked a lot as a model and she would like to do more of this.
- She started an organisation in 2006 to raise money for sick children.

Which is right? Don't look at the text!
Her first album sold ***a million / a million of*** *copies.*

b 3.6 Read the text again and listen. Then answer the questions.

1 What did Rihanna do before she became a singer? She was in a schoolgirl on the Cari- bbean
2 Why did she and her mother fly to the USA?
3 Which company did she sign a record contract with? Whit Jay Z
4 How old was she Rihanna when she first met Jay-Z?
5 Which song was her biggest hit from *Good Girl Gone Bad*? Is Umbrella
6 What would she like to do in the future?

She would like a model.

c Work with a partner. Ask and answer the questions.

1 Do you like the type of music Rihanna sings?
2 Do you know any other similar singers / bands? Do you like their music?

4. She has 17 years
2. To Roger's studio

4 Grammar

Present perfect and past simple

a Look at the examples and complete the table with the present perfect of the verb *record*.

Get it right!

The verb *go* has two past participles.

✓ *She has been to Rome three times.* = She isn't in Rome now, but she was there at some time in the past.

✗ *She has ~~gone~~ to Rome three times.*

✓ *She has gone to Rome.* = She's in Rome now.

⋯› *Rihanna **has worked** a lot as a model. She **hasn't studied** at university. There **have been** eight hit singles on this album.*

Positive

I/You/We/They …
He/She/It … … an album.

Negative

I/You/We/They …
He/She/It … … an album.

***Yes/No* questions**

… I/you/we/they
… he/she/it … an album?

Short answers

Yes, I/you/we/they **have**. / No, I/you/we/they … .
Yes, he/she/it … . / No, he/she/it **hasn't.**

Information questions

How many albums … I/you/we/they / … he/she/it **recorded**?

Look at the examples of the present perfect and past simple. Then choose the correct word to complete the rule.

⋯› *She**'s worked** a lot as a model. She **started** an organisation to raise money for sick children in 2006.*

- We use the present perfect for past actions. We **say / don't say** exactly when they happened.

Grammar reference: pages 136–137

b Complete the sentences with the verbs in the present perfect.

1 His band … (play) ten concerts. has play
2 Simon … (not read) that book. hasn't read
3 … (you/see) Shakira in concert? Have you saw
4 We … (not study) Psychology. haven't studied
5 Maya … (go) to Egypt. She loved it. has gone
6 … (they/eat) sushi before? Have they ate

c Choose the present perfect or the past simple.

has done

MC Inferno is only a teenager, but he [1]*did / has done* a lot. In 2005 he [2]*bought / has bought* his own studio and then [3]*started / has started* a record label. He [4]*began / has began* listening to hip-hop when he was 13. First he [5]*learned / has learned* the lyrics to his favourite rap albums, and then he [6]*wrote / has written* his own words. MC Inferno [7]*played / has played* at many clubs and festivals in Liverpool. In 2006 he [8]*won / has won* a music competition called 'Streetwaves'.

5 Speak

a You are going to act out an interview between a rock star and a journalist.

Student A: You are a rock star. Make notes about:

- your name / the name of your band
- when you started singing / playing
- the names of your hit songs / albums
- the cities / the countries you have played in
- a typical day for you
- your future plans

Student B: Turn to page 125.

b Work with a partner. Student B interview Student A.

c Tell the class about any interesting questions or answers.

6 Vocabulary

Music online

a 3.7 Match the two parts of the sentences. Then listen and check.

1 H

1 **Cover art** is
2 When you **download** music
3 You sing into a **microphone**
4 A **playlist** is a selection of
5 A **record label** is a company
6 **Tracks** are songs
7 When you **update** a website
8 When you **upload** music you

A you add new information to it.
B on an album.
C you copy it from the internet to your computer.
D to record your voice.
E copy it from your computer to the internet.
F that records and sells music.
G songs created in a digital audio programme.
H the picture on the cover of a CD.

Check it out!

- Sometimes the same word can be a **noun** and a **verb**.

noun	verb
a **download**	to **download**
a **record**	to **record**
a **programme**	to **programme**

b Do you know any more words for music online? Write them in your Workbook (page 120 Exercise 3w).

c Work in a group. Ask and answer the questions. Then tell the class.

1 What are the best websites to download music from?
2 Where can you upload music or photos to?
3 Which albums do you think have great cover art?
4 Have you ever sung into a microphone? Where and when?
5 Which tracks would you choose to make the best playlist in the world?

7 Listen

a What do record labels do? Make a list of what record labels do to help artists that make music for them.

b 3.8 Listen and write the things that students learn to do at Sharp Records.

organise concerts | record songs | upload music | design cover art | create a webpage | sell records

c 3.8 Listen again and choose the correct answer: A, B or C.

1 Sharp Records teaches ...about the music business.
A school teachers
B young people in the UK
C musicians all over the world

2 Sharp Records began the project ...
A at a secondary school.
B at a university.
C with the *Sugababes*.

3 Fans can listen to tracks ...
A in a recording studio.
B in concert.
C online.

4 Charisse has not ...
A made a music video.
B written her own lyrics.
C been on TV.

5 Simo used to ...
A like rap.
B make his own tracks on his computer.
C sing on his own.

Get it right!

We spell *a record* and *to record* the same, but we pronounce them differently.
a record /ˈrekɔːd/
to record /rɪˈkɔːd/

8 Grammar

Present perfect with *for* and *since*

a Look at the examples and complete the table with *have/has* and *for* and *since*.

> *I've worked* on the project **for** three years.
> ***How long have*** Sharp Records run the project?
> Charisse has been with Sharp Records **for** two years now, **since** she was 14.
>
> **Questions**
>
> | | | | |
> |---|---|---|---|
> | **How long** | … | I/you/we/they | **lived** in |
> | | … | he/she/it | London? |
>
> **Answers**
> … five years.
> … 2005.
>
> Choose the correct words to complete the rules.
> - We use ***for*** / ***since*** with the present perfect and a specific point in time.
> - We use ***for*** / ***since*** with the present perfect and a period of time.
> - With ***for*** and ***since***, the action started in the past and ***is finished*** / ***is still happening***.

Grammar reference: pages 136–137

Get it right!

- *for + a year / a long time / ages.*
- *since + 2008 / I was a child / I was 11.*
- ✓ *I have had this computer for a long time.*
- ✗ *I have had this computer ~~since~~ a long time.*

b Copy and complete the table with the words.

8 o'clock three minutes 2009 a long time
a month five weeks I was three years old
last week March Saturday morning six years
Tuesday ten seconds

for	since
three minutes	*8 o'clock*

c Put the words in the correct order.

1 you / been / How long / at school today / have ?
2 How long / have / studied / English / you ?
3 have / had / How long / you / this / book ?
4 known / have / you / How long / your best friend ?
5 in your home / has / your family / lived / How long ?

Get it right!

✓ *How long have you lived in London?*
✗ *~~Since when do you live in London?~~*

d Answer the questions in Exercise 8c about you. Write two answers for each question, one with *for* and one with *since*.

Interaction 7 DVD

Talking about songs

a 3.9 Listen to Ben and Sarah choosing a song to upload onto their website. Do they agree on a song?

b 3.9 Listen again. Who says each phrase, *B* (Ben) or *S* (Sarah)?

What do you think of … ?
Oh, I don't.
I love it.
I think it's great.
So do I.
I think it's rubbish.

c 3.10 Turn to page 124. Listen to the sentences and repeat them. Practise the pronunciation of the stressed *I* (for contrast) and unstressed *I*.

d Work with a partner.
Student A: Turn to page 127.
Student B: Turn to page 130.

Portfolio 7

An album review

a Read the two album reviews. Did the reviewers like the albums?

b In an album review we use facts (*Natasha Khan is British*) and opinions (*That song is great*). Read the sentences and write *F* for facts and *O* for opinions.

1 This is their second album.
2 I love her voice.
3 The Jonas Brothers are American.
4 I think this is their best album.
5 There are 11 tracks on the album.
6 It's good for when you want to relax.
7 I like every song on the album.

c We use adjectives to give our opinions. Write the adjectives in the table.

~~amazing~~ boring disappointing fantastic great OK rubbish terrible the best not bad

Positive	Neutral	Negative
amazing		

d Write a review of an album. Include:

- the name of the album
- the names of some tracks
- some facts about the artist/album
- your opinions about the album

Don't include a star rating!

e Swap reviews with a partner. Read your partner's review and give their album a star rating (1–5 stars).

Star Music Mag

File Edit View Insert Format Tools Actions Help

http://www.starmusicmag.com/august/reviews.php

HOME | NEWS | REVIEWS |

Star rating: ✪✪✪✪

Two Suns is the second album from Bat for Lashes. I love Natasha Khan's voice, it's so mysterious! There are 11 tracks on the album and one extra iTunes bonus track you can download. My favourites are 'Daniel' and 'Two Planets'. Her lyrics are interesting and make me feel sad and happy. It's not party music but it's a good album for when you want to relax and forget about everything. I'm going to see her in concert soon and I can't wait!

by Mark (London, UK)

Star rating: ✪✪✪✪✪

I've been a Jonas Brothers fan since I saw them on the Disney Channel. The American brothers are a great pop boy band and I think *A Little Bit Longer* is their best album. Listen to it and you'll see why they're so popular. There are 14 tracks on the album and they're all different. Lots of guitar in 'Burnin' up', slower songs like 'When you look me in the eyes' and great dance tracks like 'Live to party'. I like every song. Buy a copy now, you won't be sorry!

by Jade (Brisbane, Australia)

Email us your album review to www.starmusicmag.com

Thursday, May 11 Going

GIG

DJ IQ

At 15, turntablist DJ IQ had his own radio show; at 17 he'd scooped the DMC young DJ title. Now 21 years old, the North-West London lad has been graduating from decks to production desk. As well as putting in the hours with solo gigs and as Jehst's tour DJ, he has also been building up an impressive list of production credits with high-profile British artists.

Those MCs are now on hand to return the favour: *Live! From The Sofa*, out this week on Mancan/Dented Records, is IQ's follow-up to last year's Brainfood album and boasts guest vocalists that resemble a who's who of British hip hop.

As for this live showcase, IQ has a stage-busting line up that should make the album's posse cut Eight Bars Of Fire a highlight. This should be a British hip-hop night to savour.
Tonight, Notting Hill Arts Club, 21 Notting Hill Gate W11, 6pm to 2am, free before 8pm, £5 after. Tel:020 7460 4459 Tube: Notting Hill Gate

Brand New Bookings!

Below is a list of London's biggest upcoming gigs. Go to timeout.com/booking ahead for details of hundreds more live music events for the rest of the year and beyond.

May

1 **McFly** Hammersmith Apollo, £22.90
13 **Dan Auerbach** Islington Academy, £14
15-16 **St Etienne** Bloomsbury Ballroom, £20

June

9 **EXTRA Beyoncé** 02 Arena £49.50 (Also May 25-6, June 8)
11, 16-19 **The Script** Shepherds Bush Empire, £18.50
17 **Jarvis Cocker** The Troxy £tbc
26 **Seal** Hammersmith Apollo, £45-£30

July

1 **Crosby, Stills & Nash** Royal Albert Hall, £65-£45
14 **Of Montreal** Shepherd's Bush Empire, £15.50

August and beyond

Aug 22-23 **V FESTIVAL: Oasis + The Killers + Elbow + MGMT + Razorlight + Fatboy Slim** + more Hylands Park, Chelmsford, £152.50 (w/e ticket with camping), £132.50 (w/e ticket without camping), £73.50 (day ticket).
Nov 27 **Gong** Forum, £20
Dec 12 **Status Quo** Wembley Arena, £33.50

Venues

12 Bar Club *22-23 Denmark Place, off Denmark street, WC2H 8NL 020 7240 2120. ⊖ Tottenham Court Road*
100 Club *100 Oxford Street, W1D 1LL, 020 7636 0933 ⊖ Tottenham Court Road*
229 *229 Great Portland Street W1W 5PN, 020 7323 7229 ⊖ Great Portland Street*
93 Feet East *150 Brick Lane, E1 6QL, 020 7247 3293 ⊖ Liverpool Street*
Ace Café *Ace Corner, NW10 7UD, 020 8961 1000 ⊖/rail Stonebridge Park*
Apple Tree *45 Mount Pleasant WC1X 0AE, 020 7837 2365 ⊖ Farringdon*

1 Culture UK: London music scene

a Look at the information about different music events in London and answer the questions.

1 Match the artists with the venues for their concerts.

Artists DJ IQ Beyoncé Mc Fly The Killers St. Etienne

Venues The O2 Arena V Festival, Hylands Park Bloomsbury Ballroom Hammersmith Apollo Notting Hill Arts Club

2 When do people start singing at the Hip Hop Karaoke night?

3 If you want to play at the Underage Festival what two things do you have to do?

4 What type of event is *breakin' convention*?

5 Which DJ has had his own radio show?

b Copy and complete the puzzle and find the mystery word.

1 A place where a concert or music event happens.

2 Someone who plays or sings with you in a music band.

3 Someone who plays music on the radio or at discos

4 When music is played to an audience e.g. at a concert.

5 Another word for a song on a CD.

6 Singing a song into a microphone for fun.

7 A live performance by a musician or a band.

8 Something given to the winner of a competition.

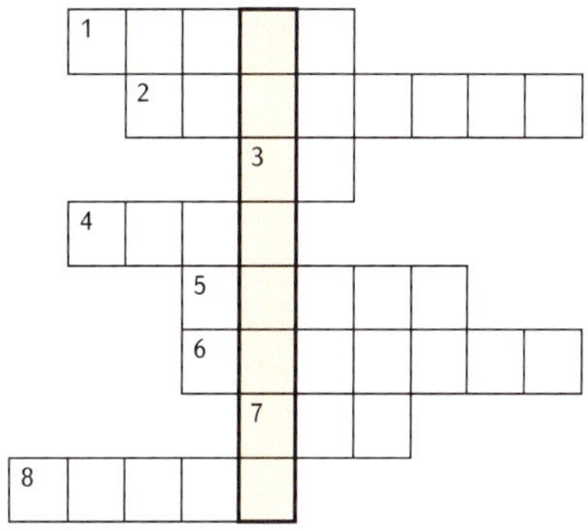

c Work with a partner. Look at the music events on in London. Which events would you like to go to? Why?

2 Your noticeboard

A poster: music concerts in your country

a Work in a group. Make a list of concert venues in your country.

b Use the internet or music magazines to find information about the concert and music venues. Find the following information:

- venues
- artists(s)
- date(s)
- price
- where you can buy tickets

c Make a poster about concert and music venues in your country. Include the information from Exercise 2b and pictures of the venues or artists.

8 Believe it or not

Zero conditional
First conditional
Vocabulary: Adjectives of personality; Special days
Interaction 8: Responding to news

1 Read and listen

a Read the text quickly. Which of these things are included in the texts?

animal   year you were born   month you were born   lucky colour   lucky number

Chinese horoscopes

What personality do you have if you're a dog, a pig or a rat? Find your animal and lucky number from the year you were born and read about yourself.

Pig 猪
1983, 1995, 2007 6 7
OK, pigs, you have lots of friends, you're sociable and easy-going, but everyone knows that pigs are lazy! If you're a pig, you don't like hard work.

Rat 鼠
1972, 1984, 1996 1 6
It's great being a rat! They're intelligent, hard-working and sociable. But it's not all good news – rats don't plan well for the future and they talk too much!

Ox 牛
1973, 1985, 1997
Are you patient? Are you strong? If you're an ox, you are. You're serious and hard-working, but you need to have more fun! Go to a party or a theme park!

Dog 狗
1982, 1994, 2006 8
If you're a dog, you're kind, sensitive and easy-going. But it's not all good. Sometimes you're impatient, especially if there's a problem.

Tiger 虎
1974, 1986, 1998 1 3
These fun, natural leaders are really self-confident and love adventure. In fact, tigers are fine if everything is OK. Problems make them feel anxious.

Rooster 鷄
1981, 1993, 2005 6 8
Roosters are hard-working but you birds sometimes find it difficult to relax. Take a break, roosters – sit down, listen to some music and chill out!

Rabbit 兔
1975, 1987, 1999 4
We all know rabbits are lucky! But did you know that big ears mean you are good listeners too? You're sensitive, but sometimes you don't live in the real world.

Monkey 猴
1980, 1992, 2004 6 8
Watch out for monkeys! They're intelligent and friendly, but they can be dishonest and they like laughing at people.

Dragon 龍
1976, 1988, 2000 9
If you're a dragon, you're a natural leader. Dragons are full of energy and self-confidence. But people say you're insensitive!

Sheep 羊
1979, 1991, 2003 8 9
Wake up, sheep! You're so relaxed, you're nearly asleep! Yes, you're sensitive, but you don't like making decisions. You prefer to follow everyone else.

Horse 馬
1978, 1990, 2002 9
Calling all friendly horses. You might be sociable and easy-going, but be careful when you're angry! You can be really insensitive.

Snake 蛇
1977, 1989, 2001 3 9
Snakes are quiet, intelligent people who always know what to do. But why are you so mean with money?

b 3.11 Read the text again and listen. Which animals …

1 have lots of friends. (4 animals)
2 work hard. (3 animals)
3 have lots of confidence. (2 animals)
4 are clever. (3 animals)
5 listen and understand when you have a problem. (3 animals)

c Work in a group. What is your Chinese horoscope? Do you agree with the description of you? Why? / Why not?

2 Vocabulary Adjectives of personality

a 3.12 Match the adjectives with the definitions. Then listen and check.

Someone who …

1 C hard-working

1 does a lot of work
2 is relaxed and doesn't worry about things
3 talks a lot
4 always tells the truth
5 likes to meet and spend time with other people
6 feels uncomfortable with other people
7 gives money, time or help to others
8 listens to others and understands them
9 doesn't mind waiting and is kind when people make mistakes
10 makes good decisions or shows good sense

A easy-going
B generous
C ~~hard-working~~
D honest
E patient
F sensible
G sensitive
H shy
I sociable
J talkative

Get it right!

quiet or quite?

✓ *She's quite clever.*
✓ *Shh! Be quiet!*
✗ *Shh! Be ~~quite~~!*

b 3.13 Match the opposites with the adjectives in Exercise 2a. Then listen and check.

anxious dishonest insensitive lazy mean
impatient quiet self-confident silly unsociable

Check it out!

We sometimes use **prefixes** to make **opposites**.

lucky → **un**lucky
patient → **im**patient
sensitive → **in**sensitive
honest → **dis**honest

c Do you know any more adjectives of personality? Write them in your Workbook (page 121 Exercise 1).

d Which three adjectives best describe your personality? Write them down. Show the adjectives to your partner. Does he/she agree? Why? / Why not?

3 Pronunciation

Syllables DVD

a 3.14 Listen to the adjectives and write the number of syllables.

1 dishonest
2 easy-going
3 fun
4 talkative
5 honest
6 impatient
7 insensitive
8 friendly
9 hard-working
10 mean

b 3.15 Listen, check and repeat.

c 3.16 Listen and repeat.

He's so hard-working, self-confident, fun, friendly, sociable, easy-going and talkative!

4 Grammar

Zero conditional

a Look at the examples and choose the correct words to complete the rules.

*If you'**re** a dog, you'**re** kind. **If** you'**re** a pig, you **don't like** hard work.*
*What personality **do** you **have if** you'**re** a dog, a pig or a rat?*

- The zero conditional talks about things that are **always** / **sometimes** true.
- We make the zero conditional with *if* + present simple, + **present** / **past** simple.

Grammar reference: page 137

b Complete the sentences with the present simple of the verbs.

1 are, is

1 If you … (be) an ox, your lucky number … (be) eight.
2 If we … (visit) our grandmother, we always … (take) the train.
3 If I … (not understand) my Maths homework, my sister … (help) me.
4 He … (play) football after school if he … (not have) a lot of homework.
5 Elizabeth is very shy. If she … (go) to a party, she … (not talk) to anyone.
6 What … (happen) if you … (mix) soap and water?

c Complete the sentences about you.

1 If I want to talk to my friends, I …
2 If I argue with my parents, I …
3 If I don't have a lot of homework, I …
4 If I go to a party, I …

Check it out!

- We can write the same conditional sentence in two ways.
  If she's in London, she visits us.
  (**with** a comma)
  She visits us if she's in London.
  (**no** comma)

5 Speak

a Work with a partner. Ask your partner the questions and write his/her answers: A, B or C.

PERSONALITY QUIZ

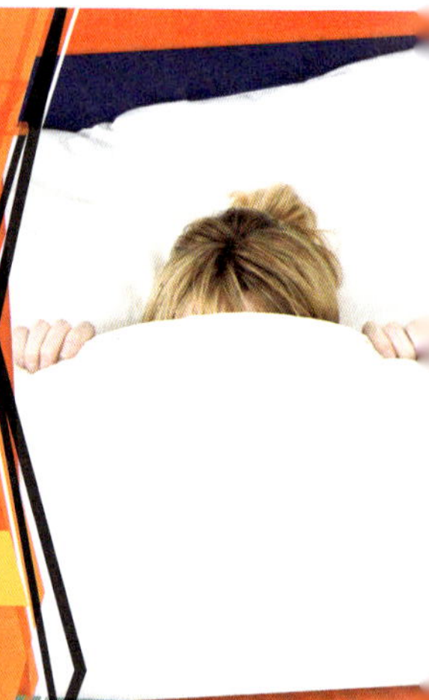

1 If you wake up early, do you …
A go to school early to see your friends?
B go back to sleep?
C do some homework?

2 If somebody gives you some money, do you …
A go shopping the same day?
B buy a present for a friend?
C save it?

3 If someone tells you a secret, do you …
A tell everybody?
B tell your best friend?
C tell nobody?

4 If you have some free time, do you …
A go out with friends?
B relax and listen to music?
C help your parents at home?

5 If you go to a party, do you …
A talk to everybody?
B talk to one or two friends?
C talk to nobody?

b Look at your partner's answers. Are they mostly As, Bs or Cs? Read the Key on page 143. Do you agree with it?

c Write another personality quiz question for your partner. Tell the class your partner's answer.

Culture Vulture

Did you know that the date of Chinese New Year changes every year? The day is between January 21 and February 20. When do you celebrate the New Year? Do you know any other holidays that can change date?

6 Vocabulary

Special days

a 3.17 Match the special days with the pictures. Then listen and check.

A 3 Diwali

1 Christmas Day
2 Day of the Dead
3 ~~Diwali~~
4 Eid
5 Hanukkah
6 New Year's Eve
7 Thanksgiving

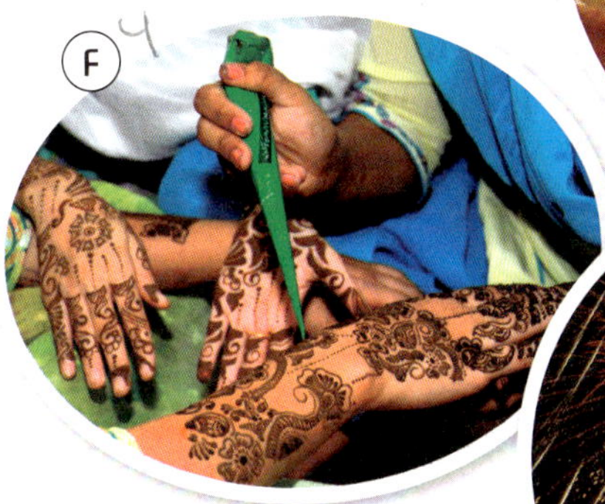

Check it out!

New Year's **Eve**
= the day **before** New Year's Day
Christmas **Eve**
= the day **before** Christmas Day

b 3.18 Listen to the five people. Which celebrations in Exercise 6a are they talking about?

c Work in a group and answer the questions.

1 Which special days do people celebrate in your country?
2 Do you celebrate any other special days?
3 What is your favourite special day? Why?

7 Listen

a A superstition is when we believe things are lucky or unlucky. Look at the pictures. Do you think the things are lucky or unlucky?

b 3.19 Listen to people talking about superstitions around the world. Match the countries with pictures A–E.

Argentina China Japan
Russia Turkey

c 3.19 Listen again. Are the sentences *right* (✓) or *wrong* (✗)? Correct the wrong sentences.

1 In China people clean their houses after the New Year festival.
2 In Turkey people think that black cats are sometimes unlucky.
3 White snakes bring bad luck in Japan.
4 The number five is unlucky in Japan.
5 Russians don't like looking in broken mirrors.
6 You shouldn't pick up coins from the ground in Argentina.

d What superstitions are there in your country? Do you believe them?

8 Grammar First conditional

a Look at the examples and choose the correct words to complete the rules.

> *If you **find** a white snake, you**'ll be** lucky.*
> *You**'ll have** bad luck **if** you **don't touch** your hair.*
>
> - We use the first conditional to talk about possibilities in the **future** / **past**.
> - We make the first conditional with *if* + **present simple** / **infinitive** and *will* or *won't* + infinitive **with** / **without** *to*.

Grammar reference: page 137

b Match the two parts of the sentences.

1 D

1 If you break a mirror,
2 Your teacher will be angry
3 I'll make you a cake
4 If you don't work harder,
5 When I leave school,
6 What will you wear

A I'll go to university.
B you won't pass your exam.
C if you go to the party?
D you'll have bad luck.
E if you want.
F if you don't do your homework.

Check it out!

***If** I see him, I'll tell him.* =
I'm **not sure** I'll see him.
***When** I see him, I'll tell him.* =
I'm **sure** I'll see him.

c Complete the questions with *will*/ *won't* and the verbs.

1 If you … (not pass) your exams, what … you … (do)?
2 Who … you … (meet) if you … (go out) this weekend?
3 If you … (not have) any homework this evening, what … you … (do)?
4 Where … your family … (stay), if they … (go) on holiday this year?

d Work with a partner. Ask and answer the questions in Exercise 8c.

Get it right!

If you find …
✓ *If you find a snake, you'll be lucky.*
✗ *If you ~~will~~ find a snake, you'll be lucky.*

Interaction 8 DVD

Responding to news

a 3.20 Listen to Sophie's conversations and number the pictures in order.

b 3.20 Listen again and match 1–5 with A–E.

1 Well done!
2 I'm sorry.
3 Good luck!
4 Congratulations!
5 Oh, no!

A You must be really upset.
B That's brilliant news!
C That's excellent!
D That's awful.
E I'm sure it'll be fine.

c 3.21 Turn to page 124. Listen to the sentences and repeat them. Practise sounding sincere!

d Work with a partner.
Student A: Turn to page 127.
Student B: Turn to page 130.

A

B

C

D

E

Portfolio 8

Messages

a Look at the different types of message. Match A–D with 1–4.

1 a formal invitation to a celebration of a special day
2 a congratulations message
3 a good luck message
4 an informal invitiation

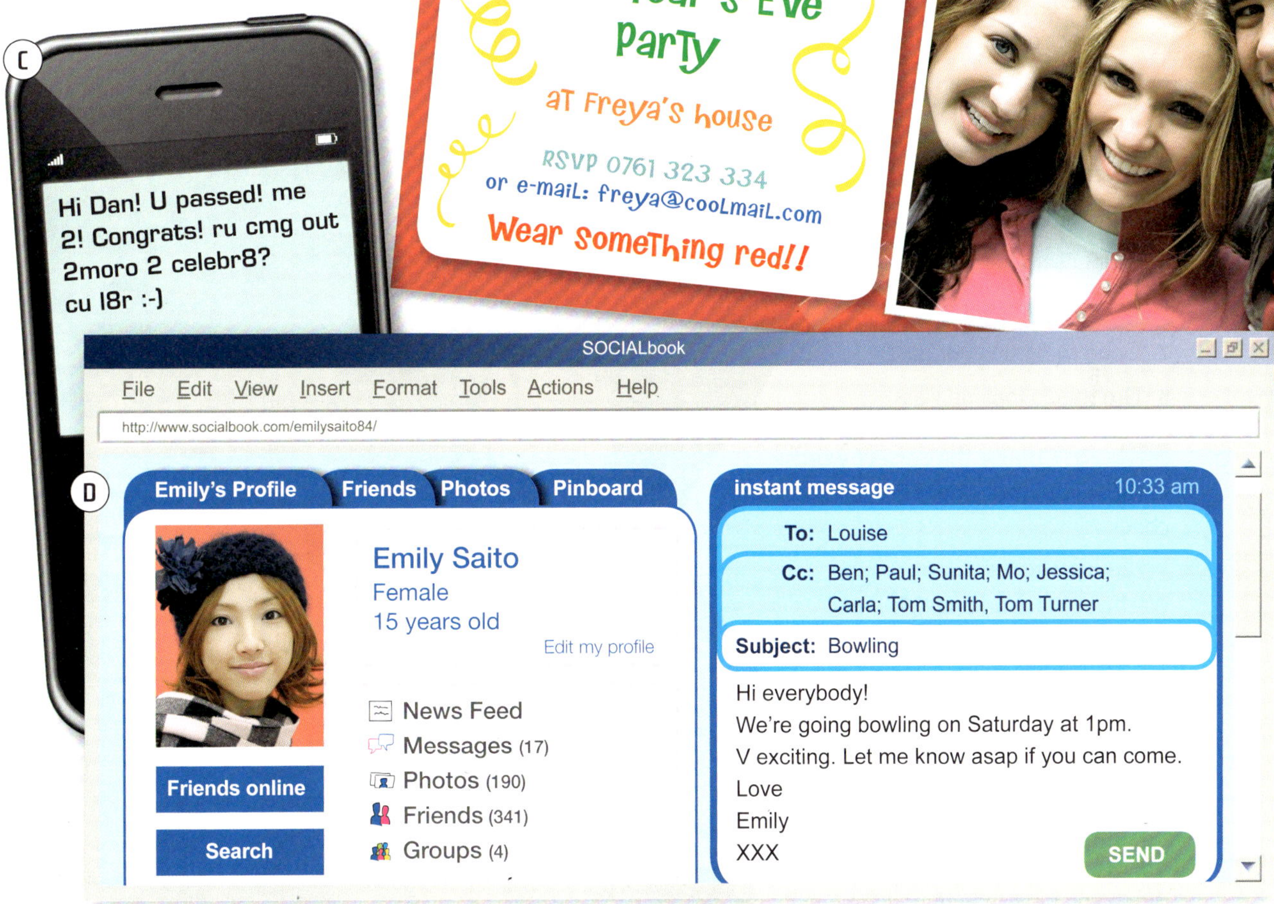

b Match the abbreviations with their meanings.

1 H

1 RSVP
2 cu l8r
3 ru
4 b4
5 2moro
6 v
7 XXX
8 asap

A are you
B before
C kisses
D very
E see you later
F as soon as possible
G tomorrow
H please reply (French: *réspondez s'il vous plaît*)

Check it out!

- Sometimes we leave out words in short messages.
  Back soon. = I'll/We'll be back soon.
  Gone to shops. = I've/We've gone to the shops.

c Take out the unnecessary words and use abbreviations to make short messages.

1 I'll be back home before 7pm.
2 I've gone to the supermarket.
3 I'll see you very soon.
4 I've left some chicken in the fridge for you.

d Work with a partner. Write a congratulations text message and a good luck email to your partner. Use abbreviations and short phrases like the ones in Exercise b.

e Read your partner's messages and reply.

Superstition

1 Song

a 3.22 Look at the pictures and listen. Which things in the song are in the picture?

b 3.22 Listen again and put the lines in the correct order.

1 Thirteen-month-old baby,
2 Very superstitious,
3 Seven years of bad luck,
4 Writing on the wall,
5 Ladder's about to fall,
6 Very superstitious,
7 Good things in your past.
8 Dropped a looking glass,

c 3.23 Choose the correct words in the rest of the song. Then listen and check.

Very superstitious,
Wash your face and *hair* / *hands*
Let me cause a problem,
Do all that you *can* / *can't*

Keep me daydreaming,
Keep me going *strong* / *on*
You don't wanna save me,
Sad is the *song* / *belong*.

When you believe in *things* / *dreams*,
That you don't understand,
Then you suffer!
Superstition ain't the *way* / *road*.

Check it out!

- We often use **short forms** in songs.
  want to → wanna isn't → ain't

d What is the song's message? Do you agree with it?

1 If you are superstitious, your life will go well.
2 If you are superstitious, you'll be unhappy.
3 If you wash a lot, you won't be superstitious.

Song Superstition

2 Sound check

a 3.24 Match the lines with the correct stress pattern, A or B. Then listen and check.

A ●•••● B ●•••●•

1 Very superstitious, A
2 Writing on the wall, B
3 Very superstitious, A
4 Ladder's 'bout to fall, B

b 3.25 Listen again to the verse. Copy the sentences and <u>underline</u> the stressed syllables.

Thir-teen month old ba-by, Se-ven years of bad luck,
Dropped a loo-kin' glass, Good things in your past.

c 3.25 Listen again and repeat.

MOTOWN RECORDS

If you like soul music, you'll know the Motown record label. It started in 1959 in Detroit, also called the **Mo**tor **town**. Motown's African American artists became famous all over the world. The Motown sound was a mixture of soul and pop.Famous Motown artists included Diana Ross, Stevie Wonder and The Jackson Five. Nowadays the label produces different styles of music, including rap, hip-hop and rock. Current Motown artists include Shontelle and the Kaiser Chiefs.

3 Musical notes

a 3.26 Listen and write the types of music from the 1960s and '70s in the order you hear them.

R&B Soul Funk Pop

b Which groups were famous in your country in the 1960s and 70s?

Get it right! 7 and 8

Common errors

1 *been* or *gone?*

We use *have / has + been* if someone has returned from a place (they are not there now).

✓ **A:** *Do you know Berlin?*

✓ **B:** *Yeah, **I've been** there many times.*

✗ **B:** *Yeah, I've ~~gone~~ there many times.*

We use *have/has + gone* if someone is still there.

A: *Where's Nacho?*

✓ **B:** *He's **gone** to the supermarket. He'll be back soon.*

a Complete the phone call with *been* or *gone*.

Hi Mum – yeah, we're having a great time! Now, we're sitting outside a café, but we've done so many things – Well, we've [1]… to the Louvre Museum and to Notre Dame Cathedral, and Jen and I have just [2]… up the Eiffel Tower – Yeah, Jen's with me now. She says hello - Alicia? No, she isn't here. She's [3]… to get the tickets for the Rihanna concert. Yeah, I'll say hello for you – No, Martin's [4]… to buy Rihanna T-shirts for us all. – OK, I'll call you later. Bye.

b 3.27 Listen and check your answers.

2 …since Monday

We use the present perfect, not the present simple or the past simple, with *since*.

✓ *I **haven't bought** an album since 2009.*

✗ *I ~~don't buy~~ / ~~didn't buy~~ an album since 2009.*

Remember to use *for* + a period of time and *since* + the start of a period.

✓ *I've been here **for** two days / **since** Monday.*

✗ *I've been here ~~since~~ two days.*

Work with a partner. Say a word or expression from the box and your partner makes a sentence with *since / for* and the word. Do it quickly!

2010 last week my birthday five days
a long time I was five years old
December Thursday two minutes

3 First conditional

We use the present simple, not *will*, after *if* in first conditional sentences.

✓ *If you **break** a mirror, you'll have seven years bad luck.*

✗ *If you ~~will~~ break a mirror, you'll have seven years bad luck.*

a Correct the sentences that are wrong.

1 You'll have good luck if you see a black cat.
2 If you won't go to the party, I won't speak to you!
3 She'll go to university if she will work hard.
4 If you will go to the supermarket for me, I'll give you five euros.
5 The teacher will be happy with you if you tell the truth.

b Work with a partner and complete the sentences with your own ideas.

1 If …, I'll buy you an ice cream.
2 Your teacher will be angry if … .
3 If …, you'll have a lot of friends.
4 You won't pass your exams if … .

4 Say it right!

Consonant Clusters

a 3.28 Some words end in more than one consonant. Listen and write the consonants at the end of these words in your notebook. (Be careful – some are plural!)

1 ta _ _ _
2 proje _ _ _
3 a _ _
4 te _ _ _
5 consona _ _

b 3.29 Listen and repeat these words. Make sure you pronounce all the consonants at the end of the words. Then read the words to a partner.

1 crisp
2 crafts
3 effect
4 scientists
5 gift
6 biggest

Review 7 and 8

1 Grammar

a Complete the sentences with the verbs in the present perfect.

see read not buy meet work not go

1 I … six of the Harry Potter books.
2 … you … the new film about aliens?
3 They … to Africa before. They're really excited.
4 We … your cousin before. He's very nice.
5 I … a present for Vicky. What do you think she'd like?
6 She … all over the world with her company.

[ ] 6

b Choose the correct words.

1 We've been at school *for / since* two hours.
2 They've lived in that house *for / since* 1998.
3 Jan's had her bike *for / since* four months.
4 I've known my best friend *for / since* ten years.
5 Have you seen Fran *for / since* Monday?
6 Mark's been at the hospital *for / since* 8 o'clock.

[ ] 6

c Match the two parts of the sentences.

1 If you press this,
2 She has breakfast at 6.30 am
3 If the weather's bad,
4 He always does well
5 Teaching dogs to sit is easy
6 I practise the guitar in my room

A we don't go to the country at the weekend.
B if he works hard.
C the door opens.
D if she goes to work by train.
E if my family are out.
F if you give them biscuits.

[ ] 6

d Put the words in the correct order.

1 tell / I / Justin / If / I'll / him / see
2 she / to / concert / When / we'll / the / comes / go
3 it's / eat / outside / cold / won't / If / we
4 They / he / homework / won't do / doesn't / if / their / help / them
5 Will / don't go / we / Laura / to her party / be angry / if?
6 will / doesn't / do / if / bus / What / come / you / the?

[ ] 6

2 Vocabulary

a Complete the sentences with the words.

album hit to record lyrics to perform studio

1 Her new single is a … in Europe.
2 I know all the … to their songs.
3 They're going … at four big festivals this summer.
4 Have you heard their latest … ?
5 Be quiet! They're working in the … .
6 She wants … some songs with that new producer.

[ ] 6

b Write the missing letters in your notebook.

1 One song in your personal music system: t _ _ _ _
2 To put information from your computer onto the internet: u _ _ _ _ _
3 To add new information to a website: u _ _ _ _ _
4 A company that makes and sells albums: r _ _ _ _ _ _ _ _ _ _
5 To put songs or videos from the internet onto your computer: d _ _ _ _ _ _ _
6 A selection of songs in your personal music system: p _ _ _ _ _ _ _

[ ] 6

c Match the adjectives with the descriptions.

hard-working impatient sensitive talkative easy-going generous shy sociable honest sensible

1 Sophie talks all the time.
2 Jack likes buying presents for people.
3 Mia spends a lot of time doing her homework.
4 Ryan doesn't worry about anything. He's always relaxed.
5 Emily doesn't like answering questions in class.
6 Ethan never lies, he always tells the truth.
7 Molly likes meeting new people.
8 Adam always thinks about how other people feel.
9 Louise is always prepared and knows what to do.
10 Chris is terrible at waiting for anything.

[ ] 10

d Put the letters in the correct order and make special days.

1 ukHankah
2 mastrisCh yaD
3 lawiDi
4 weN arYes vEe
5 givThknasing
6 yDa fo het Ddae

[ ] 6

9 What does she look like?

Question tags
Defining relative clauses
Vocabulary: Describing appearance; On TV
Interaction 9: Identifying people

1 Vocabulary

Describing appearance

a Work with a partner. Take turns to describe a picture and guess which one it is.

She's got blonde hair.

Picture C?

b 3.30 Match the pictures with the sentences. Then listen and check.

1 She's got **short**, **straight** hair and she's **beautiful**, like a lot of models.
2 It's really **cute**! Look at its **little** nose and **big**, **round** eyes!
3 **A:** She's quite **fat**.
B: It's rude to say fat. You should say **overweight**.
4 He's **bald**, but I think he's really **good-looking**.
5 He's got **pointed** ears and a **long** chin. He looks strange, but he's not **ugly**.
6 She's **pretty** and she's got **long**, **wavy** hair.

c Which adjectives of appearance are:
1 negative?
2 often used for men?
3 often used for women?

d Do you know any more words for describing appearance? Write them in your Workbook (page 122 Exercise 1).

Check it out!

look like =
have the same appearance
*He **looks like** his father.*
*She **looks** nothing **like** her sister!*

Get it right!

✓ *She's got short hair.*
✗ *She's got ~~the hair short~~.*

2 Speak

a Work with a partner. Match the dogs with their owners. There is one extra picture.

b Take turns to describe an owner or a dog and to guess the picture.

She's got long, curly red hair.
It's brown and white and it's got short ears.

3 Listen

a 3.31 Listen to the interview. What is the speaker's opinion: 1, 2 or 3?

1 Many people look like their pets.
2 Many people don't have pets.
3 Many people have the same personality as their pets.

b 3.31 Listen again and choose the correct words in the text.

1 pets

Appearance
- A lot of people look like their [1] friends / pets
- An American scientist took photos of [2] dogs / cats and their owners
- People matched the photos of pets and owners together [3] correctly / incorrectly
- Most people think their pets are [4] ugly / beautiful

Personality
- The happiest pet owners are people who have [5] dogs / fish
- Cat owners are [6] sensitive / insensitive
- People who own snakes are the most [7] independent / intelligent

c Work with a partner. Answer the questions.

1 Do you know anyone who looks like their pet? Describe them.
2 What pet have you got / would you like? Why?
3 Do you agree with Dr Jill White? Why? / Why not?

4 Grammar

Question tags

a Look at the examples and complete the table with the correct form of verbs *be* and *do*.

Check it out!

- With other tenses or modal verbs, repeat the **auxiliary** or the **modal** verb in the question tag.
  *You**'ve got** a car, **haven't** you?* *He **can** swim, **can't** he?*
  *She **shouldn't** go out, **should** she?* *It **won't** rain, **will** it?*

*People who keep snakes are very intelligent, **aren't they?***
*I don't look like a snake, **do I?*** *People don't really look like their pets, **do they?***

Positive statements: *be*	**Negative statements: *be***
I'm late, **aren't I?**	I'm not late, **am I?**
You/We/They're late, … **you/we/they?**	You/We/They aren't late, … **you/we/they?**
He/She/It's late, … **he/she/it?**	He/She/It isn't late, … **he/she/it?**

Positive statements: other present simple verbs	**Negative statements: other present simple verbs**
I/You/We/They take photos, **don't I/you/we/they?**	I/You/We/They don't take photos, … **I/you/we/they?**
He/She/It takes photos, … **he/she/it?**	He/She/It doesn't take photos, … **he/she/it?**

Choose the correct words to complete the rules.

- We can use question tags to check information or to invite someone to **agree** / **disagree** with us.
- After a positive statement, we use a **positive** / **negative** question tag.
- After a negative statement, we use a **positive** / **negative** question tag.

Grammar reference: page 138

b Match the statements with the question tags.

1 C

1 He's really good-looking,
2 Her fish looks like her,
3 We can't pay in dollars,
4 Jon doesn't like big dogs,
5 She's got a long nose,
6 I haven't been here before,

A can we?
B does he?
C isn't he?
D have I?
E doesn't it?
F hasn't she?

c Complete the sentences with question tags.

has she?

1 She hasn't got straight hair, …
2 They are bald, …
3 I'm really late, …
4 You will come to dinner tonight, …
5 We haven't tried this before, …
6 I should go now, …

5 Pronunciation Question tags DVD

a 3.32 Listen to the pronunciation and look at the different meanings.

1 She's a vet, isn't she? = I'm not sure. Is she a vet? *(checking information)*

2 She's a vet, isn't she? = I'm sure she's a vet. *(asking for agreement)*

b 3.33 Listen to the sentences. Choose the correct meaning: A or B

1 He's cute, isn't he?
A Not sure B Sure

2 They're beautiful dogs, aren't they?
A Not sure B Sure

3 She won't lose the race, will she?
A Not sure B Sure

4 We have got enough money, haven't we?
A Not sure B Sure

5 She doesn't like curly hair, does she?
A Not sure B Sure

6 They can see us, can't they?
A Not sure B Sure

c 3.33 Listen, check your answers and repeat.

6 Vocabulary On TV

a 3.34 Complete the descriptions with the words in the box. Then listen and check.

advertisement channel chat show comedy series documentary drama series quiz show soap opera the news

1 quiz show

1 A … is a game where people answer questions to win prizes.
2 On a … famous people answer questions about themselves and their work.
3 A … is a TV station that shows lots of different programmes.
4 A … is a programme that gives facts and information about a subject.
5 A … is funny and has the same characters every week.
6 … s are on TV between programmes. They try and sell things.
7 A … is serious and has the same characters every week.
8 … is a programme that reports recent events and things happening now.
9 A … is a drama that continues over a long period of time. The characters are the same in every programme.

Get it right!

✓ *This is my favourite series.*
✗ *This is my favourite ~~serie~~.*

b 3.35 Listen and choose the correct answer.

1 the news / advertisement
2 documentary / comedy series
3 quiz show / drama series
4 chat show / advertisement
5 soap opera / chat show
6 documentary / soap opera

c Do you know any more TV words?
Write them in your Workbook (page 122 Exercise 4).

d Work in a group and answer the questions.
You have three minutes.

Culture Vulture

Did you know that the popular British soap opera *Coronation Street* was first shown on TV in 1960 and continues today. Are there any soap operas on TV in your country? Do you watch any soap operas? Do you like them?

7 Read and listen

a Describe the people in the picture. Who do they look like?

b Read the text quickly and match the headings with the paragraphs.

- A free gift
- Life as a lookalike
- A special TV documentary
- Sorry, you can't come in here!

LOOKALIKES GO TO HOLLYWOOD

Camilla Shadbolt and Andy Harmer

1

Andy Harmer and Camilla Shadbolt look very similar to David and Victoria Beckham. They wear the same clothes, style their hair in the same way and even have the same tattoos as the international superstars. As a result, schools, companies and media organisations ask Andy and Camilla to appear in public as lookalikes, instead of the actual Beckhams. They have also appeared in films and several TV advertisements as Victoria and David. The couple have worked as lookalikes since 1997 and people who see Andy and Camilla at events or on TV often think that they are the real celebrities.

2

Before David and Victoria moved to America in 2007, the two professional lookalikes went to Los Angeles and made a documentary. The TV company wanted to know how popular the Beckhams would be in Hollywood before they moved there. But Victoria and David didn't know about the idea for the programme.

3

While they were in LA, Camilla and Andy went to an expensive jewellery shop. The shop assistants who served Camilla thought she was the real Victoria. They told her to have anything she wanted for free, so Camilla took a black pearl necklace which cost thousands of dollars. The shop wanted 'Victoria' to wear it because it would be good for their business, but Camilla knew it was wrong to keep the necklace and decided to return it.

4

The lookalikes went to a nightclub in LA where lots of celebrities go. The nightclub manager thought they were the real Beckhams and gave them champagne. Later, they went to a restaurant which is popular with top Hollywood stars like Penélope Cruz and Brad Pitt. However, this time they weren't so lucky as the restaurant manager knew they weren't the Beckhams and told them to leave immediately.

When David and Victoria heard about the documentary, they were very angry with Camilla and Andy. They asked the TV company who made the programme not to show it. However, it was shown on a British TV channel a few months later.

> **Which is right? Don't look at the text!**
> *People who see Andy and Camilla* ***in*** */* ***on*** *TV …*

c 3.36 Read the text again and listen. Are the sentences *right* (✓), *wrong* (✗) or *doesn't say* (-)?

1. Lookalikes copy famous people's hair and clothes.
2. When people see Camilla and Andy, they always know that they are not the Beckhams.
3. Andy and Camilla made the documentary to see if they were more popular than the Beckhams.
4. The real Victoria went to the jewellery shop before Camilla.
5. Camilla didn't keep the necklace.
6. Camilla and Andy had dinner with Penelope Cruz.
7. Camilla and Andy were sorry about the documentary.

d Work with a partner and answer the questions.

1. Do you know anyone who looks like a famous celebrity?
2. What do you think the advantages and disadvantages of being a celebrity lookalike are?
3. Would you like to be a lookalike? Why? / Why not?

8 Grammar Defining relative clauses

a Look at the examples and complete the table with the pronouns *where*, *which* or *who*.

The shop assistants ***who*** *served Camilla thought she was the real Victoria. Camilla took a necklace* ***which*** *cost thousands of dollars. The lookalikes went to a nightclub in LA* ***where*** *Paris Hilton often goes.*

I saw a man. He looks like my uncle.	→	I saw a man … looks like my uncle. who
She has a car. The car is black.	→	She has a car … is black. wich
There's a house. Tom was born there.	→	There's the house … Tom was born. where

Defining relative clauses give us information about the person, thing or place we are talking about. Choose the correct words to complete the rules.

- We use *who* for **places** / **people** / **things**. that (person, object)
- We use *which* for **places** / **people** / **things**.
- We use *where* for **places** / **people** / **things**.

Grammar reference: pages 138–139

b Choose the correct word.

1 A drummer is someone *who* / *which* plays the drums.
2 They're the girls *which* / *that* went to the party on Friday.
3 A comedy is a type of film *who* / *which* is funny.
4 This is the shop *that* / *where* I bought my shoes.
5 That's the newspaper *who* / *that* I read every day.
6 We're the people *who* / *where* live in that house.

Check it out!

We often use ***that*** for **people** or **things** in defining relative clauses.
He's the boy ***that*** *knows Kim.*
= He's the boy **who** knows Kim.
This is the computer ***that*** *I use.*
= This is the computer **which** I use.

c Complete the sentences about you.

1 The person who I talk to most is … 2 One object which I use every day is … 3 A place where I would like to go is …

Interaction 9 DVD Identifying people

a 3.37 Listen to Danny and Lily at a party. Look at the picture and say who Danny knows.

b 3.37 Listen again and complete the phrases with the words.

1 who's

that's	mean	one
~~who's~~	with	looks

1 Who's the guy … wearing a baseball cap?
2 Do you … the DJ?
3 He … a bit shy.
4 The … who's dancing?
5 The girl … short, dark hair.
6 Oh, … Sara.

c 3.38 Turn to page 124. Listen to the sentences and repeat them. Practise stressing the important information at the end of the sentence.

d Work with a partner.
Student A: Turn to page 128.
Student B: Turn to page 131.

Portfolio 9 Describing a person in a letter

a Read the letter and look at the pictures. Who is Robert?

1

2

3

Dear Chris,

It was great to [1]*hear / here* from you the other day. I'm really excited about joining [2]*you're / your* band. We're still meeting on Saturday afternoon, aren't we?

Where [3] *would / wood* you like to meet? I know the café where you met my friend Jack, so we could meet [4] *their / there* if you like. Is 4 o'clock OK? Here's a description of myself so you [5]*no / know* who I am.

Some people say that I look a bit like the star of that new American comedy series *Too late!*, but nobody has ever asked me [6]*for / four* my autograph! You know the guy I mean, don't you? The one who's really funny! I've got short, brown hair and brown eyes. I'm tall and quite skinny and I'll [7]*where / wear* blue jeans and a [8]*read / red* T-shirt.

Please [9] *write / right* to me and send me a description of yourself so that I know who you are. Can't wait [10]*too / to* [11]*meat / meet* you all.

[12]*See / Sea* you on Saturday,

Robert

Check it out!

Homophones are words that sound the same but are spelled differently.

- hear – here there – their

b Read the letter again and choose the correct words.

c Imagine you are Chris. Reply to Robert's letter and answer his questions. Include the following information:

- if you can meet on Saturday
- where to meet and at what time
- a description of yourself
- what you are going to wear

d Swap your letter with a partner. Did he/she spell everything correctly?

The Memory Birds

JACK! HAVE YOU SEEN JACK? CAN YOU HELP ME?
JACK! HOLLY!
OH GOOD, YOU KNOW WHO I AM.
DID THE BIRDS GET YOU TOO, MIA?
WHO'S SHE?
THE BIRDS DIDN'T GET ME. I'M HERE TO TAKE YOU HOME. BUT FIRST YOU HAVE TO REMEMBER.
REMEMBER WHAT?
HOLD ON.
LISTEN TO ME, ALL OF YOU. TRY TO REMEMBER! WHAT ARE YOUR NAMES? TELL ME YOUR NAMES.
YOU ARE PEOPLE. YOU ARE FREE AND YOU HAVE NAMES! TELL ME WHAT THEY ARE!
YOU'RE LAURA.
I'M LAURA ... LAURA ...
YOUR NAME IS SARAH.
I'M SARAH ...
I'M DAVID.
J ... JACK. ... MIA?
MIA? IS THAT YOU? MIA? WHAT JUST HAPPENED? WHAT'S GOING ON?
JACK! COME ON, LET'S GO.
BOOOM!
WELL DONE, MIA. YOU DID IT. I KNEW YOU COULD.
SIX MONTHS LATER.
I STILL CAN'T BELIEVE WHAT HAPPENED.
PEOPLE FORGOT TO ASK QUESTIONS.
I DIDN'T. AND I'M NEVER GOING TO STOP!

10 Getting around

Verb + *-ing* and verb + infinitive
Infinitive of purpose and *for* + noun
Vocabulary: Travel verbs; Going on a trip
Interaction 10: Booking a flight

1 Read and listen

a Look at the pictures. How are the people travelling? Where do you think they are?

b Student A: Read the text about Rob Thomson. Student B: Read the text about Rosie Swale-Pope. Answer the questions about your text.

1 How did he/she travel?
2 Which countries did he/she visit?
3 How long was the trip (in kilometres)?
4 How long did it take (in time)?
5 What problems did he/she have?
6 What record did he/she set?

New Zealander **Rob Thomson**, 28, began cycling from Japan to England in July 2006. But when he got to Switzerland he stopped cycling, because it was too easy, and went on by skateboard. Rob loved skateboarding and after he reached England he didn't want to stop. He took a boat to the Caribbean, then skateboarded across the USA. After that he flew to China and continued to travel across Asia by skateboard.

On the 12,159 km trip he needed to use three pairs of shoes, three skateboards and three sets of wheels. He thought the friendliest people he met were in the USA and Uzbekistan. In China one family killed a sheep for dinner and cooked the insides for him! Some parts of the journey were difficult. He travelled in temperatures of 45ºC in China, and –23ºC in Turkey. In Texas a lorry, which was carrying a house, nearly crashed into him.

When journalists asked him why he made the journey, Rob said he enjoyed learning new things. He arrived back in New Zealand two and a half years after starting his trip. Now he has the world record for the longest journey by skateboard.

In a five-year period, **Rosie Swale-Pope** ran over 32,000 km around the world. From her home in Wales, she went through Europe, Russia, Siberia, Alaska, Canada, the USA, Greenland and Iceland. But this wasn't her first long journey. In the 1970s, Rosie sailed round the world with her family and her second child was born on the boat.

Rosie decided to make the trip at the age of 57, after her husband died. She wanted to make people think more about their health. In 2003 she started running. She had a small cart to carry her food, clothes and a tent. The journey was hard and there were some serious problems. She was knocked down by a bus, she had to camp in temperatures of –62ºC, she was attacked by wolves and bears and she fell on ice and broke several ribs. At one time the only thing she had to eat was uncooked spaghetti. On the journey lots of men asked her to marry them because they thought she was very strong!

She finished running in August 2008 and wrote a book about her journey: *Just a Little Run Around the World*. She is the first person to travel around the world on foot and by boat.

c Work with your partner. Tell him/her about Rob or Rosie. Use your answers to Exercise 1b.

This is about Rob's trip. He went round the world by bicycle and by skateboard. He went to …

Which is right? Don't look at the text!
*Lots of men asked her to **marry with** / **marry** them.*

d 4.1 Read the texts again and listen. Whose trip do you think was more interesting? Why?

2 Grammar

Verb + *-ing* and verb + infinitive

a Look at the examples then copy and complete the table with the verbs *want* and *finish*.

after he reached England he ***didn't want to stop***
She ***finished running*** *in August 2008.*

Verb + *-ing*	Verb + infinitive with *to*
hate	*agree*
like	*learn*
not mind	*hope*

Grammar reference: page 139

b Find the verbs in the texts on page 84 and add these verbs to complete your table in Exercise 2a.

enjoy decide need stop

Check it out!

- Some verbs can take the *-ing* form or the infinitive with *to*. The meaning doesn't change.
  Rob ***began*** *cycl****ing***. = Rob **began to** cycle.
  He ***continued*** *travell****ing***. = He **continued to** travel.
  She ***started*** *runn****ing***. = She **started to** run.

c Choose the correct words.

1 I don't mind *to go* / *going* to the beach when it's cold.
2 Kate wants *to get* / *getting* a job in France next year.
3 They agreed *to look after* / *looking after* our dog at the weekend.
4 Mario needed *to work* / *working*, so he didn't go to the disco.
5 We really enjoy *to watch* / *watching* tennis on TV.
6 When did you learn *to drive* / *driving*?

d Complete the sentences with the correct form of the verbs.

be buy climb help ~~study~~ work

1 to study

1 We wanted … Japanese three years ago, but we couldn't find a teacher.
2 Suzanne hates … in the house alone.
3 I don't mind … you get things ready for the party.
4 You need … some new trainers.
5 They were tired, but they continued … up the mountain.
6 Joe hopes … with a voluntary group in Africa.

e Complete the sentences about you: three true sentences and one false sentence.

1 In the summer I love …
2 This evening I hope …
3 Yesterday I learned …
4 At the weekend I enjoy …

f Work with a partner. Tell your partner your sentences. Can he/she guess the false sentence?

3 Speak

a You are going to go on a trip around the world with your partner.
Student A: Put the words in the correct order.
Student B: Turn to page 125.

1 you / Where / go / like / would / to ?
2 travel / do / you / to / How / want ?
3 going / to / we / Where / sleep /are ?
4 to / do / we / take / need / What ?

b Work with a partner. Discuss and answer the questions.

c Tell the class about your trip. Whose trip is the most interesting? Who has the best plan?

We decided to go to …
We want to travel by …
We're going to sleep in …

4 Vocabulary Travel verbs

a 4.2 Match the verbs with the pictures. Then listen and check.

catch drive get into / get out of
get on / get off ride take off / land

1 train: catch, drive, get on / get off

1

land

2

3

drive

4

5

Get it right!

ride a motorbike

✓ *My brother can drive a car.*
✓ *My brother can ride a motorbike.*
✗ *My brother can ~~drive~~ a motorbike.*

b Complete the sentences with the correct form of the travel verbs in Exercise 4a.

1 I must go. I have to … a bus at five o'clock.
2 Are you ready? We … at the next station.
3 She … her car and drove away. get into
4 Did you … your motorbike all around South America? drive
5 They … the taxi and went into the airport. get into
6 Mum and Dad have got on the plane. We're going to watch it … .
7 Come on, … the train. It's leaving! get on

c Do you know any more travel verbs? Write them in your Workbook (page 123, Exercise 1).

d Work in a group. Answer the questions.

1 Have you ever ridden a motorbike or driven a car?
2 Have you ever missed a bus, train or plane?
3 Do you ever catch a bus or train? Why?/ Why not?

Culture Vulture

Did you know that in the UK you can drive a car or ride a 125cc motorbike at 17? How old do you have to be in your country? Do you agree with the age limits?

5 Pronunciation DVD

Diphthongs: /eɪ/, /əʊ/ and /aɪ/

a 4.3 Listen to the /eɪ/, /əʊ/ and /aɪ/ sounds in these words.

/eɪ/ sail /əʊ/ road /aɪ/ ride

b 4.4 Copy the tables. Then listen and tick (✓) the correct sound.

	/eɪ/	/əʊ/	/aɪ/
sail	✓		
road		✓	
ride			✓
boat			
plane			
bike			

	/eɪ/	/əʊ/	/aɪ/
fly			
train			
motorbike			
cycle			
railway			
slow			

c 4.5 Listen, check your answers and repeat.

d 4.6 Listen and repeat.

I rode my bike in Spain and drove a train in China.

6 Grammar

Infinitive of purpose and *for* + noun

a Read the text about Camilla. Change the words in **bold** but don't change the meaning. Use the words in the box.

for a to take

In 2008, 15-year-old Camilla Hempleman-Adams became the youngest British woman to ski to the North Pole. She was preparing **for** her school exams at the time, but decided to do the trip because she was worried about the effects of climate change. Her father, also an explorer, went with her on the trip. Camilla really enjoyed skiing to the North Pole, but she had to use earplugs to sleep because everybody snored in the tent and it was too noisy. She also didn't like the food and went **to have a** pizza as soon as she got home!

Choose the correct words to complete the rules.

- We use *to* + ***verb*** / ***noun*** to explain why a person does something.
- We use *for* + ***verb*** / ***noun*** to explain why a person does something.

Grammar reference: page 139

b Match the two parts of the sentences.

1 C

1 We drove to Liverpool yesterday
2 She went to the newsagent's
3 They bought some cheese and tomatoes
4 I'm going to my room
5 Did you have a party
6 He's gone to the café

A to make a pizza.
B for your birthday?
C to visit my grandparents.
D for a magazine.
E for a drink.
F to do my homework.

c Complete the sentences with *for* or *to*.

1 to

1 They went to the supermarket … buy some food.
2 She went to the concert … see her favourite band.
3 Did you leave early … go to the football?
4 I'm staying at home tonight … study for my exam tomorrow.
5 He went to Spain … a holiday.
6 We're going to the sports centre this afternoon … a swim.

d Complete the sentences about you.

1 I go to school to …
2 I'd like … for my birthday.
3 Sometimes I go into town to …

7 Listen

a Look at the box. What would you do at an airport, a train station or a bus station?

buy a ticket ask for information about times
go through security show someone your bag
take everything out of your pockets

b 4.7 Listen to two conversations. What types of transport are the passengers using?

c 4.7 Listen again and choose the correct answer: A, B or C.

Conversation 1

1 The passenger has to show his …
A credit card.
B passport.
C boarding pass.

2 The passenger's plane leaves at …
A 10:15.
B 10:35.
C 11:05.

3 The passenger has … in his pocket.
A a video game
B sunglasses
C a mobile phone

Conversation 2

4 The passenger wants to pay …
A by credit card.
B with cash.
C by cheque.

5 The bus to Chicago leaves from …
A bus stop 7.
B bus stop 17.
C bus stop 70.

6 The bus driver wants …
A her passport.
B her ticket.
C her luggage.

d Work with a partner. Have you ever travelled on your own? Where did you go? If not, would you like to travel on your own? Why? / Why not?

8 Vocabulary Going on a trip

a 4.8 Match the two parts of the sentences. Then listen and check.

1 F

1 You can buy a bus or train ticket
2 All trains to London
3 When I travel, I take my clothes
4 There is **security** in airports to protect
5 When you travel to a different country,
6 A **timetable** is a list of times
7 A **window seat** on a bus, train or plane
8 When you travel by plane, you go to the

A you need a **passport** or identity card.
B leave from **platform** 3.
C is next to the window.
D **check-in desk** first and show your ticket.
E people while they are travelling.
F online or from the **ticket office**.
G in a big **suitcase**.
H when buses and trains arrive and leave.

b Do you know any more words for going on a trip? Write them in your Workbook (page 123 Exercise 4).

c Work with a partner. Take it in turns to describe a word from Exercise 8a. Your partner guesses the word.

A: *It's a thing to carry clothes in when you travel.*
B: *A suitcase.*

Get it right!

miss = not catch
✓ *I missed the bus.*
✗ *I ~~lost~~ the bus.*

Interaction 10 DVD

Booking a flight

a 4.9 Listen and choose the correct information about Andy's flight.

b 4.9 Listen again and put the questions in the order you hear them.

F, …

A Do you want to check in online or at the airport?
B When you come back, which flight do you want?
C Where do you want to go to?
D Which flight do you want going out?
E When do you want to go?
F Where do you want to go from?
G When do you want to come back?

c 4.10 Turn to page 125. Listen to the questions and repeat them. Practise the pronunciation of *do you* (/dʒə/) + verb.

d Work with a partner.

Student A: Turn to page 128.
Student B: Turn to page 131.

Portfolio 10

An email about travel plans

a Read Jessica's email to her cousin Shannon. Which activities in the pictures does she mention in the email?

A

palplace

File Edit View Insert Format Tools Actions Help

http://www.palplace.com/new_message.php

messages photos videos links

New message from Jessica received at 3:29 pm today

Hi Shannon

How are you. I arrived in Britain from Canada yesterday and Im staying with Uncle Tom and Aunt Mary for a couple of days in London. tomorrow were going to the city centre to go sightseeing.

Id like to visit you in Devon next week. I want to go to the beach and see Sarah and Matt. Ive got some questions that I need to ask you. Can I catch a train from London to Plymouth. Where can I buy a ticket. How do I get from the station in Plymouth to your house. I dont mind catching a bus or getting a taxi.

See you soon

Jessica

B

C

D

b Read the email and correct ten punctuation mistakes.

Check it out!

- Use **apostrophes** for contractions: *I'd* (*I would*) and possessives (*John's dog*)
- Use **?** at the end of questions and **.** at the end of sentences.

c Jessica asks four questions in her email. What are they?

d Match the answers with Jessica's questions.

1 You can buy a ticket from the train station.
2 I'm fine, thank you.
3 Don't worry, I can pick you up from the train station in Plymouth.
4 You can catch a train from Paddington Station in London.

e Imagine you are going to visit your partner in his/her town. Write an email to your partner about your travel plans.

1 Tell your partner …
- when you are going to arrive in the country.
- when you'd like to visit him/her.
- what you want to do there.

2 Ask your partner about transport and tickets to their town.

f Read your partner's email and write a reply.

Is South Africa for you?

South Africa is a large and very beautiful country. It is in the south of the African continent and is about the size of France and Spain put together. It is easy to get to by plane and a great place for tourists to travel around with excellent roads and buses. So what can you hope to find in South Africa?

Animal safari

For most people, a safari is a holiday of a lifetime and a fantastic opportunity to see wild animals in their natural habitat. The Madikwe Safari is perfect for families. If you want to see all the 'big five' animals (elephants, leopards, lions, rhinos and zebras) in one day then this is the trip for you. But only if you don't mind getting up early! The day begins at six o'clock in the morning and you start watching the animals before breakfast. Then you spend the middle of the day at the swimming pool and get into the jeep again in the evening to watch more animals.

Don't forget to take:

- **Warm clothes and sun cream.** The temperature is freezing cold in the morning and at night and boiling hot in the middle of the day.
- **A camera for everyone.** The whole family will want to take thousands of photos.

African adventure

The Khamkirri Reserve is for people who like adventure. It is near the red Kalahari Desert and is a great place for activities like quad biking or mountain biking. But if you love having five-star service on holiday, then this isn't for you. You will sleep in tents, and sometimes there is no running water or electricity. Expect to eat lots of meat too. A typical dish is kudu, a kind of antelope, which you cook yourself on a barbecue. This is a perfect opportunity to enjoy the beautiful African sky. Watch it change from blue to orange and red at sunset, then black with millions of stars at night.

Don't forget to take:

- **Old clothes.** The red sand is impossible to wash out!
- **A music player with good headphones.** You don't want to hear strange animal noises at night!

Help the animals

Edeni is a South African game reserve near the Kruger National Park. If you love learning about animals, then this five-week trip is for you. You can watch the lions, leopards, cheetahs, wild dogs and elephants interact. It's dangerous, so most of the time you will be in a car, but you will follow the cheetahs on foot. Watch out for spiders and snakes at the campsite too. This is a very exciting experience, but not if you're frightened of wild animals.

Don't forget to take:

- **As little as possible.** You will need to carry everything you take.
- **Cream for insect bites.** There are a lot of mosquitoes in the rainy season.

1 Culture World: South Africa

a Read the article quickly and match the holidays 1–3 with the people A–C.

1 Animal safari **2** African adventure **3** Help the animals

(A)

Jill and her brother Nick love animals. They're both studying to be vets and like adventure.

(B)

The Miller family want to go on a special holiday this year.

(C)

Marc's very sporty and adventurous. He loves travelling and camping in different places.

b Read the article again. Are the sentences *right* (✓), *wrong* (✗), or *doesn't say* (–)?

1. South Africa is as big as France.
2. There are 50 flights a day to South Africa.
3. On the 'Animal safari' you see the same animals in the morning and in the evening.
4. You don't stay in a hotel on the 'African adventure'.
5. You can try local food on the 'African adventure'.
6. You should take old clothes on the 'African adventure' because you might lose them.
7. On the 'Help the animals' holiday you watch spiders and snakes from a car.
8. You won't be in a car while you observe the cheetahs.

c Find words in the article that mean …

1. people who visit a country or place (paragraph 1)
2. a strong vehicle to travel off roads (paragraph 2)
3. the time in the evening when the sun goes down (paragraph 3)
4. a natural area of land where wild animals live (paragraph 4)

2 Your project A holiday advert

a Work in a group. Make a list of places where people can go on holiday in your country. How can they travel there? Where can they stay? What can they do there?

b Make an advertisement for a holiday at one place in your country. Use the information in Exercise 2a. Illustrate the advertisement with pictures.

Get it right! 9 and 10

Common errors

1 He looks strange

Look (+ adjective) means *to appear* or *seem*.

✓ *He* ***looks*** *strange.*

✗ *He looks ~~like~~ strange.*

Look like (+ noun) means to be similar in appearance to somebody or something else.

✓ *She* ***looks like*** *her sister.*

Correct the sentences that are wrong.

1 She looks like younger than 28.
2 He looks like George Clooney. He's really good-looking!
3 Your bedroom looks very clean today! Congratulations!
4 Our new teacher looks like very patient. We're very lucky!

2 Question tags

In English we don't use *no* as a question tag.

✓ *It's going to rain,* ***isn't it?***

✗ *It's going to rain, ~~no~~?*

Be careful with *have to*.

✓ *We have to go now,* ***don't we?***

✗ *We have to go now, ~~haven't we?~~*

a Complete the phone call with the correct question tag.

Hi Lucy, I can't hear you very well. You're coming home soon, 1 … ? What? You're staying for another week! You can't really be serious, 2 …? But you have to prepare for your exams, 3 …? You want to do well, 4 … ? You aren't going to fail, 5 … ? And, what about Jen? Sorry, what? Ah, so she's staying too, 6 … ? So, I guess her parents are angry too, 7 … ? What? Ah, OK, so they're happy about it then. Well, I'm not! You have to come home now! Lucy, Lucy, you are still there, 8 …. ? Lucy?

b 4.11 Listen and check your answers.

3 The man who …

Don't use a personal pronoun (*he*, *she*, *they*, etc.) after *who* or *that* in defining relative clauses.

✓ *That's the man who lives in the big house.*

✗ *That's the man who ~~he~~ lives in the big house.*

a Join the two sentences. Use *who* or *that*.

1 This is the boy. He wants to buy your scooter.
2 I know a girl. She can help you with your homework.
3 There are some students. They always come to class late.
4 I have a friend. He's going to Japan next week.

b Work with a partner. Say a phrase from Box A. Your partner completes it with *who* or *that* and the correct phrase from Box B.

A

That's the programme …
She's the girl …
He's the boy …
They're the people …

B

They looked after our dog.
He went to the party.
It's about animals.
She's got a long nose.

4 Say it right!

-tion

a 4.12 Many words in English end in *–tion*. We pronounce this /ʃən/. Listen and repeat these words.

station invention organisation
description information

b 4.13 Work with a partner and read these sentences. Then listen and check.

1 I don't know the location of the station.
2 She showed her invention at the exhibition.
3 You can get information on our organisation from Reception.
4 You have to write a description for the competition.

Review 9 and 10

1 Grammar

a Complete the sentences. Choose the correct answer: A, B or C.

1 She's very pretty, ... ?
A is she **B** isn't she **C** does she
2 You haven't got £2, ... ?
A haven't you **B** don't you **C** have you
3 He doesn't go to our school, ... ?
A does he **B** don't you **C** is he
4 We've seen this before, ... ?
A didn't we **B** have we **C** haven't we
5 They can't sing very well, ... ?
A can they **B** can't they **C** do they
6 You will help me, ... ?
A will you **B** are you **C** won't you

[ ] 6

b Match the two parts of the sentences.

1 They met the actor
2 This is the café
3 A soap opera is a drama series
4 Our dog is the one
5 She's the teacher

A where they have great milkshakes.
B which goes on for a very long time.
C that's in the new comedy series.
D who gives us lots of homework.
E which is swimming in the pond.

[ ] 5

c Choose the correct words.

1 Ewan hates *to wash up / washing up*.
2 They like *to do / doing* their English homework.
3 We hope *to visit / visiting* Indonesia next summer.
4 She doesn't mind *to help / helping* us today.
5 Did you finish *to paint / painting* him?

[ ] 5

d Complete the answers with ***to* + verb** or ***for* + noun**.

learn some bread visit my birthday make a walk

1 A: Why did you buy that chocolate? B: ... a cake.
2 A: Why are they going to Italy? B: ... Italian.
3 A: Why did she go to the shops? B: ... .
4 A: Why is he going to France? B: ... his family.
5 A: Why are they going to the park? B: ... .
6 A: Why did she give you that money? B: ... .

[ ] 6

2 Vocabulary

a Match the adjectives with the descriptions.

overweight cute good-looking beautiful wavy ugly bald

1 A very pretty woman.
2 A person with no hair.
3 Someone who weighs too much.
4 An attractive man.
5 An attractive small dog.
6 Hair that is between straight and curly.
7 A very unattractive person.

[ ] 7

b Put the letters in the correct order and make TV words.

1 thac wosh
2 eth senw
3 ziqu hows
4 nalchen
5 maard reesis
6 dyemoc erises
7 tryamencodu
8 tisvermenadet

[ ] 8

c Choose the correct words.

1 The plane *takes off / gets off* at ten o'clock.
2 Can you help your grandmother *get off / get into* the car?
3 They took a photo of her *getting on / getting out of* a taxi.
4 What time do you have to *catch / get into* your bus?
5 This is our stop. Are you ready to *get out / get off*?
6 We're going to meet them at the airport. Their plane *lands / gets on* at 5.30.
7 Quick! We're going to *miss / catch* the train!

[ ] 7

d Answer the questions with the words in the box.

window seat security passport platform check-in desk timetable ticket office suitcase

1 What do you look at to find out your bus times?
2 Where do you buy a train ticket?
3 Where do you sit if you want to see the view?
4 What do you put your clothes in when you go on a trip?
5 Where do you go when you arrive at an airport?
6 Where do you stand before you get on a train?
7 What do you need to take to a foreign country?
8 Where do you go after check-in and before you can get on the plane?

[ ] 8

11 Lights, camera, action!

Present simple passive
Past simple passive
Vocabulary: Films; Materials
Interaction 11: Choosing a film

1 Read and listen

a Read the text quickly. Which job is the text about?

Film stunts

When we watch films, we see our favourite film stars jump away from explosions, drive fast motorbikes in dangerous chase scenes, and fly through the air like superheroes. Or do we? Famous actors are good at their jobs but they often aren't trained for the dramatic stunts their characters perform in action films. This is where the job of a stunt man or stunt woman comes in. Experts in dangerous action, stunt people are often filmed walking into fire or crashing cars, because it's their job! These days, in many films computer-generated imagery, or CGI, is also used to create very realistic special effects. Some actors also like the challenge of filming their own action scenes. Angelina Jolie did her own stunts in the film *Wanted* and Daniel Craig likes doing as many of his own stunts as possible.

Car chases

Car chase scenes can't usually be filmed more than once because they are very expensive. More airbags are added to cars for extra safety. Stunt people drive the cars and the real actors are filmed inside a different car. The two shots are then put together in the studio so you see the actor driving fast down a mountain, and not the stunt driver.

Stunts with fire

Stunt people wear lots of special clothes to protect them when they film a fire scene. They carry a small oxygen tank and there are always doctors on the film set in case there are accidents.

High falls

Many high falls are done with CGI because they are so dangerous. However, when stunt people are used they never fall directly onto the ground. They fall onto large airbags with an extra airbag placed inside the first one to make it safer. Sometimes bungee jump ropes are used too.

Do you think you could be a stunt person? If you like martial arts or other extreme sports, don't mind working long hours and enjoy danger, then the answer could be *Yes*!

> **Which is right? Don't look at the text!**
> *Famous actors are good **at** / **in** their jobs.*

b 4.14 Read the text again and listen. Are the sentences *right* (✓), *wrong* (✗) or *doesn't say* (–) ?

1 Directors use CGI for all film stunts.
2 Stunt people have a very dangerous job.
3 Car chases in films take a long time to shoot.
4 In car chases real actors sit next to stunt people inside the car.
5 In stunts with fire, there are always doctors on the film set.
6 Stunt people always use bungee jump ropes when they fall.

c Work in a group and answer the questions.

1 Which films do you think have good stunts or special effects?
2 Would you like to be a stunt person? Why? / Why not?

2 Vocabulary Films

a 4.15 Match the words with the letters in the picture. Then listen and check.

A 5 location

1 camera operator **2** director **3** extra **4** film star **5** ~~location~~ **6** make-up artist **7** script **8** set **9** stunt person

b Complete the sentences with words in Exercise 2a.

1 film star

1. Keira Knightley is a famous … .
2. Steven Spielberg is the … of the *Indiana Jones* and *Jurassic Park* films.
3. A … often does all the dangerous things in a film.
4. The … films the actors while they are acting.
5. The actors have to learn their words from a … .
6. The … for the film *Notting Hill* is an area in London.
7. Usually films are made on location or on a … in a studio.
8. A … changes an actor's appearance.
9. An … appears in a film, but he/she doesn't say anything.

c Do you know any more film words? Write them in your Workbook (page 124 Exercise 1).

d Work in a group. Ask and answer the questions.

1. Who are your favourite film stars / directors?
2. Would you like to work in films? What would you like to do?

Culture Vulture

Did you know that there are Oscars for 'Best Visual Effects'? Winners include *The Lord of the Rings*, *The Golden Compass* and *Avatar*. Do you think special effects and make-up are important in films? Why? / Why not?

3 Pronunciation DVD

-ed in regular past participles: /t/, /d/ and /ɪd/

a 4.16 Listen to the sentences and choose the correct pronunciation of the *-ed* ending: /t/ /d/ /ɪd/.

1. The main characters are **played** by actors.
2. Many films are **based** on books.
3. The story can be **adapted** by scriptwriters.
4. A film is **recorded** on location.
5. The scenes aren't always **filmed** in the correct order.
6. The filming is **watched** by the director.
7. A different opening to the film is sometimes **included** on the DVD.
8. The film is **finished** in the studio.

b 4.17 Listen and check your answers.

c Work with a partner. Read the sentences in Exercise 3a with the correct pronunciation.

d 4.18 Listen and repeat.

The film is directed, produced and filmed by the same person.

#1 The cars are drove by people
The emails are send by people from computers
on

4 Grammar

Present simple passive

a Look at the examples and complete the table with the verb *do*.

> *Computer-generated imagery* ***is used*** *for special effects.*
> *Real actors* ***are filmed*** *inside a different car.*
> *Usually car chases* ***aren't repeated****.*

Positive
This stunt … … on location.
Some stunts … … by actors.

Negative
This stunt **isn't done** on location.
Some stunts … … by actors.

***Yes/No* questions**
… this stunt … on location?
… these stunts … by actors?

Short answers
Yes, it … . / No, it **isn't**.
Yes, they **are**. / No, they … .

Information questions
Where … this stunt … ?
Where … these stunts … ?

Choose the correct words to complete the rules.

- We make the passive with the verb **be** / **do** and the past participle.
- We use the passive when we **know** / **don't know** who does the action, or when it **is** / **isn't** important who does the action.

Grammar reference: page 139

b Complete the sentences with the verbs in the present simple passive.

1 are made

1 800 films … (make) in India every year.
2 In *Quantum of Solace* James Bond … (play) by Daniel Craig. is played
3 The *Pirates of the Caribbean* films … (not base) on a book, but on a Walt Disney theme park ride. aren't based
4 What … (Keira Knightley's first film /call)?
5 The songs in the film *Hannah Montana* … (sing) by Miley Cyrus. are sons
6 Some films … (not show) at the cinema. You can only watch them on DVD. aren't showed
7 In the film *WALL-E*, a robot … (create) to clean Earth.
is created

Get it right!

by

- Use *by* after the passive to say who does the action.

✓ *Action scenes are often done by stunt people.*
✗ *Action scenes are often done ~~for~~ stunt people.*

c Rewrite these sentences in the present simple passive.

1 People drive cars on the left in Britain.
2 People send emails from computers and mobile phones.
3 People speak English in Australia.
4 People drink lots of green tea in Japan.
5 People download films from the internet.

Get it right!

800 films are made …

✓ *800 films are made in India every year.*
✗ *800 films ~~they~~ are made in India every year.*

5 Speak

a Work with a partner. Student A: Put the words in the correct order.

Student A

1 are / you / invited to / parties / How often ?
2 sports / played / What / at / your school / are ?
3 your country / are / Which / visited most / tourist attractions / in ?
4 your birthday / is / How / by / your family / celebrated ?

Student B: Turn to page 125.

b Work with your partner. Take it in turns to ask and answer the questions in Exercise 5a.

c Change partners. Tell your new partner two things Student A / Student B told you.

Three languages are spoken in Leila's family: Spanish, French and English.

6 Vocabulary Materials

a 4.19 Match the words with the pictures. Then listen and check.

A 8 wood

1 cardboard **2** cotton **3** glass **4** leather
5 metal **6** plastic **7** rubber **8** ~~wood~~

b Do you know any more materials? Write them in your Workbook (page 124 Exercise 3).

c Work with a partner. Answer the questions.

1 How many different materials can you see in the classroom?
2 What materials are you wearing today?

d Work in a group. Take it in turns to describe an object and guess what it is.

scissors bag jeans table coin jacket
sunglasses watch pen TV shoes box

A: *They're small and made of metal and plastic. They're for cutting.*
B: *Scissors!* A: *Yes. Your turn.*

A

B
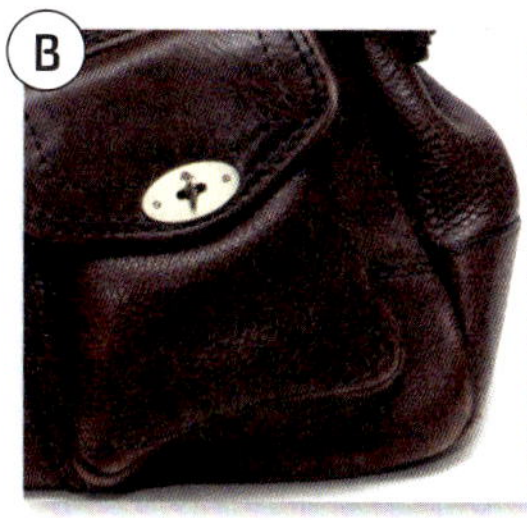
C
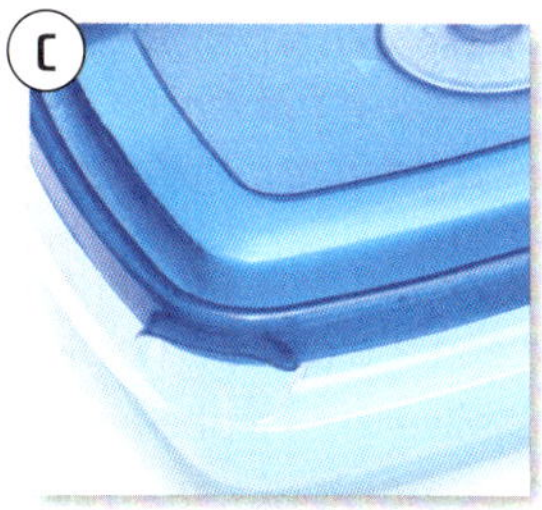
D

E

F
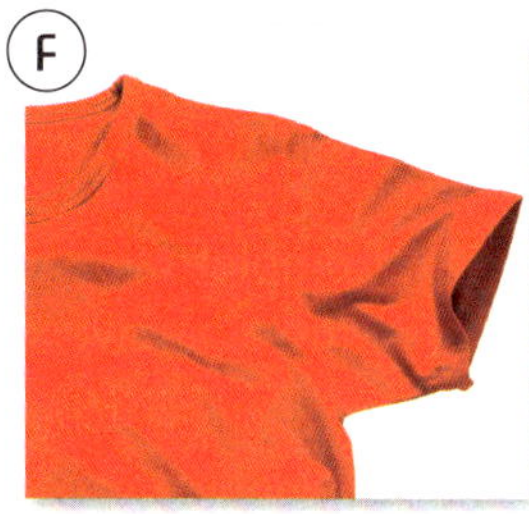
G

H

Get it right!

To describe purpose, use *for* + *-ing*.
✓ *That pen is for writing on CDs.*
✗ *That pen is for ~~write~~ on CDs.*

7 Listen

a 4.20 James Bond, the famous British spy, has used a lot of different gadgets (things with a special purpose) in the Bond films. Listen and write the materials you hear.

metal leather plastic rubber wood glass

b 4.20 Listen again and choose the correct answer: A, B or C.

1 What was James Bond's first gadget?
A an exploding gun **B** a leather briefcase
C a gold knife
2 What was Ian Fleming's job?
A a writer **B** a scientist **C** a filmmaker
3 What were the false fingerprints in the Bond film made of?
A plastic **B** metal **C** rubber
4 When was a real underwater car invented?
A in 1978 **B** in 1988 **C** in 2008
5 In which film did Bond wear X-ray glasses?
A *Goldfinger* **B** *Diamonds are Forever*
C *The World is Not Enough*

c Work with a partner. Have you seen any good gadgets in films? What were they made of? What were they used for?

8 Grammar Past simple passive

a Look at the examples and choose the correct words to complete the rules.

> *The Bond books **were written** by Ian Fleming.*
> *The underwater car **wasn't invented** in the 1960s.*
> ***Was** the briefcase **used** in real life?*
>
> - We make the past passive with the verb **be** / **do** in the past simple and the past participle.
> - We use the past passive to describe actions in the passive voice that are **finished** / **not finished**.

Grammar reference: page 140

b Complete the sentences with the verbs in the past simple passive.

1 Plastic watches … (invent) in 1971. were invented
2 Perfume … (produce) 4,000 years ago. was produced
3 Pizza is from Italy but the first pizza restaurant … (not open) in the USA until 1905. wasn't opened
4 T-shirts were first made in 1913, but they … (not sell) in shops until the 1950s. weren't sold

c Complete the questions with the verbs in the past simple passive. Then choose the correct answer.

1 Where and when … sunglasses first … (wear)? were

2 Where and when … the first film … (show)? were showed

3 Where and when … traffic lights first … (use)?

4 Where and when … blue jeans first … (make)? were / made

A In Paris in 1907. 2
B In the USA in 1873. 4
C In China in the fifteenth century. 1
D In London in 1868. 3

d 4.21 Listen and check your answers.

Interaction 11 DVD

Choosing a film

a 4.22 Mehmet and Karen are at a film festival. Which film do they decide to see?

Charter College
16th Film Festival

Venue: Arts Centre – Room 1

6:00 STAR WARS
The classic science-fiction film with Harrison Ford.

8:15 HAIRSPRAY
Zac Efron stars in this very funny musical comedy.

Venue: Main Hall

6:15 CASINO ROYALE
Daniel Craig's first Bond film. An exciting, action-packed movie.

8:30 NIGHT AT THE MUSEUM
A security guard left alone in the Natural History Museum one night gets a shock! Comedy chaos follows!

b 4.22 Listen again and match the parts of the sentences.

1 D

1 What do you	**A** *Star Wars*?
2 How about	**B** see that.
3 What else	**C** good.
4 What's	**D** fancy going to see?
5 Sounds	**E** is on?
6 Let's	**F** *Night at the Museum* about?

c 4.23 Turn to page 125. Listen to the sentences and repeat them. Practise sounding enthusiastic.

d Work with a partner.
Student A: Turn to page 128.
Student B: Turn to page 131.

Portfolio 11 A film review

a Read the review of Ruby's favourite film. Would you like to see the film?

MOVIE INSIDER

File Edit View Insert Format Tools Actions Help

http://www.movieinsider.net/competitions/favfilm.php

MY FAVOURITE FILM!

This month's winner: Ruby Thomson from Cardiff wins a month's entry pass to her local cinema!

My favourite film is *Donnie Darko*, a dark comedy, which is sometimes funny and sometimes frightening. It's a fantastic film. It stars Jake Gyllenhaal and other famous actors like Drew Barrymore and Patrick Swayze.

The film is set in an ordinary American town. Donnie Darko (Jake Gyllenhaal) is a teenager with a normal life but a lot of psychological problems. One night he meets a terrifying man dressed as a rabbit. When a plane creashes into Donnie's house, the man saves his life and then tells him that the world will end in 26 days. The film is about the next 26 days. It's a teenage love story, a thriller, a sci-fi film, and a comedy, all in one film.

Donnie Darko was made in 2001. It was written and directed by Richard Kelly, who was only 25 when he made it. It has won loads of independent film awards, but no Oscars. The soundtrack is really good, and includes 1980s pop songs. Watch this film now and see what you think of it.

SEND US A REVIEW OF YOUR FAVOURITE FILM

YOU COULD WIN NEXT MONTH'S PRIZE!

b Put the information in the film review in the correct order.

C, …

A director
B year made
C name of the film
D awards
E the story (or the beginning of the story)
F the stars

c Write a review of your favourite film.

- Include the parts of a film review from Exercise b.
- Include other interesting information (e.g. special effects).
- Don't include 'spoilers' (e.g. the ending).

d Swap reviews with a partner. Does the review include all the necessary information?

Carr Manor High School enjoying Film Academy 2007

Leeds Young People's Film Festival presents

FILM ACADEMY
Education Programme

Leeds Young Film is part of Leeds City Council's Development Directorate. We create and sustain opportunities for young people to develop their creativity and education through exploration of the moving image and interactive arts, from greater access to international film culture to experience of film making, career development and showcasing.

MediaFish

Explore Experiment Experience. Film.

MediaFish is a cooperative of young people who are passionate about film and everything to do with it. We provide a variety of free film screenings to cater for everyone's needs. If you love film, you will love MediaFish.

Presented by Leeds Young People's Film Festival

- Home
- About
- Film Prog
- Events
- News
- Membership

Welcome to MediaFish, Leeds only film club run exclusively for and by young people.

MediaFish is back with the 11th Leeds Young People's Film Festival!

To make sure you find out about the film festival first go to www.leedsyoungfilm.com and join the mailing list.

Latest Ne

Film entry is now closed for the Leeds Young People's FIlm Festival

Day by Day Diary

Time	Title	Venue	Age	Page
Thursday 2 April				
6.30pm	Opening Night Gala – Monsters vs Aliens	Hyde Park Pic House	PG*	7
Friday 3 April				
7.00pm	Media Diploma Screening	Hyde Park Pic House	15	27
9.00pm	Let the Right One In	Hyde Park Pic House	15	8
Saturday 4 April				
10.00am	Leeds Dreams Open Day	Leeds Film Academy	11+	26
11.00am	Dr Mel Gibson – Talking Comics	Hyde Park Pic House	8+	23
11.15am	Leeds Dreams Open Day	Leeds Film Academy	11+	26
1.00pm	Leeds Dreams Open Day	Leeds Film Academy	11+	26
2.00pm	NYFA Under 14 years	Hyde Park Pic House	PG	9
2.15pm	Leeds Dreams Open Day	Leeds Film Academy	11+	26
4.00pm	NYFA 15-19	Hyde Park Pic House	12+	10
6.45pm	Frank Cottrell Boyce On Set Masterclass	Hyde Park Pic House	12+	10
8.00pm	Bleach: Memories of Nobody	Hyde Park Pic House	PG	11

NATIONAL YOUNG FILMMAKERS' AWARD

Leeds Young People's Film Festival

ENTRY FORM

The National Young Filmmakers' Award is a competition for short films made by young people (up to 19 years old) in the UK. Selected films will be entered into a competition where a jury consisting of young people and industry professionals will award £250 in two age categories to the films that are chosen.

THE FILM

Film title ....

Year of production ....

Running time (mins) ....

Type of film

- Fiction ☐
- Documentary ☐
- Animation ☐

Screening format

DVD ☐	Beta-SP ☐	16mm ☐
Mini-SP ☐	Digi-Beta ☐	Other ☐

Programme outline

Arts award accreditation is available for participants completing more than 15-20 hours in Film Academy.

FILM THEORY

How to watch a film – looking at film criticism, including types and genres, narrative and character. Includes screenings of a variety of films and film clips with discussion and group activities.

ANIMATE!

An introduction to the world of animation- Make your animation, using digital software, edit it, add sound effects and music, then share it with the group.

1 DAY FILM CHALLENGE

An introduction to film making – Learn about the various roles involved in making a film from start to finish, including editing and adding a soundtrack. Take away a copy of your finished film on DVD.

FILM JOURNALIST

How to appreciate a film and tell others about it. With professional film writer and journalist.

SCRIPT TO SCREEN

How to develop an idea for a film into a script from start to finish-excellent for literacy skills / experience.

FILM ACADEMY

SEND YOUR ENTRY NOW IF IT'S READY!

1 Culture UK: Leeds

a Look at the information about the Leeds Young People's Film festival and answer the questions.

1. When does the festival start?
2. Which venues are used for the festival on Saturday 4th April?
3. How old do you have to be to enter the NYFA short film competition?
4. Who chooses the winners of the NYFA short film competition?
5. Which course on the programme teaches you how to make an animated film?
6. If you want to watch and learn about different types of films, which course on the programme should you do?
7. At the end of which course on the programme do you get to keep your own film?
8. How much does it cost to watch the films shown by MediaFish?

b Copy and complete the puzzle and find the mystery word.

1. A type of film made with moving pictures.
2. You enter this to win a prize.
3. To give money or a prize in a competition.
4. A book you use to record important dates and events.
5. When you enter a competition sometimes you complete an ... form.
6. Another word for a 'picture'.
7. A general term for children and teenagers

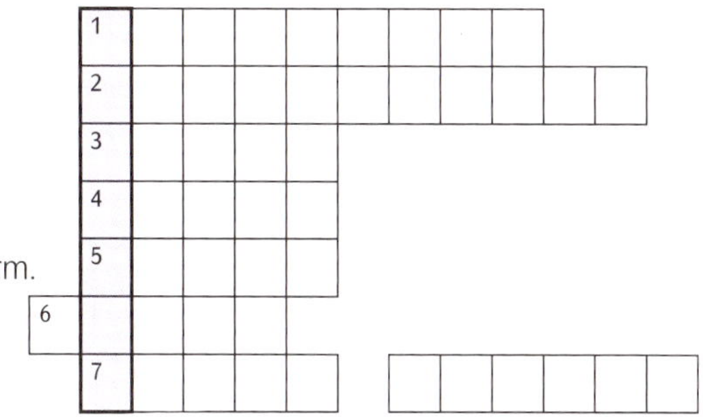

2 Your noticeboard

Making a short film

a Work in a group. Imagine you are going to make a short film for young people. Decide on information about the film and the jobs.

The film

- the type of film you want to make
- the title of the film
- location(s)
- the story
- the main characters

The jobs

- What jobs will each person in your production team do? (director, camera operators, writer, make-up artist)
- Who will the actors be? (stars, extras, stunt people)

b Make a poster about your film. Include the information from Exercise 2a.

12 Money talks

Second conditional
***Someone*, *anyone*, *everyone*, *no one*, etc.**
Vocabulary: Money; Money verbs
Interaction 12: Reacting in difficult situations

1 Read and listen

a Read the text quickly. What kind of programme do you think *The Secret Millionaire* is?

TV Mag's Pick of the week

BBC1
…fast News 0–10.35
…ing Cooks .35–11.00
…ness Lunch .00–12.00
…breakdown 2.00–12.30
…or It! 2.30–1.00
O'clock news .00–2.00
…tor's Surgery 2.00–2.30
…imal Park 2.30–3.00
…iz Time 3.00–3.30
…ow It Alls 3.30–4.00
…apstars 4.00–4.30

The Secret Millionaire

'If you were a millionaire, would you give your money to someone you didn't know?'

For many people the answer to this question would be 'No, I wouldn't' or 'If I were a millionaire, I'd buy a big house'. But what about the Secret Millionaire?

In the documentary series *The Secret Millionaire*, real millionaires look for someone to give some of their cash to. For ten days the millionaires live and work as normal people in some of the poorest areas of the UK. At the end of their visit, the millionaires tell everyone who they really are and give away thousands of pounds. They have to decide how many people to give money to and how much to give to each person.

Ben Way, the secret millionaire. Channel 4. Wednesday 9pm.

In the first programme, Ben Way, aged 26, is the secret millionaire. Ben started his first business on his fifteenth birthday and he soon became the youngest company director in the UK. While he was a teenager, he made £25 million and was one of the first *dot com* (internet business) millionaires. At the age of 21, he was on the UK's 'Richest people under thirty' list next to Robbie Williams. Although Ben had lots of financial difficulties and after that lost all his money, amazingly, he is now a millionaire again. He wants to use his money to help other people change their lives.

In this week's programme, Ben leaves his private plane and expensive home in central London and goes to live in Hackney, one of the poorest parts of the city. He lives in a room in a small flat and works with young people in a youth centre. Ben makes lots of friends: the manager of the youth centre, an ex-boxing champion who helps young people and a student who wants to be a fashion designer. But who does he give his money to?

Breakf… 9.00
Morn…
Bus… 1…
DIY 12.…
Go Fo… 12.3…
Lunch 1.0…
Natu… 2.0…
Wed… 2.3…
Musi… 3.00…
It Only… 3.30…
Total W… 4.0…
No…

> **Which is right? Don't look at the text!**
> ***During* / *For*** *ten days the millionaires live and work as normal people.*

b 4.24 Read the text again and listen. Choose the correct answer: A, B or C.

1 Ben Way is …
   A a student. **B** a company director.
   C the manager of a youth centre.

2 For ten days the secret millionaire …
   A works at home. **B** gives away lots of money.
   C works with people he/she doesn't know.

3 After ten days the secret millionaire …
   A gives away some of his/her money.
   B starts a new business. **C** goes on holiday.

4 Ben wanted to be the secret millionaire because he …
   A likes secrets. **B** is from Hackney.
   C wants to help people.

c Work in a group and answer the questions.

1 Is there a TV series like *The Secret Millionaire* in your country? NO
2 Are there any famous teenage millionaires in your country? Who are they?

2 Vocabulary Money

a 4.25 Match the words with the pictures. Then listen and check.

A 4 credit card

1 cash **2** cash machine
3 coins **4** ~~credit card~~ **5** notes
6 PIN (Personal Identification Number)
7 purse **8** receipt **9** wallet

A

B

C

D

E

F
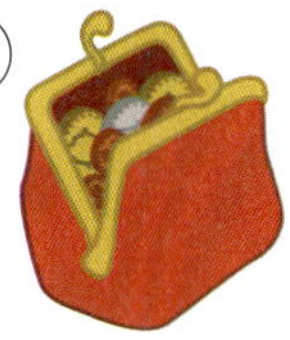

G

H

I

b Complete the sentences with the words in Exercise 2a.

1 wallet

1 Have you seen my … ? It's got all my bank cards in it.
2 Would you like to pay in cash or by … ?
3 I'm going to the … to get some money.
4 Don't tell anyone your … , it's a secret!
5 I keep all my coins in my … .
6 A: I bought this camera here last week but it broke yesterday.
B: Have you got the … ?

c Do you know any more money words? Write them in your Workbook (page 125 Exercise 1).

d Work with a partner. Ask and answer the questions.

1 Where do you keep your money?
2 Do you usually use cash or a credit card?
3 Do you usually keep receipts when you buy something?

Get it right!

✓ *If I won the lottery, I'd buy a big house.*
✗ *If I ~~would win~~ the lottery, I'd buy a big house.*

3 Grammar Second conditional

a Look at the examples and choose the correct words to complete the rules.

__If__ I __won__ the lottery, I__'d buy__ a big house.
__If__ you __were__ a millionaire, __would__ you __give__ your money to someone you didn't know? No, I **wouldn't**.

- We use the second conditional to talk about **real** / **unreal** situations.
- The verb after *if* is in the past simple, but it is used to talk about the **past** / **present and future**.
- After *would(n't)* we use the infinitive **with** / **without** *to*.

Grammar reference: page138

b Complete the sentences with the correct form of the verbs.

1 were, would buy

1 If I … (be) a millionaire, I … (buy) a sports car.
2 She… (tell) you the answer if she … (know) it.
3 What … (you/say) if you … (meet) someone famous?
4 If I … (find) a wallet, I… (not keep) it.
5 Ben and Sally … (walk) to school if they … (not live) so far away.
6 If you … (not go) to school, what … (you/do)?

Check it out!

- We often use ***I/he/she/it* + *were*** with the second conditional.
If I __were__ you, I'd go home.
If she __were__ here, she'd talk to us.

c Complete the sentences about you.

1 If I went to a different school, …
2 If I lived in another country, …
3 I'd be very happy if …
4 If I spoke perfect English, …

4 Pronunciation Long sentences DVD

a 4.26 Listen to a way of practising pronunciation in long sentences.

If I were a millionaire, I'd take my friends on holiday.

b 4.27 Listen and check. Start at the end.

1 If I could learn | an instrument, | I'd choose the guitar.
2 If Lady Gaga | played here, | I'd go and see her.
3 If you went | to the party, | you'd have | an amazing time.
4 If you could live | anywhere, | where would | you live?

c Work with a partner. Take turns to say the sentences. Start at the end and say the sentences in sections. Repeat after your partner.

1 If I went to Paris with my friends, I'd visit the Eiffel Tower.
2 If I were a sports star, I'd be a Brazilian footballer.
3 If you won the lottery, would you travel around the world?
4 If you could fly, would you visit the moon?

5 Speak

Work with a partner. You are going to play snakes and ladders. You will need a coin. Read the rules before you start.

Rules

1 Take turns to throw the coin. If you throw a head, move forward one space, If you throw a tail, move forward two spaces.
2 If you land on a snake head, go down the snake, if you land at the bottom of a ladder, go up the ladder.
3 If you land on a question you must answer it. If you answer correctly, stay on the square. If you answer incorrectly, go back one square.

6 Vocabulary Money verbs

a 4.28 Match the two parts of the sentences. Then listen and check.

1 Can I **borrow** £10? | A I'll give it back to you tomorrow.
2 Shall I **lend** you £10? | B You can give it back to me tomorrow.

3 We had to **pay for** | A £20 on books.
4 We had to **spend** | B five books.

5 Did she **waste** that money? | A Yes, she put it in the bank.
6 Did she **save** that money? | B Yes, she spent it on rubbish!

7 Did you **win** a lot of money | A in the competition?
8 Did you **earn** a lot of money | B as a waitress?

b Complete the sentences with the verbs.

borrow earn lend pay for
save spend waste ~~win~~

1 win

1 If you buy a lottery ticket, you might … some money.
2 Don't … your money on clothes you don't wear.
3 People often … money from a bank if they want to buy something expensive.
4 How much money did you … in your job last month?
5 If you … the cinema tickets, I'll buy the popcorn.
6 My brother wants to … his money to buy a car.
7 Can you … me some money until tomorrow?
8 She likes to … money on nice presents for her family.

c Do you know any more money verbs? Write them in your Workbook (page 125 Exercise 4).

d Work in a group. Ask and answer the questions.

1 What do you spend money on?
2 Do you ever waste money? How?
3 Have you ever won any money?
4 Do you earn any money? How?

Check it out!

borrow = take for a short time
lend = give for a short time
*Can **I borrow** £5?* = Will ***you lend me*** £5?

Culture Vulture

Did you know that British teenagers spend about £1,000 a year on mobile phones, MP3 players and music downloads? What do teenagers in your country spend money on? Do you think they spend money well or waste money?

7 Listen

a 4.29 Listen and match the speakers with the people they would like to be for a day.

1 Damien 2 Colleen 3 Bobby
4 Nicole 5 Steve

b 4.29 Listen again. Are the sentences *right* (✓) or *wrong* (✗)? Correct the wrong sentences.

1 Damien would like to start his own dot com company.
2 Colleen doesn't like Jessica Alba's clothes.
3 Bobby would like to watch Jenson Button drive.
4 Nicole would like to meet her cousin's university friends.
5 Steve loves the Jonas Brothers' music.

c Work with a partner. If you could be anyone for a day, who would you be? Why?

8 Grammar

someone, *anyone*, *everyone*, *no one*, etc.

a Look at the examples and complete the table.

*If you could be **anyone** for a day, who would you be?*
*I wouldn't want to be **anyone** famous.*
*I'd be **someone** rich and famous.*
*There's **nobody** who drives like him.*
***Everyone** would want to do that, wouldn't they?*

	Some- **Specific**	*Any-* **Not specific**	*Every-* **All**	*No-* **Negative**
People	… somebody	… anybody	… …	no one …
Things	something	…	…	…
Places	…	anywhere	everywhere	…

Choose the correct words to complete the rules.

- We often use *any-* words in questions and **positive** / **negative** statements.
- When we use *no-* words we always use a **positive** / **negative** verb.
- With *some-*, *any-*, *no-* and *every-* words we use the **singular** / **plural** form of the verb.

Grammar reference: page 140

b Complete the words with *some*, *any*, *no* or *every*.

1 Every

1 …body knows that the world is round!
2 She was very quiet. She didn't say …thing at the meeting.
3 I looked …where for my sunglasses but I couldn't find them.
4 … one knows my secret. I haven't told anyone.
5 I don't mind where we go. …where you want.
6 …body has eaten all my chocolates! Who was it?

c Complete the sentences with the words in the box.

anybody ~~anything~~ Everyone nowhere somebody something

1 anything

1 It doesn't cost … . It's free.
2 She didn't speak to … all night.
3 You look hungry. I'll get you … to eat.
4 There's … at the door. I'll go and see who it is.
5 There's … in England as nice as my town!
6 … was at the party last night.

d Work with a partner. Tell your partner about …

1 somewhere you like going at the weekend.
2 everything you want for your next birthday.
3 someone you talk to every day.
4 something interesting you've seen on the internet.

Interaction 12 DVD

Reacting in difficult situations

a 4.30 Listen to Liam and Sandra. What does Sandra want?

1 She wants Liam to pay her back some money.
2 She wants to give Liam some money.
3 She wants Liam to lend her some money.

b 4.30 Listen again and write the number of the phrases you hear.

1 Can I talk to you for a moment?
2 Have you got a minute?
3 You know that/those …
4 Umm, let me think.
5 Er, let me see.
6 Well, the thing is …
7 I would if I could, but …

c 4.31 Turn to page 125. Listen to the sentences and repeat them. Practise sounding 'diplomatic'.

d Work with a partner.
Student A: Turn to page 128.
Student B: Turn to page 131.

Portfolio 12

A 'for and against' essay

a Read Kelly's 'for and against' essay about being a teenage millionaire. Do you agree with her? Why? / Why not?

Is it a good thing to be a teenage millionaire?

There are good things and bad things about being a teenage millionaire. 1… , you are very independent if you have money. You can also be generous and spend money on your family and friends. 2… , if you have money, you'll have more opportunities. You can travel around the world or start your own company.

3… , there are some disadvantages. Someone who has won all their money on the lottery doesn't have to work hard, but most millionaires have to work really hard to earn their money. He or she might not have any free time. 4… if you have a lot of money, it is sometimes difficult to know who your real friends are. Perhaps people only want to be with you because of your money.

5… , I think that it's better not to be a teenage millionaire. You might not enjoy working all the time and you need to be with people who are your true friends. I'm going to work really hard and I hope to be a millionaire when I'm 30!

b Complete the text with the phrases.

On the one hand In conclusion Another point is that
On the other hand What is more

c Read the essay again and find examples of …

1 personality adjectives *(paragraph 1)*
2 the present perfect *(paragraph 2)*
3 the zero conditional *(paragraph 2)*
4 the first conditional *(paragraph 1)*
5 a defining relative clause *(paragraph 3)*
6 a verb + *-ing* and a verb + infinitive *(paragraph 3)*

Check it out!

We normally structure an argument the following way:
First paragraph: arguments **for**
Second paragraph: arguments **against**
Third paragraph: your **conclusion/opinion**

d Choose one of these questions and write a 'for and against' essay (about 150 words). Use the phrases in Exercise b and the structure in the Check it out! box.

Is it a good thing …

1 to be a teenage celebrity?
2 to start work when you're 16?
3 to have a national lottery?

Money, money, money

1 Song

a 🔊 **4.32** Listen to the beginning of the song and write the words you hear.

work poor sad pay rich
sleep money happy dreams

b Work with a partner. Look at the words that you wrote in Exercise 1a. What do you think the song is about?

c 🔊 **4.32** Listen again and match the two parts of the sentences.

1 E

1	I work all night,	**A**	I have to pay
2	to pay the bills	**B**	bad
3	Ain't it	**C**	if I got me a wealthy man
4	And still there never seems to be	**D**	I'd fool around and have a ball …
5	That's too	**E**	I work all day,
6	In my dreams I have a plan	**F**	a single penny left for me
7	I wouldn't have to work at all,	**G**	sad

Chorus

8	Money, money, money	**H**	all the things I could do
9	Money, money, money	**I**	it's a rich man's world
10	Aha-ahaaa	**J**	must be funny, in the rich man's world
11	If I had a little money	**K**	always sunny, in the rich man's world

d 🔊 **4.33** Listen to the last verse of the song. How does the singer decide to get rich?

1 by working hard
2 by going to a casino
3 by marrying a rich man

e Do you think the singer's plan is a good one? Do you think rich people are happier than other people? Why? / Why not?

Song Money, Money, Money

2 Sound check

a Look at the stress pattern. Copy the first line of the chorus and underline the stressed syllables.

●•●•●• Money, money, money

b 4.34 Match the lines from the chorus with the stress patterns A–D. Then listen and check.

1 Must be funny — A ••●●●
2 In the rich man's world — B ●•●•●•
3 All the things I could do — C ●•●•••••
4 If I had a little money — D ●•●•

c 4.34 Listen again and repeat.

3 Musical notes

a 4.35 Listen to some other types of music that were popular in the 1970s. Write the types of music in the order you hear them.

disco   prog rock   reggae   heavy metal

b Which types of the music above do you like? Would you listen to any normally? Which music was popular in your country in the 1970s?

ABBA

ABBA were a Swedish pop group which was internationally famous from the mid 1970s until the early 80s. The name comes from the first letters of the names of the people in the group: **A**gnetha, **B**jörn, **B**enny, and **A**nni-Frid. They were famous for their disco sound and crazy costumes! The band sang in English but also translated a lot of their most popular songs into Spanish. ABBA's music is still very popular and millions of records are sold every year. The successful musical of their best-loved songs, *Mamma Mia!*, is touring around the world. It was made into a very successful film in 2008.

Get it right! 11 and 12

Common errors

1 Everyone wants to ...

Make sure you use these words correctly.

✓ *I did**n't** understand **anything** in the email.*

✗ *I didn't understand ~~nothing~~ in the email.*

✓ Everyone *wants* to sit next to Paco.

✗ *Everyone ~~want~~ to sit next to Paco.*

✓ *I turned round, but **no one** was there.*

✗ *I turned round, but ~~anyone~~ was there.*

✓ *I didn't see **anyone** there.*

✗ *I didn't see ~~any person~~ there.*

Correct the sentences.

1 Does any person know the answer to this question?
2 Nobody do really well in this class.
3 I tried to phone home but anybody answered.
4 He didn't say nothing at all at the party.
5 Everybody are going to meet at the cinema later.

2 Second conditional

Use the past simple, not *would*, after *if* in second conditional sentences.

✓ *If I **had** a bank card, I'd go on holiday to Egypt.*

✗ *If I ~~would have~~ a bank card, I'd go on holiday to Egypt.*

a Correct the sentences that are wrong.

1 If I earned money at the weekend, I'd be able to buy a bike.
2 I'd pay in cash if I would have some.
3 If I would know my PIN number, I would be able to get some money out of the bank.
4 I would take the bus if I had some cash.

b Work with a partner and complete the sentences with your own ideas.

1 If … , I would be really sad.
2 You wouldn't say that to me if … .
3 If … , we would be friends.
4 I would go with you if … .

3 Can I borrow…?

Make sure you use these words correctly.

✓ *I only **spent** five euros last weekend. I was really careful. (✗ I only ~~wasted~~…)*

✓ *Don't **waste** your money buying sweets. They're bad for you. (✗ Don't ~~lose~~…)*

✓ *Jake delivered pizzas to **earn** money for his holidays. (✗ … to ~~win~~ money …)*

✓ *Can I **borrow** your pen?. (✗ Can I ~~lend~~…)*

a Choose the correct word.

A: Dad, I haven't got any money.
B: What do you mean? You [1] *win / earn* £100 every weekend working at Pizza One!
A: I know, but I had to [2] *spend / waste* £80 on those cool trainers I told you about.
B: You didn't need them! I would say you [3] *spent / wasted* £80 on those 'cool' trainers!
A: OK, OK. So, I had £20 left and I [4] *lost / wasted* that going to that awful film with Danny.
B: Well, that was stupid. You'll have to stay at home this evening then!
A: Aw Dad, can I [5] *borrow / lend* £20? I promise to try and save some money next weekend.

b 4.36 Listen and check your answers.

4 Say it right!

Word stress

a Some words in English look like words in your language, but the stress isn't always on the same syllable. Which syllable is stressed in these words?

1 favourite
2 immediately
3 interesting
4 usually
5 chocolate
6 occasions

b 4.37 Listen, check and repeat.

c Work with a partner. Write a sentence with two of the words from Exercise 4a. Your partner reads the sentence out loud.

Review 11 and 12

1 Grammar

a Complete the sentences with the verbs in the present simple passive.

1 More cars … (produce) in Japan than anywhere else in the world.
2 98% of Antarctica … (make) of ice.
3 200 babies … (be born) every minute.
4 800,000 laptops … (lose) in airports every year.
5 About 60% of all bank robbers … (catch) by the police.

5

b Complete the questions with the verb in the past simple passive.

1 A: When … computer programmes … (invent)?
B: In 1843, by Ada Byron.
2 A: How many snakes … (use) in the film *Raiders of the Lost Ark*?
B: 7,500.
3 A: When … the first album … (record)?
B: In 1948, by Columbia records.
4 A: When … scissors first … (use)?
B: About 4,000 years ago, in Egypt.

4

c Complete the sentences with the correct form of the verbs.

1 If I had some money, I … (buy) a very big TV.
2 Grace would cycle to school if she … (have) a bike.
3 He … (not know) what to say if he met someone famous.
4 What would you do if you … (win) the lottery?
5 If I … (be) you, I'd phone home.

5

d Choose the correct words.

1 We need *someone / anyone* to play the drums in our band.
2 I don't know *nothing / anything* about it. Don't ask me!
3 Are you going *anywhere / everywhere* nice this summer?
4 *Nobody / Anybody* can go in there. The door's locked.
5 *Everyone / Someone* needs to be alone sometimes.

5

2 Vocabulary

a Put the letters in the correct order and make film words

1 tnstu oepsnr
2 milf rats
3 rpcist
4 crietdor
5 xreat
6 akme pu trsait
7 tes
8 ioaltocn

8

b Complete the sentences with materials.

1 The g… bottles and the p… containers go in different bins.
2 We need some c… boxes to carry the books.
3 You can't put things made of m… in the microwave.
4 Our next model is Mike, wearing a c… T-shirt and a l… jacket.
5 I've got her some g… earrings for her birthday.
6 The desk and chair in my room are made of w… .

8

c Copy and complete the puzzle and find the mystery word.

1 It's made of plastic and you use it to buy things.
2 Money made of paper.
3 You put a card in and it gives you money.
4 It's used for keeping small amounts of money.
5 Money made of metal.
6 A secret number for your bank account.
7 It's used for keeping larger amounts of money.

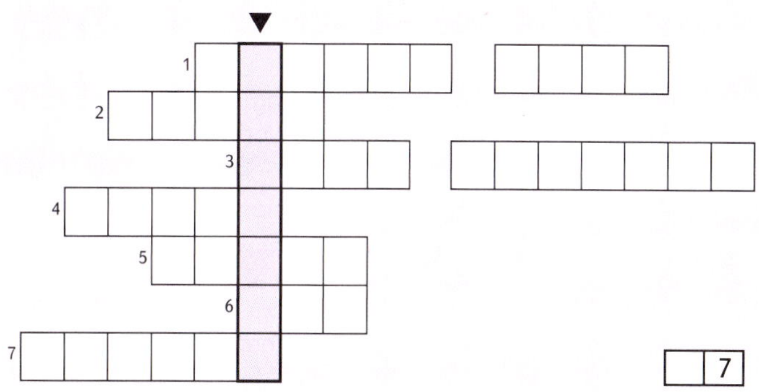

7

d Choose the correct words.

1 He *earned / won* a lot of money while he was working at the restaurant.
2 Can you *borrow / lend* me some money until tomorrow?
3 They *waste / pay for* a lot of money on stupid things.
4 She *spends / saves* money every week and puts it in the bank.
5 My brother *borrowed / lent* some money from me, but he hasn't paid me back.
6 I'll *pay for / spend* the card if you get the present.

6

Skills 4 Real

UNITS 1–4

1 Speaking

Work with a partner. Answer the questions.

1 Do you, or any teenagers you know, have a job in the evening after school, at the weekend or in the school holidays?
2 What do you/they do?
3 Is it common for teenagers to have a part-time job in your country?

2 Reading

a Look at the job adverts and read Tom's fact file. Then answer the questions.

1 Which jobs do you think Tom would be good at? Why?
2 Which jobs could he apply for? Why?

Name: Tom Smith
Age: 17
Qualifications: 10 GCSEs in Maths, Chemistry, Physics, Biology, English, Physical Education, Geography, History, French, Art.
Studying for AS Levels in Maths, Biology, Chemistry and Psychology.
Likes: sport (especially football), Science, meeting new people. He is a volunteer tennis coach for Year 7 pupils at his Secondary School
Dislikes: cooking, drum n' bass music
Driving licence: Yes

---

jobfinder - the best employment network in the UK

File Edit View Insert Format Tools Actions Help

http://www.jobfinder.co.uk/searchresults_page1.html

1 **Job Details**

Job Title:	Kids party entertainer
City / Town:	Nottingham
Company name:	Mad Science: East Midlands
Company sector:	Adventure, Catering/ Hospitality/Leisure, Childcare/Care Work, Education, Entertainment, Promotions/Events
Pay:	£20–£25 per session

Job Description

We are looking for bright, confident, engaging people to present science-themed birthday parties to children between the ages of 5–12. Applicants must be available to work weekends. You must be comfortable around children and have an in-depth knowledge of science. This is a perfect opening for any candidates wishing to pursue a career in teaching or performing arts.

Qualifications Required

A science AS level is required.

Candidates must have access to a vehicle and hold a full UK driving licence.

You must be eligible to work in the UK.

You must be able to speak English fluently.

APPLY HERE

File

http://ww...

2 **Vacancy details**

Assistant Soccer Coach

Company:	Kings Camps
Location:	UK Nationwide
Benefits:	On Application
Start:	April, July and August
Duration:	1 or 2 weeks

Description

If you're mad about football and want to pass on your enthusiasm and love of the game to children, then coaching at International Soccer Schools could be for you.

The Assistant Soccer Coach is responsible for assisting a coach in leading a group of children aged 5–7 years through a range of football coaching, themed activities and games. You will be responsible for the health, safety and enjoyment of the group in your care.

Requirements

Fun, vibrant and bubbly personality with a passion for football. Experience of working with children from 5 years upwards. Experience of coaching and leading children in football and other sports desirable.

share more +

---

jobfinder - the best employment network in the UK

File Edit View Insert Format Tools Actions Help

http://www.jobfinder.co.uk/searchresults_page3.html

3 **Job Details**

Job Title:	Waiting and kitchen staff
City/Town:	Restaurants nationwide
Company name:	Zizzi
Company sector:	Catering/Hospitality/Leisure
Pay:	£ on application

Job Description

Zizzi restaurants advertise for waiting staff and kitchen staff through their website. For both waiting staff and kitchen staff send your CV directly to the restaurant you are interested in. You can find the restaurant finder on the Zizzi website to obtain the full address details.

To find out more, click "APPLY" and visit the Zizzi careers site.

Qualifications Required

You must be eligible to work in the UK.

You must be able to speak English fluently.

APPLY HERE

jobfinder - the best employment network in the UK

File Edit View Insert Format Tools Actions Help

http://www.jobfinder.co.uk/searchresults_page4.html

4 Staff for Nozstock Festival – volunteer and get in free!

Description Free entry for volunteer workers at festival!

From July 31 – August 2, Nozstock Festival (Tickets £60 in advance, £70 on the gate) welcomes over 4000 festival-goers to Bromyard, Herefordshire, with live bands, soloists, and DJs playing music from rock and indie to ska and hip-hop alongside a dance-feast of drum n' bass and hard dance on 8 stages.

We are offering festival-goers the opportunity to come and work with us for free entry to the festival. Many opportunities are available for friendly stewards and café assistants. No experience is required and training will be provided. So don't worry, as long as you can point on a map or make coffee, we are the festival for you!

If you are interested in joining the Nozstock team, email work@nozstock.com before July 10th and we will send you an application form.

Region West, Herefordshire	**Country** United Kingdom
Hourly Rate £0.00	**Minimum Age** 17
Requirements n/a	**Email** www.nozstock.com

b Match the words with the meanings:

1 the people who work for an organisation
2 providing food and drinks for people
3 all the jobs you do during your life
4 things that are needed or demanded
5 someone who helps to organise a big event
6 someone who teaches people to improve at a sport

A catering
B requirements
C staff
D coach
E career
F steward

c Work with a partner. Discuss which of the four job adverts you would / would not like to apply for and why.

3 Listening

a 4.38 Listen to three people talking about part-time jobs. Make notes about each person.

1 Do you think it's a good idea for teenagers to have a part-time job?
2 What did you use to do as a part-time job when you were a teenager?
3 What was the best thing about the job?
4 What was the worst thing about the job?

b 4.38 Listen again and check your answers.

c Work with a partner. Who do you think had the best part-time job when they were a teenager? Who had the worst? Why?

4 Writing

a Write an advert to advertise your ideal part-time job. Think about:

- the qualities you need
- the experience you need
- duties/hours
- how much you will earn

b Swap your advert with a partner. Read your partner's advert. Would you like to do the job? Why? / Why not?

Skills 4 Real

UNITS 5–8

1 Speaking

Work with a partner. Answer the questions.

1 How often do you use a computer? What do you use it for?
2 Do think you know a lot about computers? Why? / Why not?
3 Can everyone in your family use a computer? Who can? / Who can't?

Are you internet-savvy?

Web whizz-kid or hopeless online? Find out here...

Start:

Have you set up your own personal blog?
- Yes
- No

Do you watch all your fave programmes online?
- All the time!
- No, never

You've got a question. Google it or ask a mate?
- Google it
- Ask a pal

Are any of the letters on your computer keyboard worn?
- Yes
- Not really

For a school project, do you hit the books or the net?
- Net
- Library for me!

Do you enter competitions or do quizzes online?
- Yes
- Never

Do you know what an HTML code and uploading are?
- Of course!
- Not really

Do you check your email or networking account daily?
- Yes, always
- No

Someone offers you a 'cookie'. You ...
- Click to accept it
- Hope it's the choc-chip type!

A Cyber-chic
You know how to do anything you need to online – you could even show your IT teacher a thing or two! Whether it's blogging, chatting or downloading, you know your way around the internet like most people know their way around their local shop. Try to use your web skills to your advantage – you could end up as a web designer or a celebrity blogger one day. But don't neglect your real life for cyber-reality. Face-to-face interaction is just as important too!

B PC pal
You can use email and access your favourite websites, but you're not a complete web devotee. There's nothing wrong with that, but are you maximising the fun you could be having online? Ask your mates to recommend a site, or Google your fave band, a TV programme, or a must-see movie. It's a great way to find new music, too. Just experiment by visiting some different sites and you'll soon become more confident.

C Software scared
Whoa, do you even know how to switch on your computer? Maybe you're a passionate bookworm, or perhaps you're just scared of giving cyber-space a go, but the fact is, you can't avoid using the web forever. Start off with something simple like setting up an email account, and you'll find that 'puters are pretty useful. They make researching school projects a doddle, and there are loads of other fun things you can do on the internet as well. So, try it today!

2 Reading

a Do the quiz and answer the questions. Do you agree with your profile? Why? / Why not?

b Look at the profiles and decide if these speakers are 'cyber-chic' (A), 'PC pal' (B) or 'software scared' (C).

'I use the computer to keep up with my friends, but I prefer playing sport to surfing the net in my free time.'

'I'm not keen on the net. I prefer to ask my teacher for extra info if I need help with my homework.'

'I'm making my own music at the moment and uploading it on to the net. That way everyone can listen to it!'

'I'm a real web devotee and the keys on my laptop are already worn out after only a year.'

c Read the quiz again and match the words with the correct definition: A, B or C.

1 savvy
- **A** knowing a little
- **B** knowing nothing
- **C** knowing a lot

2 worn
- **A** tired
- **B** damaged by a lot of use
- **C** dressed

3 face-to-face
- **A** in person
- **B** online
- **C** on the phone

4 devotee
- **A** friend
- **B** fan
- **C** expert

5 bookworm
- **A** someone who hates books
- **B** someone who reads a lot
- **C** something which eats paper

6 doddle
- **A** something very easy
- **B** something very silly
- **C** something very difficult

d Write three more questions for the quiz. Work with a partner and ask your questions. Do you think your partner is internet-savvy?

3 Listening

a 4.39 Listen to three people talking about computers. Make notes about each person for each question.

1. What do you use the internet for?
2. Have you ever bought anything online?
3. Do you use social networking sites?
4. Do you download music or films?

b 4.39 Listen again and check your answers.

c Work with a partner. Ask and answer the questions in Exercise 3a.

4 Writing

a Work with a partner. You're going to design a webpage to encourage people who are 'PC pals' or 'software scared' to use the internet more. Think about:

- why the internet is useful
- why the internet is fun
- who can help you become more confident about using the internet.

b Swap your webpage with other students. Which webpage do you prefer? Why?

Skills 4 Real
UNITS 9–12

1 Speaking

Work with a partner. Answer the questions.

1 Which TV programmes do you watch:
- with your friends?
- with your family?
- in the morning/evening?

2 Is anyone in your family a 'telly addict'?

3 Do you think television is good in your country? Why? / Why not?

2 Reading

a Read the TV guide quickly. Which programmes would/wouldn't you like to watch? Why?

TV listings Wednesday 23rd

Supernatural

The thrilling story of the Winchester brothers continues in a new fourth series of the fantasy drama. Starring Jensen Ackles and Jared Padalecki.

Fantasy. Today at 10:05pm on ITV1

Supernatural

America's Got Talent

More from the first semi-final in LA, where an all-male dance troupe and a 10-year-old martial artist are among those hoping to wow judges David Hasselhoff, Sharon Osbourne and Piers Morgan.

General Show/Game Show. Today at 9:00pm on ITV2

Hollyoaks

Hollyoaks follows the dramatic lives of a group of students at Hollyoaks Community College in Chester. The show has become known for its gorgeous young cast and melodramatic storylines. Hollyoaks has fans all over the world, broadcasting to Canada, Norway, Sweden, Finland, Ireland, USA, Turkey and parts of Eastern Europe.

Today at 7:00pm on E4

Hollyoaks

PICK OF THE WEEK

Transworld Sport

Action and features, focusing on mainstream activities and minority interest events, from football, tennis and golf to BMX biking, surfing and kite-boarding.

General Sports. Today at 10:00pm on Sky Sports 3

Transworld Sport

Animals at Work

Einstein the Imitator: A talented parrot enters a competition, a Labrador goes in search of bats, and a goat solves a smelly problem. With John Barrowman. Last in the series.

General/Children's/Youth. Today at 4:05pm on BBC1

T in the park: Musical Festival

Highlights of the T in the Park festival held at Balado, Perth and Kinross, including performances by the Ting Tings, Franz Ferdinand, Little Boots, Paolo Nutini, Glasvegas, Florence and the Machine and Doves. Edith Bowman, Reggie Yates and Nick Grimshaw present.

General Music/Ballet/Dance. Today at 7:00pm on BBC Three

T in the park

Sacha Baron Cohen: Hero of Comedy

An insight into the life and career of Ali G, Borat and Bruno creator Sacha Baron Cohen. The programme charts the comedian's rise from appearances on *The 11 O'Clock Show* to his international success in Hollywood and recognition in *Time* magazine's list of 100 People Who Shape Our World.

Comedy/Documentary. Today at 10:30pm on C4

b Read the TV guide again. Which programme ...

1 has different music groups playing outside?
2 is the final programme for a period of time?
3 is about two people from the same family?
4 is about the real life of a funny actor?
5 shows a type of cycling?
6 has lots of young actors in it?
7 is filmed in Los Angeles?

c Find the words in the TV guide that mean:

1 not real or true, something that exists in your imagination
2 a group of dancers
3 the best parts of something, for example a concert or sports event
4 indicating the main person in a film or TV programme
5 someone who entertains people by being funny or telling jokes
6 all the actors in a film or TV programme

3 Listening

a 4.40 Listen to three people talking about television. Make notes about each person.

Abi

Sumara

Ben

1 When do you watch TV?
2 What are your favourite types of programmes?
3 What types of programmes do you never watch?
4 Do you like adverts?
5 How much TV do you watch a week?

b 4.40 Listen again and check your answers.

c Work with a partner. Ask and answer the questions in Exercise 3a.

4 Writing

a You are a programmer for a TV channel. You want to plan an evening of television with something for everyone. Make the programmes sound as appealing as possible. Include the following information:

- the title, time and type of programme
- a short summary of the programme
- names of TV/film stars or other famous people in the programme

b Work in a group and swap your TV guides with other students. Which other TV guides do you like? Why?

Unit 4 Interactive Science: Food for thought

1 Think!

Work with a partner. Where do these foods go in the food pyramid?

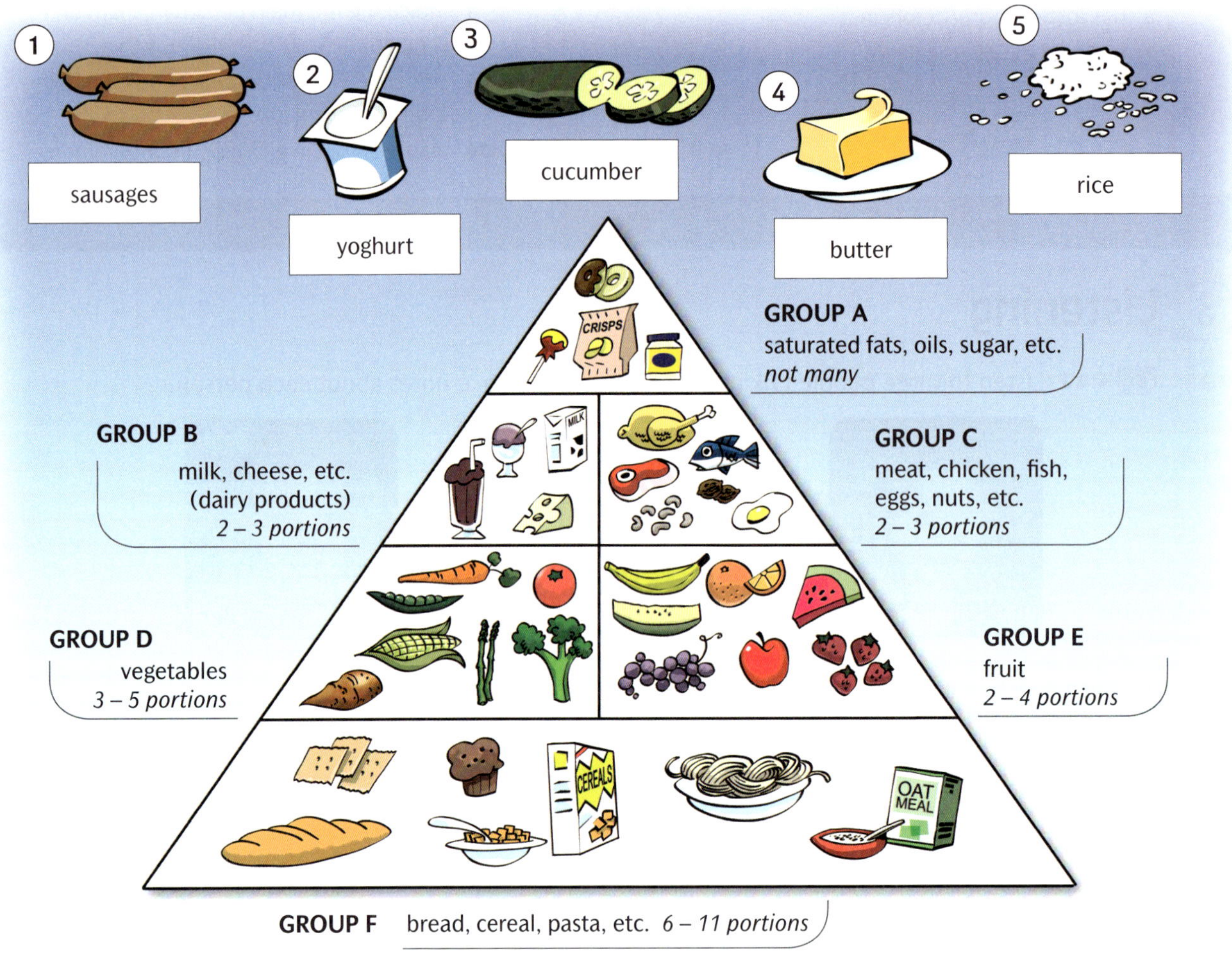

Did you know?

Popeye did not eat spinach for its iron content, but for the vitamin A it contains. The popular cartoon character had a very good effect on the spinach industry when he was invented, because more young people began to eat it.

2 Listening

a 4.41 Listen to the radio programme and check your answers.

b 4.41 Listen again and make sentences.

1 Butter		**A** iron and protein.
2 Rice		**B** calcium.
3 Yoghurt	contain(s)	**C** carbohydrates and vitamin B.
4 Sausages		**D** nutrients like vitamin A, vitamin C and minerals like potassium.
5 Cucumbers		**E** saturated fats.

3 Speaking

Look at the pictures. Have you ever eaten any of these things? Would you like to? Why/why not?

paella, Spain

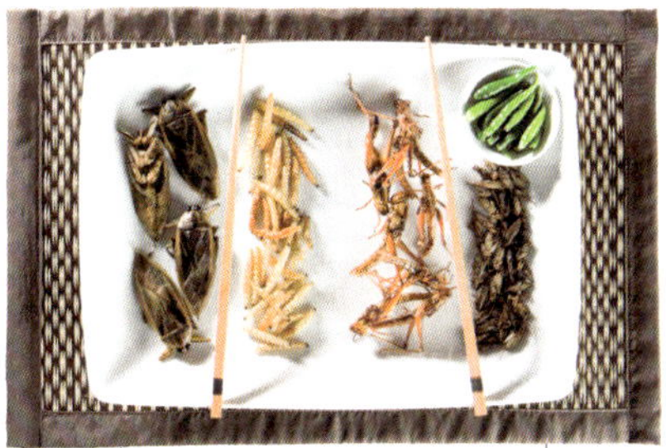

fried insects, China

fried crab claws, USA

4 Reading

a Read the text quickly. Has your answer to Exercise 3 changed?

Grasshopper soup for lunch?

How do you feel about eating insects? You eat shrimps and crabs in your paella, don't you? Well, insects, shrimps and crabs are all arthropods! So why not eat insects too?

Did you know that insects contain more protein and less fat than meat? For example, hamburgers contain about 18% protein and 18% fat. A cooked grasshopper contains about 60% protein and just 6% fat. And insects are full of vitamins and minerals too.

A Dutch scientist, Arnold Van Huis, wants us to eat more insects. There is a meat crisis because the world population is growing. He says that insects are the solution. They cost very little to produce and don't need much water or space. They also produce very few greenhouse gases so are good for the environment.

And eating insects isn't as strange as you think. They were a favourite dish for the ancient Romans and ancient Greeks and they are still a traditional food in many parts of the world. Van Huis says:

'Most of the world already eats insects. It is only in the western world we don't. Psychologically, we have a problem with it. I don't know why, as we eat shrimps, which are comparable.'

So, next time you feel like a snack, how about roasted grasshoppers or fried scorpions?

Blog comments

› I've eaten caterpillars in Zimbabwe. They're delicious!
Jack, UK

› I tried grasshoppers on holiday in Thailand. They tasted like chicken. Very good!
Jo, Canada

Arthropods: a member of a group of invertebrate animals with jointed legs, a body that is divided into sections and an exoskeleton. It includes insects, spiders and crustaceans.

b Read the text again. Write *T* (true) or *F* (false).

1 Shrimps and crabs are insects.
2 Grasshoppers are better for you than hamburgers.
3 Arnold Van Huis says that eating insects is a solution to some of the world's problems.
4 People didn't eat insects in the past.
5 They eat insects in the western world.

Did you know?

The technical word for eating bugs is 'entomophagy'.

5 Final task

A friend is coming for lunch. Decide what you're going to eat and make sure it is balanced and healthy. Use the food triangle to help you. You can also look on the internet.

Unit 8 Interactive Geography: Population

1 Think!

a Work with a partner. Look at the outlines of the three **largest** countries in the world. Do you know which countries they are? Can you put them in order of size?

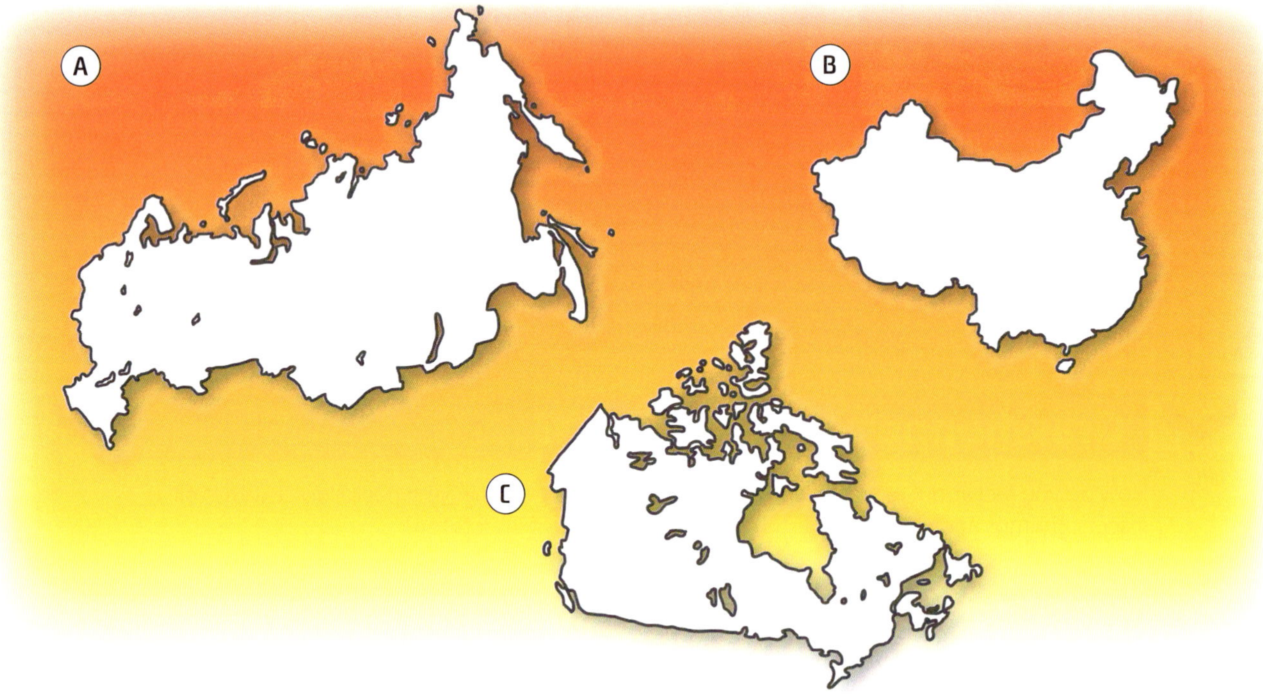

b Match the population figures with the three **most populated** countries in the world.

1 1,341,860,000	**A** India
2 1,193,000,000	**B** United States
3 311,920,000*	**C** China

* January 2011

Did you know?

Every year, the world population increases by more than 80 million people.

2 Listening

a 4.42 Listen to Emma and James doing the tasks in Exercises 1a and 1b and check your answers.

b 4.43 Listen to Emma and James talking about population. Match the geographical terms with their definitions.

1 absolute population	**A** the number of people that inhabit an area
2 population density	**B** a large number of people per square kilometre
3 densely populated	**C** very few people per square kilometre
4 sparsely populated	**D** the relation between the number of people and the size of the area they inhabit.

c Work with a partner and answer the questions.

1 Which two countries does Emma compare?
2 Which of the two countries is bigger?
3 Which of the two countries has a bigger population?
4 Which of the two countries has a higher population density?

Did you know?

Every second, five people are born and two people die.

3 Reading

Work with a partner. Read the geography magazine article and do the quiz.

What do you know about the population of Spain? Do our quiz and find out. (Answers at the bottom of the page)

a The facts

- Spain is [1]*405.987 / 505.987 / 605.987* km^2.
- The absolute population of Spain is more than [2]*30 / 46 / 80* million inhabitants.
- Women in Spain have an average of [3]*1.39 / 2.65 / 3.12* children. This is one of the lowest birth rates in the world.
- Life expectancy in Spain is very high. Women live to an average age of [4]*73 / 79 / 84* and men to [5]*71 / 77 / 82*.
- The province with the lowest population density is [6]*Soria / Segovia / Huesca*.
- [7]*14 / 18 / 22* % of people are 60 or older.
- [8]*14 / 18 / 22* % of people are 15 or younger.
- Most of the population lives [9]*in cities / in small towns / on the islands*.
- [10]*2 / 12 / 20* % of the population were born in another country.

b The statistics

To work out the population of an area we use this formula:

$$\text{Population density} = \frac{\text{the number of people}}{\text{the size of the area}}$$

Look at your answers to numbers 1 and 2 in Part a of this quiz and work out the population density of Spain.

Answers

1	505,987	**6**	Soria
2	46	**7**	22
3	1.39	**8**	14
4	84	**9**	in cities
5	77	**10**	12

mini-dictionary

average = the amount you get by adding two or more amounts together and dividing the total by the number of amounts

life expectancy = the length of time that a living thing, especially a human being, is expected to live

birth rate = the number of births that happen during a period of time in a particular place

4 Final task

Work with a partner. Choose a country and copy and complete the table. You can use the internet. Find maps and photos of the country you have chosen and make a poster.

name of country	
size in km^2	
absolute population	
population density	
life expectancy	
birth rate	

Unit 12 Interactive History: Trade

1 Think!

What do you think the things in the pictures below have in common?

2 Listening

a 4.44 Listen to a museum curator talking to a group of teenage visitors and check your answer to Exercise 1.

b 4.44 Listen again and answer the questions.

1 What did early people use as a unit of exchange?
2 Where were cowrie shells used as currency?
3 Where and when was the 'turtle' used?
4 Why does the curator say that the story behind trade beads is sad?
5 When was the first credit card produced?

c Work with a partner and answer the questions.

1 What is 'barter'?
2 How did barter change in the Neolithic Age?

Did you know?

African trade beads were made in Europe, especially in Venice, Germany and the Netherlands.

Did you know?

The cowrie shell was used as currency until the middle of the twentieth century.

3 Speaking

In the first quarter of the twentieth century Leonard Woolley, a British archaeologist, was excavating an ancient site in the city of Ur in Mesopotamia. He found the things in these pictures.

Work with a partner. Look at the pictures and discuss the questions.

1 What do you think these objects are made of?
2 What do they suggest about the society who lived there?
3 What do they suggest about the country's resources?

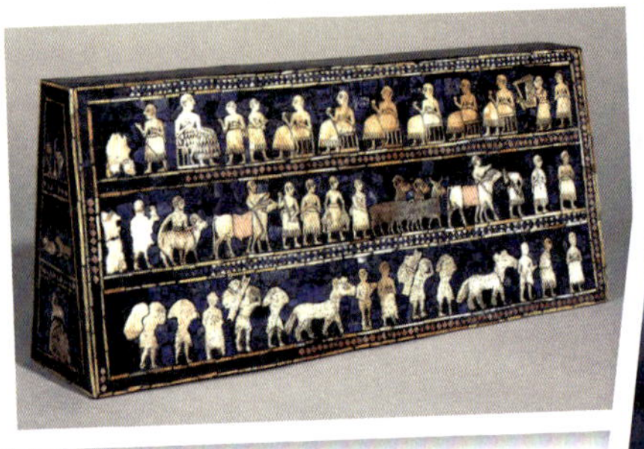

4 Reading

a Read the text and check your answers to Exercise 3.

Digging deep

In the earliest civilisations people bartered or traded. It wasn't always easy to put a 'price' on things. The things that everybody needed, such as cattle and seeds, were more valuable than other products. These things, called 'commodities', became a form of money because they had a standard value for the people who exchanged them. For example, one cow was maybe worth two goats or one bag of barley was maybe worth two bags of beans.

Trade went through a radical change when the first cities were founded around 4000-3000 B.C. in southern Mesopotamia (present-day Iraq). For the first time, people specialised in certain jobs - for example, there were potters and carpenters, and so people had different things to trade with.

Around this time the Mesopotamians invented the wheel and the sailboat. With these two inventions it was possible to move goods long distances by land or water. Some people became merchants and trade with foreign lands began. The first extensive trade routes were along the great rivers, such as the Tigris and the Euphrates.

Southern Mesopotamia had plenty of barley, meat, fish, leather and wool but very little wood, stone and metal. However, the Royal Tombs discovered in the city of Ur by Leonard Woolley contained many items, such as jewellery, made of precious metals and semi-precious stones. As Mesopotamia did not have these things, historians believe they were imported from places a long distance away, such as Iran, Pakistan and Turkey. In its trading operations, Mesopotamia used commodities, especially barley, which it exchanged for wood, stone and metal, such as gold, silver and copper.

b Read the text again and complete the table with resources mentioned in the text.

Mesopotamia		Iran, Pakistan, Turkey
…	Euphrates	…
…		…
…	Tigris	…
…		
…		

c Work with a partner. Answer the questions.

1 What are 'commodities'?

2 What changed when people began to specialise in certain jobs?

3 Why were the inventions of the wheel and the sailboat important?

4 What historical evidence is there of Mesopotamia trading with other countries?

Did you know?

When the River Euphrates changed its course, the city of Ur lost its wealth and its power.

mini-dictionary

trade = the activity of buying and selling, or exchanging, goods and/or services between people or countries

merchant = a person whose job is to buy and sell products in large amounts, especially by trading with other countries

currency = the money that is used in a particular country at a particular time

5 Final task

Work with a partner. Find out about trade in ancient Egypt. Use the internet. Present your findings on a poster. Include pictures.

Interaction: Pronunciation practice

Interaction 1 page 8

c 1.9 Listen to the sentences and repeat them. Practise sounding interested or not interested.

1 Really? I didn't know that.
2 Yeah, I know about that, I studied it in Geography.
3 Everybody knows that!
4 No way! That's incredible!
5 You're joking!
6 Wow, that's amazing!

Interaction 2 page 16

c 1.21 Listen to the sentences and repeat them. Practise the pronunciation of *use(d) to* (/juːstə/) + verb.

1 Did she use to wear special clothes for her job?
2 Did she use to work with people?
3 Leona Lewis used to be a waitress.

Interaction 3 page 26

c 1.31 Listen to the sentences and repeat them. Practise linking the words.

1 So, which picture do you think_is first?
2 What's_in picture D?
3 Is there_a boat in your picture?
4 Yes, there_is.
5 There's_a big storm …
6 … and there_are sharks_in the water.

Interaction 4 page 34

c 2.9 Listen to the sentences and repeat them. Practise the sentence stress and rhythm.

1 Is everything OK?
2 No, look, this glass is dirty.
3 Oh, sorry, I'll change it immediately.
4 Are you ready to order?
5 Enjoy your meal!
6 Oh, excuse me, but I haven't got a fork.
7 Oh, sorry about that.
8 Anything else? Coffee? Tea?
9 Could we have the bill, please?
10 Yes, no problem. Here you are.

Interaction 5 page 44

c 2.27 Listen to the sentences and repeat them. Practise stressing the important words. Speak clearly!

1 OK, **first** you have to put it in the **USB port**.
2 OK, **next**, look at the **computer screen**.
3 Now click on the **file** you want to **open**.
4 **First** you have to **close** the **files**. Then, **click** on **this icon** at the **bottom** of the **screen**.
5 **Look**, here it is at the **bottom** of the **screen**.

Interaction 6 page 52

c 2.36 Listen to the questions and repeat them. Practise the pronunciation of *do you have to … ?* (/dʒəhaftə/).

1 Do you have to wear special clothes?
2 Do you have to have lessons?
3 How old do you have to be?

Interaction 7 page 62

c 3.10 Listen to the sentences and repeat them. Practise the pronunciation of the stressed *I* (for contrast) and unstressed *I*.

1 I love it.
2 Yeah, so do I.
3 Yes I have, but I hate it. I think it's rubbish.
4 Oh, I don't. I've listened to it loads of times and I think it's great.

Interaction 8 page 70

c 3.21 Listen to the sentences and repeat them. Practise sounding sincere!

1 Oh, no! That's awful!
2 Well, never mind!
3 I'm sorry, Marc. You must be really upset.
4 Oh, wow! Congratulations! That's brilliant news!
5 Oh, well done! That's excellent!

Interaction 9 page 80

c 3.38 Listen to the sentences and repeat them. Practise stressing the important information at the end of the sentence.

1 Who's the guy who's wearing a **baseball cap**?
2 Do you mean the **DJ**?
3 He looks a bit **shy**.
4 Do you mean the girl with **short**, **blonde hair**?
5 The one who's **dancing**?

Interaction 10 page 88

c 4.10 Listen to the sentences and repeat them. Practise the pronunciation of *do you* (/dju:/) + verb.

1 Right, so, where do you want to go from?
2 And where do you want to go to?
3 When do you want to go?
4 And when do you want to come back?
5 … which flight do you want going out?
6 And when you come back, which flight do you want?
7 Do you want to check in online or at the airport?

Interaction 11 page 98

c 4.23 Listen to the sentences and repeat them. Practise sounding enthusiastic.

1 What do you fancy going to see?
2 Um, how about *Star Wars*? It's a classic.
3 How about *Hairspray*, the musical with John Travolta? Have you seen it?
4 Sounds good. Let's see that.
5 It starts at 8:30. There's time to get something to eat first.

Interaction 12 page 106

c 4.31 Listen to the sentences and repeat them. Practise sounding 'diplomatic'.

1 Liam, have you got a minute?
2 You know that money I lent you last month …
3 Well, I really need it back.
4 Can you give it to me today?
5 Well, when do you think I could have it?

Speaking activities

Unit 1, page 7

Student B: Ask Student A.

1 Can you write your name with your right and left hand at the same time?
2 Can you move your ears?
3 Can you say five things that feel horrible?
4 Can you say five things that smell nice?
5 Can you touch your nose with your tongue?
6 What are you doing at the moment?

Unit 3, page 24

You are Kevin Stephan. The journalist is going to ask you questions about what happened with Penny Brown. Make notes about:

- What happened
- What you were doing
- What you did
- How you felt

Someone hit me. *I felt very surprised!*

Unit 5, page 42

Student B: Look at the topics. Make notes about your opinions.

computers entertainment houses sport

Unit 7, page 60

Student B: You are a journalist. Put the words in the correct order.

1 name / band / What / the / your / of / is?
2 start / did / performing / When / you?
3 songs / Have / had / hit / you / any?
4 played / you / Where/ have?
5 typical / for / What's / a / day / you?
6 future / What / plans / your / are / for / the?

Unit 10, page 85

Student B: Put the words in the correct order.

1 to / what/ we / going / eat / are?
2 much / we / to / How / will / money / take / need?
3 are / going / to / How / carry / we / things?
4 have / we / If / what / will / a problem / do? /we

Unit 11, page 96

Student B: Put the words in the correct order.

1 are / by / spoken / your family / What languages ?
2 subjects / What / your school / are / at / taught ?
3 shown / Where / films / in your town / are ?
4 Which / on holidays / are / eaten / by your family / foods ?

Interaction: Student A

Interaction 1 page 8

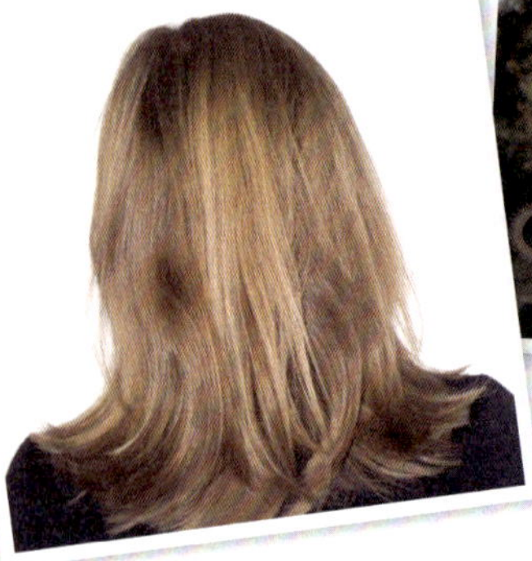

d Tell your partner some interesting facts.

Did you know that ...

1 it takes seven seconds for food to travel from your mouth to your stomach?
2 an octopus has three hearts?
3 your hair grows faster in the summer?
4 polar bears can smell food 30 km away?
5 each hair is on your head for about 5½ years?
6 cats sleep about 12 hours a day?

e Now listen to your partner's facts and show that you are interested or not interested. Use the Interaction language on the front and back cover to help you.

Interaction 2 page 16

d Answer your partner's questions about the jobs these people used to do before they were famous. Use the Interaction language to help you.

Eminem (chef) Sting (teacher) Gwen Stefani (shop assistant, sold ice cream) Johnny Depp (rock musician)

e Now ask your partner questions and guess what these people used to do before they were famous.

1 Christina Aguilera **2** Robert Pattinson **3** Madonna **4** Brad Pitt

Interaction 3 page 26

d Describe your pictures and ask about your partner's pictures. Put all the pictures in the correct order to tell the rest of the story. Use the Interaction language to help you. Don't look at your partner's pictures.

A

B

C

e Now look at all the pictures and tell the complete story with your partner. Use the past simple and past continuous.

Interaction 4 page 34

d Student A: You are the customer. Tell your waiter/waitress about the problems below. Then ask for the bill at the end of the meal.

- a dirty plate
- a place setting without a spoon
- a place setting without a napkin

e Now change roles. You are the waiter / waitress. Welcome the customer to the restaurant. Listen to the customer and help with their problems. Use the Interaction language to help you.

Interaction 5 page 44

d Look at 1–3 below. Give your partner instructions to do the tasks, but don't say what the instructions are for. Can your partner guess? Use the Interaction language to help you.

1 watch a DVD **2** download a new computer game **3** use a social networking site

e Now listen to your partner and try to guess the tasks.

Interaction 6 page 52

d Answer Student B's questions about kite surfing. Then ask Student B questions and copy and complete the fact file about paragliding. Use the Interaction language to help you.

The kite surfing experience!

It's fantastic! You stand on the water on a surfboard and a kite pulls you along.

* We're at Long Beach every weekend.
* You must wear a life jacket. We provide this.
* You must have lessons from our expert teachers first.
* Over 14s only.
* £30.00 a lesson.

Paragliding	
Clothes: ...	Lessons: ...
Price: ...	Description: ...
Place: ...	Age: ...

Interaction 7 page 62

d Write down five songs you like. Include the track / song title and the artist. Don't show your partner.

e Talk to your partner about your songs and choose one song to upload that you both like. Use the Interaction language to help you.

Interaction 8 page 70

d Tell your partner your news (you invent the details). Then listen to your partner's news and respond to it. Use the Interaction language to help you.

1 You have won something in a competition. *(What have you won?)*
2 You have got an important exam tomorrow. *(In what subject?)*
3 You have lost something. *(What have you lost?)*

Interaction 9

page 80

d You and your partner are at a party where there are some people who you don't know. Take it in turns to describe the people and write the missing names. Use the Interaction language to help you.

Interaction 10

page 88

d Your partner wants you to book a flight online for him/her. Ask your partner questions and choose the correct flight information. Use the Interaction language to help you.

Flight information

1 From
Madrid
Manchester

2 Going on:
MAY
25 26 27 28
29 30 31

3 Flights
10.30
18.30

4 To
Madrid
Milan

5 Coming back on:
MAY
25 26 27 28
29 30 31

6 Flights
09.30
16.30

7 Check in: **online** **at the airport**

e Now you want your partner to book a flight online for you. Look at your flight information and answer your partner's questions.

Your flight information

From: London to Milan

Go: June 15th (in the morning)

Come back: June 30th (in the evening)

Check in: online

Interaction 11

page 98

d You and your partner are at a film festival and you have information about different films that are on. Tell Student B about your films and listen to Student B's information. Together, decide which film you're going to see. Use the Interaction language to help you.

Venue: Queen's Hall

6:15 **Mamma Mia!**
The classic musical starring Meryl Streep. Lots of great Abba songs, dancing and Greek beaches.

8:30 **28 Hours Later**
A horror film about a terrible plague which kills nearly everybody in Britain. What happens next?

Venue: Science block – Room 3

6:00 **GHOST WORLD**
A spooky comedy about friends Thora Birch and Scarlett Johansson leaving school.

8:15 **NED KELLY**
Heath Ledger and Orlando Bloom star in an action film about a gang of robbers in Australia.

Interaction 12

page 106

d Look at the information and act out the conversations with your partner. Use the Interaction language to help you.

Conversation 1: Two weeks ago you lent your friend your new camera. Now you would like it back. Start the conversation.

Conversation 2: You borrowed four DVDs from your friend a month ago. You wanted to give them back last week, but you couldn't find them anywhere. Explain what happened and suggest a solution. Your partner starts the conversation.

Interaction: Student B

Interaction 1 page 8

d Listen to your partner's facts and show that you are interested or not interested. Use the Interaction language on the front and back cover to help you.

e Now tell your partner some interesting facts.

Did you know that …

1 you can hear a lion from 8km away?
2 your brain is more active at night than during the day?
3 a goldfish can live for 40 years?
4 you have 27 bones in each hand?
5 all mammals can jump, except the elephant?
6 the heart of a blue whale is about the size of a small car?

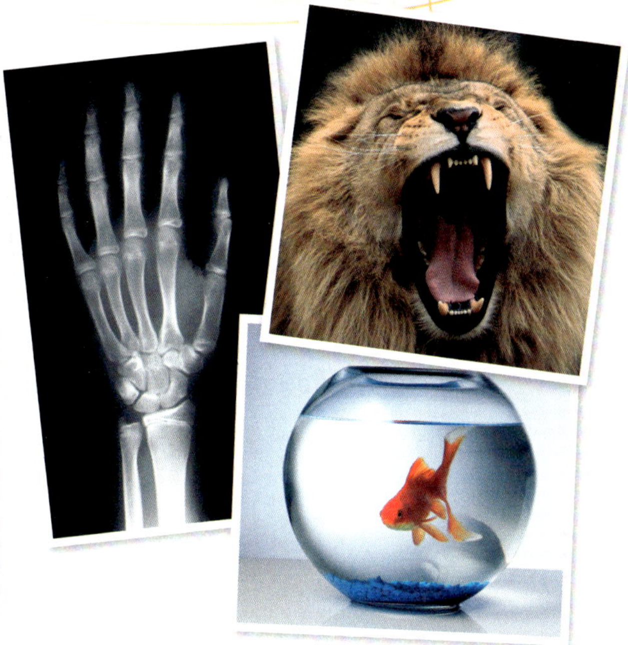

Interaction 2 page 16

d Ask your partner questions and guess what these people used to do before they were famous. Use the Interaction language to help you.

1 Eminem 2 Sting 3 Gwen Stefani 4 Johnny Depp

e Now answer your partner's questions about the jobs these people used to do before they were famous.

Christina Aguilera (TV presenter) Robert Pattinson (model) Madonna (shop assistant, sold doughnuts) Brad Pitt (driver: he drove limousines)

Interaction 3 page 26

d Describe your pictures and ask about your partner's pictures. Put all the pictures in the correct order to tell the rest of the story. Use the Interaction language to help you. Don't look at your partner's pictures.

E

F

G
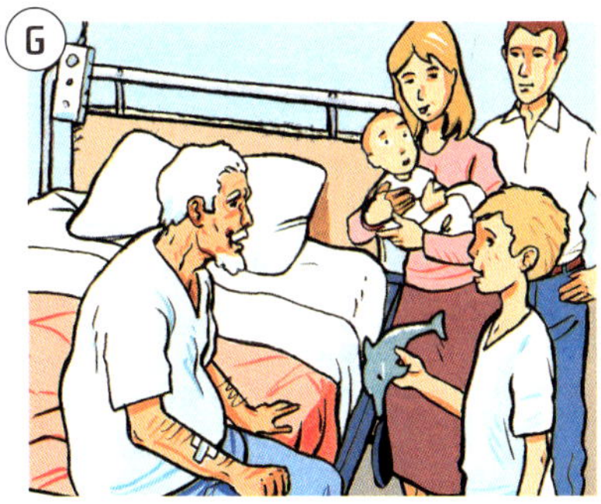

e Now look at all the pictures and tell the complete story with your partner. Use the past simple and past continuous.

Interaction 4 page 34

d Student B: You are the waiter/waitress. Welcome the customer to the restaurant. Listen to the customer and help with their problems. Use the Interaction language to help you.

e Now change roles. You are the customer. Tell your waiter/waitress about the problems below. Tell the waiter you don't have much time!

- a dirty tablecloth
- a place setting without a knife
- a dirty bowl

Interaction 5 page 44

d Listen to your partner give you instructions. Can you guess the tasks 1–3?

e Now look at 1–3 below. Give your partner instructions to do the tasks, but don't say what the instructions are for. Can your partner guess? Use the Interaction language to help you.

1 use a search engine **2** print a document **3** download a song

Interaction 6 page 52

d Ask Student A questions and copy and complete the fact file about kite surfing. Then answer Student A's questions about paragliding. Use the Interaction language to help you.

Fly with the birds – come paragliding!

It's wonderful! You can fly high in the air and look at the beautiful countryside around you.

- We're at Windy Hill every Sunday.
- You must wear warm clothes and boots.
- You don't have to have lessons. You can fly with an expert.
- Over 14s only. 14–18 year olds need a letter from their parents.
- £100 for one day.

Kite surfing

Clothes: ...	Lessons: ...
Price: ...	Description: ...
Place: ...	Age: ...

Interaction 7 page 62

d Write down five songs you like. Include the track / song title and the artist.

e Talk to your partner about your songs and choose one song to upload that you both like. Use the Interaction language to help you.

Interaction 8 page 70

d Listen to your partner's news and respond to it. Then tell your partner your news (you invent the details). Use the Interaction language to help you.

1 You are playing in a sports match this afternoon. (*What sport?*)
2 Your pet has died. (*What kind of animal?*)
3 You have passed an important exam. (*What was the exam?*)

Interaction 9

page 80

d You and your partner are at a party where there are some people who you don't know. Take it in turns to describe the people and write the missing names. Use the Interaction language to help you.

Interaction 10

page 88

d You want your partner to book a flight online for you. Look at your flight information and answer your partner's questions. Use the Interaction language to help you.

Your flight information

From: Manchester to Madrid

Go: May 26th (in the morning)

Come back: May 31st (in the afternoon)

Check in: at the airport

e Now your partner wants you to book a flight online for him/her. Ask your partner questions and choose the correct flight information.

Flight information

1 From
London
Madrid

4 To
Madrid
Milan

2 Going on:
JUNE
10 11 12 13 14
15 16 17

5 Coming back on:
JUNE
24 25 26 27 28
29 30

3 Flights
06.45
15.30

6 Flights
08.00
19.30

7 Check in: online at the airport

Interaction 11

page 98

d You and your partner are at a film festival and you have information about different films that are on. Tell Student A about your films and listen to Student A's information. Together, decide which film you're going to see. Use the Interaction language to help you.

Venue: Sir Peter Hope Room

6:00 **The Ring Two**

Sequel to the horror movie *The Ring* with Naomi Watts. Even more frightening!

8:30 **The X-files: I want to believe**

David Duchovny and Gillian Anderson are back with another exciting science fiction story.

Venue: New Theatre

6:10 **What's Eating Gilbert Grape?**

An emotional, moving drama about ordinary people with Johnny Depp and Juliette Lewis.

8:25 **Shaun of the Dead**

A very funny romantic zombie comedy about the living dead in London.

Interaction 12

page 106

d Look at the information and act out the conversations with your partner. Use the Interaction language to help you.

Conversation 1: Two weeks ago you borrowed a camera from your friend. Unfortunately you dropped it on the ground and broke it. Explain what happened and suggest a solution. Your partner starts the conversation.

Conversation 2: You lent your friend four DVDs a month ago. They belong to your brother and he wants them back. Start the conversation.

Grammar reference

1 Present simple and present continuous

Present simple

Positive			Negative			
I/You/We/They	**speak**	English.	I/You/We/They	**don't (do not)**	**speak**	English.
He/She/It	**speaks**		He/She/It	**doesn't (does not)**		

Yes/No questions				Short answers	
Do	I/you/we/they	**speak**	English?	Yes, I/you/we/they **do**.	No, I/you/we/they **don't**.
Does	he/she/it			Yes, he/she/it **does**.	No, he/she/it **doesn't**.

Information questions		
Where **do** you **work**?	What subjects **do** they **study**?	How **does** she **get** to school?

- With *he/she/it*, the verb ends in *-s*.
  he walks *it moves* *she watches* *he carries*
- We use *do/does* for questions and *don't/doesn't* for negatives.

★ For the spelling of verbs with the *-s* ending, see Rules for spelling, page 140.

- We use the present simple for permanent situations, regular or repeated actions, and facts.
  *Kelly **lives** in Berlin.* *We **play** basketball on Thursdays.* *Mike **doesn't eat** meat.* ***Do** you **like** rap music?*
- We also use the present simple to describe events in a book or film.
  *In this film, Harry **returns** to his school and **receives** a mysterious book.*

Present continuous

Positive			Negative		
I	**'m (am)**	**working**.	I	**'m not (am not)**	**working**.
He/She/It	**'s (is)**		He/She/It	**isn't (is not)**	
You/We/They	**'re (are)**		You/We/They	**aren't (are not)**	

Yes/No questions			Short answers	
Am	I	**working**?	Yes, I **am**.	No, I**'m not**.
Is	he/she/it		Yes, he/she/it **is**.	No, he/she/it **isn't**.
Are	you/we/they		Yes, you/we/they **are**.	No, you/we/they **aren't**.

Information questions		
What **are** you **doing**?	Where**'s** Helen **staying**?	Why **are** they **laughing**?

- For the present continuous we use *am/is/are* + verb + *-ing*.
- We can also use these negative forms:
  *you**'re**/we**'re**/they**'re not** work**ing*** *he**'s**/she**'s**/it**'s not** work**ing***

★ For the spelling of *-ing* words, see Rules for spelling, page 140.

- We don't normally use the continuous form for these verbs:
  like love hate want need know think believe understand
  Do you need some help? (**not** ~~*Are you needing*~~)
  I don't believe that story. (**not** ~~*I'm not believing*~~)
- We use the present continuous for actions happening now and for temporary actions.
  *Hey, look! It**'s snowing**!* *She **isn't working** today.* *What **are** you **reading** at the moment?*

★ For *taste, smell* and *sound* + adjective we also use the simple form, not the continuous.
*Those flowers **smell** lovely.*
*The sauce **doesn't taste** very nice.*

- We also use the present continuous to talk about future arrangements, often in the near future.
  *I**'m playing** tennis with Carlo tomorrow.* ***Are** you **coming** to the party on Saturday?*

2 Past simple

Positive		Negative		
I/You/We/They/He/She/It	**started**. **sang**.	I/You/We/They/He/She/It	**didn't (did not)**	**start**. **sing**.

Yes/No questions			Short answers
Did	I/you/we/they/he/she/it	**start**? **sing**?	Yes, I/you/we/they/he/she/it **did**. No, I/you/we/they/he/she/it **didn't**.

Information questions		
When **did** the concert **start**?	Where **did** they **go** yesterday?	What film **did** you **see**?

- We use the past simple for completed actions in the past.
  *I **washed** my hair yesterday. Raul **played** football last weekend. They **arrived** five minutes ago.*
- Regular verbs end in *-ed*.
  *jump → jump**ed** like → lik**ed** carry → carri**ed** drop → dropp**ed***
- Many common verbs are irregular. They don't have the usual *-ed* ending.
  *speak → **spoke** think → **thought** fall → **fell** go → **went***
  *They **flew** to Madrid on Tuesday. Irena **bought** some books yesterday.*
- We always use *didn't* + infinitive for negatives and *did* + infinitive for questions.
  *We **didn't live** here ten years ago. I **didn't speak** to Amy yesterday.*
  ***Did** you **enjoy** the film? When **did** he **go** to London?*

★ For the spelling of verbs with the *-ed* ending, see Rules for spelling, page 140.

★ For a list of irregular verbs, see page 143.

3 *used to*

Positive			**Negative**		
I/You/We/They/ He/She/It	**used to**	**play**.	I/You/We/They/ He/She/It	**didn't (did not) use to**	**play**.

***Yes/No* questions**				**Short answers**
Did	I/you/we/they/ he/she/it	**use to**	**play**?	Yes, I/you/we/they/he/she/it **did**. No, I/you/we/they/he/she/it **didn't**.

Information questions
What **did** people **use to do**? Where **did** we **use to play**? How often **did** she **use to visit**?

- We use *used to / didn't use to* + infinitive for normal or repeated actions in the past. The actions don't happen now.
  *I **used to love** this music when I was about ten.*
  *At my first school we **didn't use to get** much homework.*
  *What **did** people **use to wear** in the 19th century?*

★ Don't confuse *used to* + verb with the verb *use*.
*I **used to take** a lot of photos.*
*I **used** my phone to take these photos.*

4 Past continuous

Positive			**Negative**		
I/He/She/It	**was**	**sleeping**.	I/He/She/It	**wasn't (was not)**	**sleeping**.
You/We/They	**were**		You/We/They	**weren't (were not)**	

***Yes/No* questions**			**Short answers**	
Was	I/he/she/it	**sleeping**?	Yes, I/he/she/it **was**.	No, I/he/she/it **wasn't**.
Were	you/we/they		Yes, you/we/they **were**.	No, you/we/they **weren't**.

Information questions
Why **were** they **standing** outside? What **was** she **wearing**? Who **were** you **waiting** for?

- For the past continuous we use *was/were* + verb + *-ing*.
- We use the past continuous for an action that was in progress over a period of time in the past.
  *It was a lovely morning. The sun **was shining** and the birds **were singing**.*
  *Sorry I didn't call you. I **was working** all morning. While Mum **was cooking**, we **were doing** our homework.*
- The past continuous often describes what was happening at a certain time. The action started before that time and continued after it.
  *At this time yesterday I **was sitting** on the beach. **Were** you **watching** TV at half past seven?*
  *At 9:15 we **were** still **waiting** for the school bus.*

★ For the spelling of *-ing* words, see Rules for spelling, page 140.

5 Past simple and past continuous

- We often use the past simple and past continuous together.
  *I **was cooking** the vegetables when Julie **arrived**. The accident **happened** while we **were driving** home.*
- We use the past continuous for a longer action. We use the past simple for a shorter action.
- The past continuous action started earlier. It was already in progress when the past simple action happened.

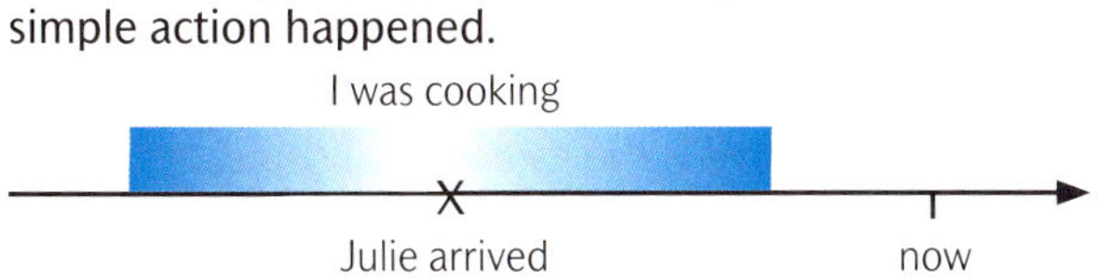

- The past simple action often interrupts the past continuous action.

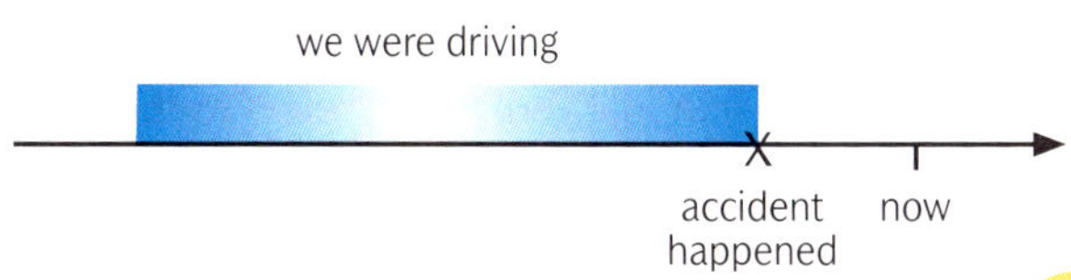

- We use *when* with the past simple and we normally use *while* with the past continuous. We can change the order of the two actions.

While *they were having lunch,* *the storm came*. *The storm came* ***while*** *they were having lunch.*

When *the storm came*, *they were having lunch.* *They were having lunch* ***when*** *the storm came*.

6 Comparative and superlative adjectives

Adjective	Comparative	Superlative
quick	**quicker**	the **quickest**
safe	**safer**	the **safest**
fat	**fatter**	the **fattest**
heavy	**heavier**	the **heaviest**

Adjective	Comparative	Superlative
honest	**more honest**	the **most honest**
intelligent	**more intelligent**	the **most intelligent**

Regular forms

- For one-syllable adjectives and adjectives ending in *-y*, we use *-er* for the comparative and *-est* for the superlative.
  *In Europe, May is warm**er** than April.* *It's sunni**er** today than yesterday.*
  *The kitchen is the warm**est** room in our house.* *Tuesday was the sunni**est** day last week.*
- For most adjectives of two or more syllables, we use *more* for the comparative and *most* for the superlative.
  *The Eiffel Tower is **more famous** than the Louvre.* *Skateboarding is **more difficult** than riding a bike.*
  *He's the **most famous** actor in Hollywood.* *Maths is the **most difficult** subject for me.*
- When we use the comparative form to compare two things, we often use *than.*
- We normally use *the* with the superlative form.

★ For the spelling of *-er* and *-est* adjectives, see Rules for spelling, page 140.

Irregular forms

- Some adjectives are irregular in the comparative and superlative.

Adjective	Comparative	Superlative
good	**better**	the **best**
bad	**worse**	the **worst**
far	**further**	the **furthest**

*I'm quite good at singing, but Alice is **better**.*
*This is the **best** song they've ever recorded.*

7 Modifiers

Duck is	**much** **a lot** **a bit**	nicer tastier more expensive	than chicken.

★ We don't use these modifiers with superlative adjectives.

- We can use *much*, *a lot* and *a bit* with comparative adjectives.
- We use *much* or *a lot* to express a big difference between things and we use *a bit* to express a small difference.
  *Travelling by bus is **much** cheaper than flying.* *Cats are **a lot** more independent than dogs.*
  *The two rooms are almost exactly the same, but ours is **a bit** smaller.*

8 *will*

Positive			Negative		
I/He/She/It/ You/We/They	**'ll (will)**	**come**.	I/He/She/It/ You/We/They	**won't (will not)**	**come**.
***Yes/No* questions**			**Short answers**		
Will	I/he/she/it/ you/we/they	**come**?	Yes, I/he/she/it/you/we/they **will**. No, I/he/she/it/you/we/they **won't**.		
Information questions					
What time **will** they **get** here?	Where **will** we **be** in ten years' time?				

★ For other modals, see *might / might not* (below), *should/ shouldn't* (pages 135–136).

- *Will* is a modal verb which refers to the future. The form *will* + infinitive is the same for all subjects.
- The negative form of *will* is *won't* (**not** ~~*willn't*~~). The question form is *will* + subject + infinitive.

Predictions

- We use *will/won't* + infinitive to make predictions about the future.
  *In the future, tourists **will go** to the moon.* ***Will** we **win** the match on Saturday?* *He **won't want** to go camping in the rain.*
- We often use *think* with *will* predictions.
  *I think you**'ll enjoy** reading this book.* *I don't think it**'ll rain** tomorrow.*

Offers and spontaneous decisions

- We use *I'll* + infinitive to make offers.
  ***I'll help** you with your homework.* *You must be hungry. **I'll get** you some bread and cheese.*
- We also use *I'll / I won't* + infinitive for decisions that we make as we speak.
  *Tim isn't answering his phone. **I'll send** him an email.* ***I won't go** out now. It's too cold.*

9 *might*

Positive			Negative		
I/He/She/It/ You/We/They	**might**	**change**.	I/He/She/It/ You/We/They	**might not**	**change**.

- Like *will*, *might* is a modal. It always goes with the infinitive of another verb, and its form doesn't change.
- The negative form of *might* is *might not*.
- It is possible to use the question form (*might* + subject + infinitive), but this is uncommon.
- We use *might / might not* + infinitive to say that something is possible but uncertain. It can refer to the present or the future.
  *Danny isn't in his room. He **might be** in the garden.* *We **might go** to the beach tomorrow, but it depends on the weather.*
  *It's only a small shop. They **might not sell** olives.* *I'll invite Sharon, but she **might not come**.*

10 *going to* for future plans

Positive				Negative			
I	**'m (am)**	**going to**	**travel**.	I	**'m not (am not)**	**going to**	**travel**.
He/She/It	**'s (is)**			He/She/It	**isn't (is not)**		
You/We/They	**'re (are)**			You/We/They	**aren't (are not)**		
***Yes/No* questions**				**Short answers**			
Am	I	**going to**	**travel**?	Yes, I **am**.	No, I**'m not**.		
Is	he/she/it			Yes, he/she/it **is**.	No, he/she/it **isn't**.		
Are	you/we/they			Yes, you/we/they **are**.	No, you/we/they **aren't**.		
Information questions							
How **are** they **going to travel**?	Where **is** he **going to meet** us?	What **are** you **going to tell** them?					

- The form is the verb *be* + *going to* + infinitive.
- We can also use these negative forms:
  *you**'re**/we**'re**/they**'re not going to** travel* *he**'s**/she**'s**/it**'s not going to** travel*
- We use *am/is/are* + *going to* + infinitive to talk about future plans and intentions.
  *I**'m going to invite** about 40 people to the party.* *We**'re not going to watch** TV tonight.*
  *Mum **is going to drive** us to the station at half past seven.*
  *When **are** you **going to see** the doctor?*

★ Future plans with *going to* are sometimes very similar to future arrangements with the present continuous. In some sentences both forms are correct.
*We**'re going to fly** to Rome on Monday.*
*We**'re flying** to Rome on Monday.*

11 *should* and *shouldn't*

Positive			Negative		
I/He/She/It/ You/We/They	**should**	**leave**.	I/He/She/It/ You/We/They	**shouldn't (should not)**	**leave**.
***Yes/No* questions**			**Short answers**		
Should	I/he/she/it/ you/we/they	**leave**?	Yes, I/he/she/it/you/we/they **should**. No, I/he/she/it/you/we/they **shouldn't**.		
Information questions					
What **should** we **do**?	How much medicine **should** I **take**?	Who **should** she **talk** to?			

- *Should* is a modal verb. It always goes with the infinitive of another verb, and its form doesn't change.
- The negative form of *should* is *shouldn't*. The question form is *should* + subject + infinitive.
- We use *should/shouldn't* + infinitive to give advice. We use *should* if we think the action is a good idea. We use *shouldn't* if we think it isn't a good idea.
  *You look tired. You **should go** to bed early tonight.* *She **shouldn't ride** her bike without a helmet.*
  ***Should** I **put** some more salt in this soup?*

12 *have to* and *don't have to*

Positive			Negative			
I/You/We/They	**have to**	**work**.	I/You/We/They	**don't (do not)**	**have to**	**work**.
He/She/It	**has to**		He/She/It	**doesn't (does not)**		

Yes/No questions				Short answers	
Do	I/you/we/they	**have to**	**work**?	Yes, I/you/we/they **do**.	No, I/you/we/they **don't**.
Does	he/she/it			Yes, he/she/it **does**.	No, he/she/it **doesn't**.

Information questions	
What **do** we **have to do** for homework?	Why **does** she **have to leave** so early?

- We use *have/has to* + infinitive for actions that are necessary. Its meaning is similar to *must* + infinitive.
  *I **have to do** the shopping for Mum today.* *Michael **has to leave** early to catch the train.* ***Do** you **have to study** later?*
- We use *don't/doesn't have to* + infinitive for actions that aren't necessary.
  *Dad can relax at the weekend because he **doesn't have to work**.* *You **don't have to wear** a coat today. It isn't cold.*
- *Don't/doesn't have to* is different from *mustn't*.
  *You **mustn't** eat that.* = Don't eat it! *You **don't have to** eat that.* = It isn't necessary to eat it, but you can if you want to.

13 Present perfect

Positive			Negative		
I/You/We/They	**'ve (have)**	**played** baseball. **written** a song.	I/You/We/They	**haven't (have not)**	**played** baseball. **written** a song.
He/She/It	**'s (has)**		He/She/It	**hasn't (has not)**	

Yes/No questions			Short answers	
Have	I/you/we/they	**played** baseball? **written** a song?	Yes, I/you/we/they **have**.	No, I/you/we/they **haven't**.
Has	he/she/it		Yes, he/she/it **has**.	No, he/she/it **hasn't**.

Information questions		
What **have** you **done**?	How many countries **has** she **visited**?	How much money **have** we **spent**?

- For the present perfect we use *have* + past participle.
- The past participle form of a verb is usually the same as the past simple.
  *She's **designed** some brilliant clothes.* *He's **made** more than 30 films.* *Have they **sold** many albums?*
  However, for some irregular verbs the past participle is different.
  *I've never **worn** a hat.* (**not** ~~*wore*~~) *Have you **seen** this painting?* (**not** ~~*saw*~~)
- *Been* is the past participle of *be*, but it can also be the past participle of *go*. The verb *go* has two past participles: *gone* and *been*.
  *Cathy has **gone** to the gym.* (= She's still at the gym now.)
  *Cathy has **been** to the gym.* (= She was at the gym, but she isn't there now.)

★ For a list of irregular verbs, see page 143.

Present perfect for experiences

- We use the present perfect to talk about actions at some time in the past up to now. We don't say exactly when they happened.
  *She'**s seen** this film three times this year.* (= from the start of this year up to now)
  *I **haven't tried** skydiving before.* (= at any time in my life up to now)
  ***Have** you **been** to Portugal?* (= at any time in your life up to now?)

Present perfect with *for* and *since*

- We also use the present perfect to talk about actions that started in the past and are still happening now.
  *I've **played** in this team for two months.* (I'm still playing in the team now.)
  *Dad **hasn't had** a holiday since April.* (He still isn't on holiday – he's still working now.)
- We use *for* + a period of time. We use *since* + a point in time when the action began.
  *Alex has been here **for two hours** / **since eleven o'clock**. I've known Lisa **for six weeks** / **since June**.*
  *We've had this car **for 12 years** / **since I was three years old**.*

Present perfect and past simple

- Past simple actions are finished – they belong to the past.
  *She **saw** the film three times last year.* (This happened last year – that time is finished.)
  *Alex **was** here for two hours.* (Then he went away – he isn't here now.)
- We use past time expressions (*yesterday*, *last week*, *in 2009*, *two years ago*, etc.) with the past simple but not with the present perfect.
  *I **didn't meet** your grandparents **yesterday**. I**'ve** never **met** your grandparents. **Did** Kate **go** to Scotland **last summer**?*
  ***Has** Kate ever **been** to Scotland? They **bought** their TV **a long time ago**. They**'ve had** their TV for a long time.*

14 Zero conditional

If	I **go** to the beach,	I always **take** my surfboard.
	plants **don't get** any water,	they **die**.
	wood **is** wet,	it **doesn't burn** easily.
	wood **is** wet,	does it **burn** easily?

Result		Condition
I always **take** my surfboard	if	I **go** to the beach.
Plants **die**		they **don't get** any water.
Wood **doesn't burn** easily		it**'s** wet.
Does wood **burn** easily		it**'s** wet?

- We use *if* when we want to show that one action depends on another.
- We use the zero conditional to talk about things that always happen in certain conditions.
- The verbs in both clauses are in the present simple.
- We can change the order of the two clauses. When the *if* clause comes first, we add a comma. When the result clause comes first, there is no comma.

15 First conditional

Condition		Result
If	I **have** time,	**I'll (will) meet** you at the café.
	she **doesn't hurry**,	she**'ll (will) be** late.
	it **rains** this afternoon,	they **won't (will not) go out**
	it **rains** this afternoon,	**will** they **go out**?

Result		Condition
I'll (will) meet you at the café	if	I **have** time.
She**'ll (will) be** late		she **doesn't hurry**.
They **won't (will not) go out**		it **rains** this afternoon.
Will they **go out**		it **rains** this afternoon?

- We use the first conditional to talk about things that are possible in the future. The action depends on a condition that is possible but not certain.
  If I see Martin, I'll tell him to ring you. (Maybe I'll see him – it's possible.)
- In the *if* clause we use a present simple verb.
  *If I **see** Martin, …* (**not** *If ~~I'll see~~ Martin*)
- In the result clause, we use *will*/*won't* + infinitive.
- We can change the order of the two clauses.

16 Second conditional

Condition		Result
If	we **bought** a boat,	we**'d (would) sail** around the world.
	he **stopped** eating chocolate,	he**'d (would) lose** weight.
	they **didn't have** a map,	they **wouldn't (would not) find** this place.
	they **didn't have** a map,	**would** they **find** this place?

Result	Condition	
We**'d (would) sail** around the world	if	we **bought** a boat.
He**'d (would) lose** weight		he **stopped** eating chocolate.
They **wouldn't (would not) find** this place		they **didn't have** a map.
Would they **find** this place		they **didn't have** a map?

- We use the second conditional to talk about unreal situations now or in the future. The action depends on a condition that is unlikely or impossible.
  If *I* ***had*** *wings, I'****d fly*** *to Australia.* (But I haven't got wings – this is impossible!)
  Jill ***would win*** *the race* ***if*** *she* ***practised*** *for it.* (But she probably won't practise, so this is unlikely.)
- In the *if* clause we use a past simple verb, but it refers to the present or future.
  If I ***had*** *wings, …* (**not** *If ~~I have~~ wings* or *If ~~I'll have~~ wings*)
- In the result clause, we use *would/wouldn't* + infinitive.
- In the *if* clause we sometimes use *I/he/she/it* ***were*** instead of *was*. This is usual when the subject is *I*.
  If I ***were*** *you, I'd see a doctor.* *If Lee* ***weren't*** (or ***wasn't***) *so lazy, he'd be a brilliant student.*

17 Question tags

	Positive statement	Question tag	Negative statement	Question tag
be **present simple**	I**'m** in the team,	**aren't** I?	I**'m not** a great singer,	**am** I?
	We**'re** early,	**aren't** we?	We **aren't** ready,	**are** we?
	He**'s** Polish,	**isn't** he?	She **isn't** from Italy,	**is** she?
Other verb forms	You**'re** working,	**aren't** you?	You **aren't** listening,	**are** you?
	He**'s** gone home,	**hasn't** he?	She **hasn't** left,	**has** she?
	It**'ll** be fun,	**won't** it?	It **won't** rain,	**will** it?
	They **can** fly,	**can't** they?	They **can't** see us,	**can** they?
	I **should** leave,	**shouldn't** I?	I **shouldn't** be here,	**should** I?
	You like olives,	**don't** you?	You **don't** eat meat,	**do** you?
	She wears glasses,	**doesn't** she?	He **doesn't** drive,	**does** he?

- We use question tags to check information or to invite people to agree with us.
  What's the time? I'm not late, ***am I?*** *It's a lovely day,* ***isn't it?*** *This doesn't taste very nice,* ***does it?***
- We add a question tag to a statement. If the statement is positive, the question tag is negative. If the statement is negative, the question tag is positive.
- If the verb in the statement is *be*, we repeat the verb *be* in the question tag.
- For other verbs, we repeat the auxiliary or modal. (An auxiliary is a form of *be*, *do* or *have* which goes with the main verb. A modal is a word like *will*, *should* and *can*.)
- A positive statement in the present simple has no auxiliary or modal. Here we use *don't/doesn't* in the question tag.

18 Defining relative clauses

Main clause	Relative clause	
That's the boy	**who**	works in the newsagent's. / I saw on the bus.
I've read the story	**which / that**	was in the school newspaper. / you wrote.
We're in the street	**where**	Maria lives.

- A defining relative clause refers to someone or something earlier in the sentence. It gives essential information about the person, thing or place we are talking about.
- We use *who* for people. We can also sometimes use *that*.
  I like <u>*people*</u> ***who*** *make me laugh.* *My uncle is* <u>*an artist*</u> ***who*** *paints birds.* <u>*The teacher*</u> ***that*** *I like best is Mrs Harrison.*

- We use *which* or *that* for things.
  *He's wearing the sunglasses **which** he bought in Brazil.* *Buses **that** go along Broad Street stop at the museum.*
  *Has anyone seen the magazine **that** I was reading?*
- We use *where* for places. It means 'in which', 'at which' or 'to which'. There must be a noun or pronoun between *where* and the verb that follows.
  *We visited all the places **where** they filmed 'The Lord of the Rings'.* (*where* = in which)
  *Barajas is the airport **where** their plane is landing.* (*where* = at which)
  *That's the restaurant **where** we often go for a Chinese meal.* (*where* = to which)

19 Verb + *-ing* and verb + infinitive

- The following verbs are followed by a verb + *-ing*:
  like love enjoy hate don't mind finish stop
  *He hates writ**ing** essays.* *Have you finished clean**ing** your room?*
- The following verbs are followed by *to* + infinitive:
  want need hope learn agree
  *We need **to buy** some bread.* *I hope **to work** as an architect one day.*
- The following verbs can take either form:
  start begin continue
  *It started **to rain** / **raining** at about ten o'clock.*
  *The plants will begin **to grow** / **growing** in the spring.*
  *She continued **to work** / **working** until midnight.*

★ However, *like/love/hate + to +* infinitive is sometimes used, especially in US English.
Also, remember that with ***would** like* (= want) we use *to* + infinitive.
*I'**d** like **to see** that film.*
***Would** you like **to come** with us?*

★ We can also use a noun or pronoun after most of the verbs in this section.
Have you finished that book?
I need some new batteries.
He hasn't started his essay.

20 Infinitive of purpose and *for* + noun

- To explain why someone does something, we can use *to* + verb or *for* + noun.

We're going to the café	***to have** lunch.*	*She's gone out*	***to get** some eggs.*
	***for** lunch.*		***for** some eggs.*

- We can also sometimes use *for* + verb + *-ing*.
  *These scissors are **for** cutt**ing** paper.* *A special camera is used **for** film**ing** underwater.*

21 Present simple passive

Positive				**Negative**			
It	**'s (is)**	**made**	of metal.	It	**isn't**	**made**	of metal.
They	**'re (are)**	**written**	in English.	They	**aren't**	**written**	in English.
***Yes/No* questions**				**Short answers**			
Is	it	**made**	of metal?	Yes, it **is**.		No, it **isn't**.	
Are	they	**written**	in English?	Yes, they **are**.		No, they **aren't**.	
Information questions							
What **are** those tables **made** of?			Where **is** Spanish **spoken**?		How **is** this machine **used**?		

- Most sentences are active. The subject does the action.
  Architects design buildings. (*Architects* is the subject and architects do the action of designing.)
  In a passive sentence the subject doesn't do the action. It is the 'receiver' of the action, which is done by something/someone else.
  Active: *Factory workers make these clothes in China.*
  Passive: *These clothes **are made** in China.* (We don't say who makes the clothes.)
  Active: *They give a prize to the best performer.*
  Passive: *A prize **is given** to the best performer.* (We don't say who gives the prize.)
- We make the present passive with the present tense of *be* + past participle.
- We often use the passive when we don't know who/what does the action, or when it isn't important who/what does the action.
- If we want to say who/what does the action, we use *by*.
  *Buildings are designed **by** architects.* *Safety equipment is worn **by** divers.* *People are sometimes killed **by** snakes.*

★ For notes on the past participle form, see Present perfect, page 136.

22 Past simple passive

Positive				Negative			
It	**was**	**invented**	in the USA.	It	**wasn't**	**invented**	in the USA.
They	**were**	**written**	100 years ago.	They	**weren't**	**written**	100 years ago.
***Yes/No* questions**				**Short answers**			
Was	it	**invented**	in the USA?	Yes, it **was**.	No, it **wasn't**.		
Were	they	**written**	100 years ago?	Yes, they **were**.	No, they **weren't**.		
Information questions							
When **was** the building **finished**?	Where **were** they **born**?	How **was** that scene **filmed**?					

- We make the past simple passive with the past tense of *be* + past participle.
  This umbrella ***was left*** *on the bus.* *Jeans* ***weren't worn*** *until the 19th century.* ***Was*** *the radio* ***invented*** *by Marconi?*
- When referring to the past, we use *be born* in the past passive form, not the present.
  Michelangelo was born in 1475. (**not** ~~*is born*~~)

23 *someone*, *anyone*, *everyone*, *no one*, etc.

	some-	*any-*	*every-*	*no-*
People	someone	anyone	everyone	no one
	somebody	anybody	everybody	nobody
Things	something	anything	everything	nothing
Places	somewhere	anywhere	everywhere	nowhere

- We use these words to talk about people, things and places without saying exactly who/what they are.
- Words with *some-* refer to a particular person/thing/place that we can't identify. We normally use *some-* in positive sentences.
  Someone*'s taken my purse!* *Let's have* ***something*** *to eat.* *The information is* ***somewhere*** *on this website.*
- We often use words with *any-* in negative sentences and questions.
  Hello? Is ***anybody*** *there?* *I don't want* ***anything*** *to drink.* *Have you seen my keys* ***anywhere****?*

  We can also use *any-* in positive sentences when we want to say 'it doesn't matter which person/thing/place'.
  This is easy. ***Anybody*** *can do it.* *I don't mind what we eat. Get* ***anything*** *you like.* *Put the boxes* ***anywhere****. I'll put them away later.*
- We use words with *every-* to mean all people/things/places.
  Everyone *needs food and water.* *Is* ***everything*** *ready?* *The park looks awful. There's rubbish* ***everywhere****.*
- Words with *no-* have a negative meaning. We always use them with positive verbs.
  Nobody *answered the phone.* *We've got* ***nothing*** *in the fridge.* *The room is full. There's* ***nowhere*** *to sit.*
- When a word with *some-*, *any-*, *every-* or *no-* is the subject of a verb, we use the singular form of the verb.

Rules for spelling

Verbs and nouns with *-s*

- Verb or noun ending in *-s*, *-sh*, *-ch*, *-x* and *-o*: add *-es*.
  *miss → miss**es*** *bus → bus**es***
  *push → push**es*** *dish → dish**es***
  *watch → watch**es*** *lunch → lunch**es***
  *relax → relax**es*** *box → box**es***
  *do → do**es*** *hero → hero**es***
- Verb or noun ending in a consonant + *-y*: ~~*y*~~ + *-ies*.
  *carry → carr**ies*** *ferry → ferr**ies***
  *fly → fl**ies*** *comedy → comed**ies***

Verbs with *-ed*

- Verb ending in *-e*: add *-d*.
  *hate → hate**d*** *invite → invite**d***
- One-syllable verb ending in a vowel + a consonant: double consonant + *-ed*.
  *stop → sto**pp**ed* *grab → gra**bb**ed*
- Verb ending in a consonant + *-y*: ~~*y*~~ + *-ied*.
  *hurry → hurr**ied*** *study → stud**ied***

Verbs with *-ing*

- Verb ending in *-e*: ~~*e*~~ + *-ing*.
  live → living *come → coming*
- One-syllable verb ending in a vowel + a consonant: double consonant + *-ing*.
  *get → ge**tt**ing* *shop → sho**pp**ing*
- Verb ending in *-ie*: ~~*ie*~~ + *-ying*.
  *lie → **l**ying* *die → **d**ying*
- Verb ending in two consonants: add *-ing*.
  find → finding

Adjectives with *-er* and *-est*

- Adjective ending in *-e*: add *-r* or *-st*.
  *nice → nice**r**, nice**st*** *large → large**r**, large**st***
- Adjective ending in *-y*: ~~*y*~~ + *-ier* or *-iest*.
  *lazy → laz**ier**, laz**iest*** *early → earl**ier**, earl**iest***
- One-syllable adjective ending in a vowel + a consonant: double consonant + *-er* or *-est*.
  *big → bi**gg**er, bi**gg**est* *fat → fa**tt**er, fa**tt**est*

Wordlist

(adj) = adjective (adv) = adverb (n) = noun (npl) = plural noun
(prep) = preposition (v) = verb (1) = Unit 1

Unit 1

Parts of the body

bone (n) /bəʊn/
brain (n) /breɪn/
chest (n) /tʃest/
chin (n) /tʃɪn/
elbow (n) /'elbəʊ/
finger (n) /'fɪŋgə/
heart (n) /hɑːt/
knee (n) /niː/
neck (n) /nek/
shoulder (n) /'ʃəʊldə/
skin (n) /skɪn/
stomach (n) /'stʌmək/
throat (n) /θrəʊt/
toe (n) /təʊ/
tongue (n) /tʌŋ/
wrist (n) /rɪst/

The five senses

ears (npl) /ɪəz/
eyes (npl) /aɪz/
hands (npl) /hændz/
hear (v) /hɪə/
mouth (n) /maʊθ/
nose (n) /nəʊz/
see (v) /siː/
smell (v) /smel/
taste (v) /teɪst/
touch (v) /tʌtʃ/

Unit 2

Jobs

architect (n) /'ɑːkɪtekt/
dentist (n) /'dentɪst/
engineer (n) /ˌendʒɪ'nɪə/
factory worker (n) /'fæktri 'wɜːkə/
firefighter (n) /'faɪəfaɪtə/
hairdresser (n) /'heəˌdresə/
journalist (n) /'dʒɜːnlɪst/
nurse (n) /nɜːs/
plumber (n) /'plʌmə/
police officer (n) /pə'liːs 'ɒfɪsə/
taxi driver (n) /'tæksi 'draɪvə/
waiter (n) /'weɪtə/

Verb/noun collocations

answer a question /'ɑːnsə ə'kwestʃən/
help a friend /help ə frend/
make the bed /meɪk ðə bed/
start work /stɑːt wɜːk/
take a photo /teɪk ə fəʊtəʊ/
wear a uniform /weər ə 'juːnɪfɔːm/

Unit 3

-ed and *-ing* adjectives

bored/boring (adj) /bɔːd//bɔːriŋ/
disappointed/disappointing (adj) /ˌdɪsə'pɔɪntɪd/ /ˌdɪsə'pɔɪntɪŋ/
embarrassed/embarrassing (adj) /ɪm'bærəst/ /ɪm'bærəsɪŋ/
excited/exciting (adj) /ɪk'saɪtɪd/ /ɪk'saɪtɪŋ/
frightened/frightening (adj) /'fraɪtnd//'fraɪtənɪŋ/
interested/interesting (adj) /'ɪntrəstɪd//'ɪntrəsˌtɪŋ/
surprised/surprising (adj) /sə'praɪzd//sə'praɪˌzɪŋ/

Ages and stages

baby (n) /ə 'beɪbi/
child (n) /ə tʃaɪld/
elderly person (npl) /'eldli 'pɜːsn/
middle-aged person (npl) /ˌmɪdl'eɪdʒd ˌpɜːsn/
teenager (n) /ə 'tiːnˌeɪdʒə/
toddler (n) /ə 'tɒdlə/

Unit 4

Adjectives

amazing (adj) /ə'meɪzɪŋ/
crazy (adj) /'kreɪzi/
delicious (adj) /dɪ'lɪʃəs/
disgusting (adj) /dɪs'gʌstɪŋ/
luxurious (adj) /lʌg'ʒʊəriəs/
memorable (adj) /'memrəbl/
trendy (adj) /'trendi/
weird (adj) /wɪəd/

Eating out

bill (n) /bɪl/
course (n) /kɔːs/
cutlery (n) /'kʌtlri/
dessert (n) /dɪ'zɜːt/
fork (n) /fɔːk/
glass (n) /glɑːs/
knife (n) /naɪf/
main course (n) /meɪn kɔːs/
napkin (n) /'næpkɪn/
plate (n) /pleɪt/
spoon (n) /spuːn/
starter (n) /'stɑːtə/
tablecloth (n) /'teɪblklɒθ/

Unit 5

Transport

boat (n) /bəʊt/
ferry (n) /'feri/
helicopter (n) /'helɪkɒptə/
lorry (n) /'lɒri/
motorbike (n) /'məʊtəbaɪk/
plane (n) /pleɪn/
scooter (n) /'skuːtə/
ship (n) /ʃɪp/
tram (n) /træm/

Computers

click on (something) (v) /'klɪk ˌɒn/
cut and paste (v) /'kʌt ənd ˌpeɪst/
disc drive (n) /dɪsk ˌdraɪv/
file (n) /faɪl/
icon (n) /'aɪkɒn/
keyboard (n) /'kiːbɔːd/
laptop (n) /'læptɒp/
memory stick (n) /'memrɪ stɪk/
mouse (n) /maʊs/
printer (n) /'prɪntə/
screen (n) /skriːn/
search engine (n) /'sɜːtʃ ˌendʒɪn/
social networking site (n) /'səʊʃəl ˌnetwɜːkɪŋ/
speakers (npl) /'spiːkəz/
USB port (n) /juː ˌes 'biː pɔːt/
webcam (n) /'webkæm/

Unit 6

Extreme sports

bungee jumping (n) /'bʌndʒi 'dʒʌmpɪŋ/
motor racing (n) /'məʊtə 'reɪsɪŋ/
mountain biking (n) /'maʊntɪn 'baɪkɪŋ/
scuba diving (n) /'skuːbə 'daɪvɪŋ/
skateboarding (n) /'skeɪtbɔːdɪŋ/
skydiving (n) /'skaɪˌdaɪvɪŋ/
snowboarding (n) /'snəʊbɔːdɪŋ/
water skiing (n) /'wɔːtə 'skiːɪŋ/

Verbs of movement

climb (v) /klaɪm/
dive (v) /daɪv/
fall (v) /fɔːl/
jump (v) /dʒʌmp/

roll (v) /rəʊl/
spin (v) /spɪn/

Unit 7

Music

album (n) /'ælbəm/
band (n) /bænd/
the charts (npl) /ðə tʃɑːts/
fan (n) /fæn/
hit (n) /hɪt/
lyrics (npl) /'lɪrɪks/
perform (v) /pə'fɔːm/
record (v) /'rekɔːd/ record (n) /rɪ'kɔːd/
single (n) /'sɪŋgl/
studio (n) /'stjuːdiəʊ/

Music online

cover art (n) /'kʌvər ɑːt/
download (v) /ˌdaʊn'ləʊd/
microphone (n) /'maɪkrəfəʊn/
playlist (n) /'pleɪlɪst/
record label (n) /'rekɔːd 'leɪbl/
tracks (npl) /træks/
update (v) /ʌp'deɪt/
upload (v) /ʌp'ləʊd/

Unit 8

Adjectives of personality

anxious (adj) /'æŋkʃəs/
dishonest (adj) /dɪ'sɒnɪst/
easy-going (adj) /ˌiːzɪ 'gəʊɪŋ/
generous (adj) /'dʒenrəs/
hard-working (adj) /ˌhɑːd 'wɜːkɪŋ/
honest (adj) /'ɒnɪst/
impatient (adj) /ɪm'peɪʃnt/
insensitive (adj) /ɪn'sentˌsɪtɪv/
lazy (adj) /'leɪziː/
mean (adj) /miːn/
patient (adj) /'peɪʃənt/
quiet (adj) /'kwaɪət/
self confident (adj) /ˌself 'kɒnfɪdənt/
sensible (adj) /'sensɪbl/
sensitive (adj) /'sensɪtɪv/
shy (adj) /ʃaɪ/
silly (adj) /'sɪliː/
sociable (adj) /'səʊʃəbl/
talkative (adj) /'tɔːkətɪv/
unsociable (adj) /ʌn'səʊʃəbl/

Special days

Christmas Day (n) /'krɪsməs deɪ/
Day of the Dead (n) /deɪ əv ðə ded/
Diwali (n) /dɪ'wɑːli/
Eid (n) /iːd/
Hanukhah (n) /'hɑːnəkə/
New Year's Eve (n) /ˌnjuː jɪəz 'iːv/
Thanksgiving (n) /ˌθæŋks'gɪvɪŋ/

Unit 9

Describing appearance

bald (adj) /bɔːld/
beautiful (adj) /'bjuːtɪfl/
big (adj) /bɪg/
cute (adj) /kjuːt/
fat (adj) /fæt/
good-looking (adj) /gʊd'lʊkɪŋ/
little (adj) /'lɪtl/
long (adj) /lɒŋ/
overweight (adj) /əʊvə'weɪt/
pointed (adj) /'pɔɪntɪd/
pretty (adj) /'prɪti/
round (adj) /raʊnd/
short (adj) /ʃɔːt/
straight (adj) /streɪt/
ugly (adj) /'ʌgli/
wavy (adj) /'weɪvi/

On TV

advertisement (n) /əd'vɜːtɪsmənt/
channel (n) /'tʃænl/
chat show (n) /tʃæt ʃəʊ/
comedy series (n) /'kɒmədi 'sɪəriːz/
documentary (n) /ˌdɒkjə'mentri/
drama series (n) /'drɑːmə 'sɪəriːz/
quiz show (n) /kwɪz ʃəʊ/
soap opera (n) /'səʊp ˌɒprə/
the news (n) /ðə njuːz/

Unit 10

Travel verbs

catch (v) /kætʃ/
drive (v) /draɪv/
get into (v) /get 'ɪntə/
get off (v) /get ɒf/
get on (v) /get ɒn/
get out of (v) /get aʊt əv/
land (v) /lænd/
ride (v) /raɪd/
take off (v) /teɪk ɒf/

Going on a trip

check-in desk (n) /'tʃekɪn ˌdesk/
passport (n) /'pɑːspɔːt/
platform (n) /'plætfɔːm/
security (n) /sɪ'kjʊərəti/
suitcase (n) /'suːtkeɪs/
ticket office (n) /'tɪkɪt 'ɒfɪs/
timetable (n) /'taɪmˌteɪbl/
window seat (n) /'wɪndəʊ siːt/

Unit 11

Films

camera operator (n) /'kæmrə 'ɒpreɪtə/
director (n) /dɪ'rektə/
extra (n) /'ekstrə/
film star (n) /fɪlm stɑː/
location (n) /lə'keɪʃn/
make-up artist (n) /ˌmeɪk ʌp 'ɑːtɪst/
script (n) /skrɪpt/
set (n) /set/
stunt person (n) /stʌnt 'pɜːsn/

Materials

cardboard (n) /'kɑːdbɔːd/
cotton (n) /'kɒtn/
glass (n) /glɑːs/
leather (n) /'leðə/
metal (n) /'metl/
plastic (n) /'plæstɪk/
rubber (n) /'rʌbə/
wood (n) /wʊd/

Unit 12

Money

cash (n) /kæʃ/
cash machine (n) /kæʃ mə'ʃin/
coins (npl) /kɔɪnz/
credit card (n) /'kredɪt kɑːd/
notes (npl) /nəʊts/
PIN (personal identification number) (n) /pɪn/ /'pɜːsnl aɪˌdentɪfɪ'keɪʃn 'nʌmbə/
purse (n) /pɜːs/
receipt (n) /rɪ'siːt/
wallet (n) /'wɒlɪt/

Money verbs

borrow (v) /'bɒrəʊ/
earn (v) /ɜːn/
lend (v) /lend/
pay for (v) /peɪ fɔː/
save (v) /seɪv/
spend (v) /spend/
waste (v) /weɪst/
win (v) /wɪn/

Irregular verbs

Verb	Past simple	Past participle
be	was/were	been
become	became	become
begin	began	begun
blow	blew	blown
break	broke	broken
bring	brought	brought
build	built	built
burn	burned/burnt	burned/burnt
buy	bought	bought
can	could	been able
catch	caught	caught
choose	chose	chosen
come	came	come
cost	cost	cost
cut	cut	cut
do	did	done
draw	drew	drawn
drink	drank	drunk
drive	drove	driven
eat	ate	eaten
fall	fell	fallen
feel	felt	felt
fight	fought	fought
find	found	found
fly	flew	flown
forget	forgot	forgotten
get	got	got
give	gave	given
go	went	gone/been
grow	grew	grown
have	had	had
hear	heard	heard
hit	hit	hit
hold	held	held
hurt	hurt	hurt
keep	kept	kept
know	knew	known
learn	learned/learnt	learned/learnt
leave	left	left
lend	lent	lent

Verb	Past simple	Past participle
let	let	let
lose	lost	lost
make	made	made
mean	meant	meant
meet	met	met
pay	paid	paid
put	put	put
read	read	read
ride	rode	ridden
ring	rang	rung
run	ran	run
say	said	said
see	saw	seen
sell	sold	sold
send	sent	sent
set	set	set
shoot	shot	shot
shut	shut	shut
sing	sang	sung
sit	sat	sat
sleep	slept	slept
speak	spoke	spoken
spell	spelled/spelt	spelled/spelt
spend	spent	spent
spin	span/spun	spun
stand	stood	stood
steal	stole	stolen
swim	swam	swum
swing	swung	swung
take	took	taken
teach	taught	taught
tell	told	told
think	thought	thought
throw	threw	thrown
understand	understood	understood
wake	woke	woken
wear	wore	worn
win	won	won
write	wrote	written

Answer Key to Personality Quiz page 68

Mostly As
You have a lot of friends and are very sociable. However, sometimes you can be impatient and insensitive and you're often very talkative.

Mostly Bs
You're friendly, generous and very relaxed. In fact sometimes you're so relaxed that people think you're lazy.

Mostly Cs
You're very hard-working, sensible and sensitive. However, sometimes you're very shy and so people think you're unsociable.

Phonemic symbols

Consonant sounds

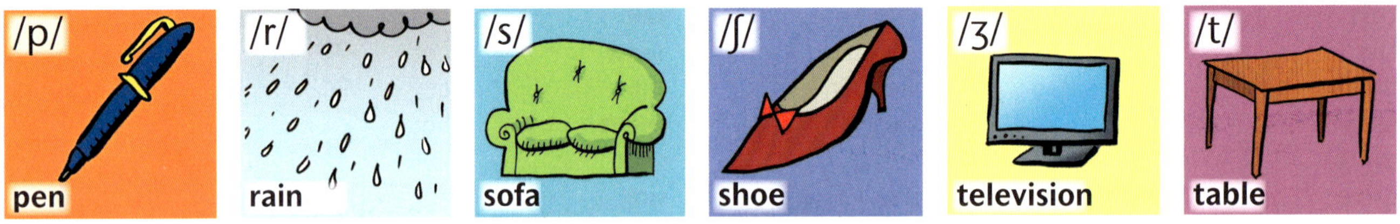

Vowel sounds

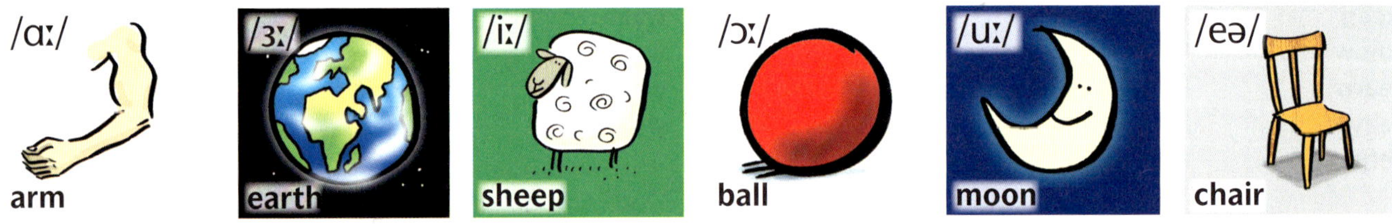

Go to the Interactive website for more pronunciation practice!

http://interactive.cambridge.org